Race and Ethnic Relations on Campus

Race and Ethnic Relations on Campus

Understanding, Empowerment, and Solutions for College Students

Eric J. Bailey, PhD, MPH

An Imprint of ABC-CLIO, LLC

Santa Barbara, California • Denver, Colorado

Library of Congress Cataloging-in-Publication Data

Names: Bailey, Eric J., 1958- author.
Title: Race and ethnic relations on campus : understanding, empowerment, and solutions for college students / Eric J. Bailey.
Description: Santa Barbara, California : Praeger, an Imprint of ABC-CLIO, LLC, [2018] | Includes bibliographical references and index.
Identifiers: LCCN 2018019877 (print) | LCCN 2018027783 (ebook) | ISBN 9781440854583 (eBook) | ISBN 9781440854576 (hardcopy : alk. paper)
Subjects: LCSH: Minorities—Education (Higher)—United States. | College integration—United States. | College students—United States—Attitudes. | United States—Race relations. | United States—Ethnic relations.
Classification: LCC LC3731 (ebook) | LCC LC3731 .B335 2018 (print) | DDC 378.1/982—dc23
LC record available at https://lccn.loc.gov/2018019877

ISBN: 978-1-4408-5457-6 (print)
       978-1-4408-5458-3 (ebook)

22 21 20 19 18   1 2 3 4 5

This book is also available as an eBook.

Praeger
An Imprint of ABC-CLIO, LLC

ABC-CLIO, LLC
130 Cremona Drive, P.O. Box 1911
Santa Barbara, California 93116-1911
www.abc-clio.com

This book is printed on acid-free paper ∞

Manufactured in the United States of America

Contents

Preface

Race and Ethnic Relations on Campus: Understanding, Empowerment, and Solutions for College Students is a new approach to addressing and better understanding many of the major controversial issues associated with race and ethnic relations for today's college students. Due to the current wave of societal racial conflicts across the United States, college students have become astutely aware of many of these issues, yet may not know how to conceptualize and deal with these issues effectively. This book confronts these race- and ethnic-relations issues directly and sets in motion a whole new way of thinking on how today's college students can do something about it.

The significance of this new book on race and ethnic relations is that it is the first and only book that provides today's college students not only a new approach to address these serious issues but, more importantly, new practical strategies to solve these issues individually and collectively. No longer can universities ignore the varying types of race- and ethnic-relations issues that arise on each campus every year. All those involved in recruiting, teaching, and graduating our next set of college students, which continues to increase in its diversity, must establish a new strategy to address the most controversial topic on college campuses today—race relations.

My personal journey with race-relations issues actually began during my early years of growing up in Wilberforce, Ohio, and going to public school in Xenia, Ohio (approximately 15 miles east of Dayton). As a very proud native Ohioan and Buckeye, I was born in Springfield, Ohio, and spent my first six years of life, including first grade, here with my mom, Jean Ethel Ballew Bailey; my dad, Roger William Bailey Jr.; and my three older brothers, Billy, Ronnie, and Dwight.

Etched into my memory of first grade in the public school in Springfield is a very special teacher. I had become extremely ill that year, and my parents had to hospitalize me. I had developed pneumonia, which required hospitalization for several days. I can't recall exactly how many days I missed from school, but what I do remember is my teacher, who came to my hospital room, sat next to me at my hospital bed, and gave me my lesson plans for the day. My teacher knew how much my parents and I valued education, and she went out her way at the end of the school day to give me my first-grade lessons. What was even more remarkable about this teacher is that she just happened to be a white Caucasian Euro-American woman!

During this time, in the United States, particularly in this part of Ohio, race relations between blacks and whites were going through some very tough times. Our worlds were mostly separate—blacks lived with and socialized with other blacks, and whites lived with and socialized with other whites. In the early 1960s, the few times that we socialized together were at school, shopping, sporting events, or work. That's why it was so unusual to see a white teacher teaching me—a black, African American kid—at the city hospital. Somehow, at that age, I knew it was an exception, something I'd never forget!

This race-relations event with my schoolteacher, along with others in Springfield, Ohio, prepared me for relations with those who were like me and those who were not. Once my parents decided to relocate to Wilberforce, Ohio (approximately 15 miles southwest of Springfield), it was a brand-new start on life for me and my family, primarily because Wilberforce and the community that we lived in (referred to as the "Valley") represented moving up in social status. In Springfield, we lived in an impoverished, low-income neighborhood, in a small house next to the city dump. By contrast, in Wilberforce, we lived in a brand-new large middle-class home next to cornfields and two historically black universities—Wilberforce University and Central State University. Needless to say, Wilberforce and the Valley symbolized to me, my family, and many others a peaceful, inspiring, educated, hopeful place to live, play, and raise a family.

Living and growing up in Wilberforce and the Valley from 1965 through the rest of my formative, young-adult, and college years (except 1968–69, in which we lived in Wyoming, Ohio)—close to our grandmother and grandfather, Lula and John Ballew, along with many of our relatives in Cincinnati on my mom's side of the family, the Pughs, Johnsons, Daniels, Ballews, and Samuels—was an unbelievably magical upbringing that any young kid would enjoy! There were so many young African American families like ours starting their lives in the Valley, which helped to establish strong bonds of support and cultural pride among all of us who lived in the Valley and throughout Wilberforce.

There were also lots and lots of kids in the Valley. In fact, several levels of age range of kids from newborns to my age range (7–8 years old) to my older brother Dwight's age (11–12 years old) to the next four-year age range, then the next four-year age range, then the college kids. Indeed, the Valley had lots and lots of kids, along with lots of vacant wooded lots to play in during these early years.

My core set of friends in the Valley consisted of Donnie Miller, Karl Miller, Lucretia Mays, Kim Kidd, Judy Walker, Mitzi Turney, and, of course, Leigh Ann Richardson. We were all in the same age range, and practically all of us developed a strong friendship bond primarily because we spent so much time together playing in the weeds, vacant lots, cornfields, and the creek.

Yet my core set of friends when I attended public school were oftentimes completely different than my Wilberforce/Valley friends. The obvious difference between my core set of friends from the public schools and my Wilberforce friends was their race. A majority of my friends at all the public schools were white, and my friends in Wilberforce and the Valley were black. It also didn't matter whether a person was mixed or not; he or she was classified as either white or black. It was not intentional, but that was the way it was. I made friends based upon our likes and dislikes, not because of one's race. Thus, my relations with other races truly started during these formative years in attending public school in Xenia, Ohio, from 1965 to 1976.

The public-school system that all of us had to attend was located in Xenia, Ohio, two miles away. Kids living in Wilberforce were bused every day (morning and afternoon) from all parts of Wilberforce to Xenia and our designated elementary, junior high, and high school. The Xenia school system had several elementary schools throughout the town, yet a majority of the Wilberforce and Valley kids attended a designated elementary school (i.e., Tecumseh Elementary), junior high school (i.e., Warner Junior High School), and high school (i.e., Xenia High School).

Once I graduated from Xenia High School in 1976, I was ready to expand my network of friends, challenge myself even more academically, and gain even more exposure to other parts of Ohio. That's why I was fortunate that my parents supported my college education to attend Miami University (Oxford, Ohio). My parents (Jean and Roger) not only wanted me to get my college education from a major public university with high academic standards, but more importantly they wanted me to get the exposure to other races that I would not achieve if I stayed locally.

Fortunately, my public-school years in Xenia and the relations that I had with kids who were racially different from me prepared me for the type of student population (predominantly all white) and the race-relations issues at Miami University. I was accustomed to being a so-called minority in a school system, yet never really thought that I was a minority just because there were only a few of us (blacks) attending the school. I simply went to school and college and developed a close set of friends based upon "likes" and "dislikes," not because of anybody's skin color.

That's why my core set of friends at Miami University (1976–80) consisted of Randy Orr, Matt Covert, and Duane McDonald. They just happened to be racially different from me, but that didn't matter. We roomed, socialized, partied, and studied together because we liked the same things and were willing to experience such different facets of each other's culture as music and food. That's what is so fantastic about going to college—it presents the opportunity to interact, socialize, and engage with people who are completely different from you (racially, ethnically, socially, economically, and politically).

In addition to my friends at Miami University, I also had my football friends at the university. Interestingly, they were almost entirely African Americans. My core friends consisted of Duane McDonald, Howard Daniel, Ronnie Brinson, Rickie Neal, Kurt Springs, and Donnie Treadwell. For two and a half years (1979 and 1980), I played football for the Miami University football team. I was a walk-on who made the team as a defensive cornerback. Although I predominately played on the scout team, I did see action in an actual game as a special team's player during my senior year. It was the thrill of a lifetime playing in a Division I major college football game, and I owe all that opportunity and experience to my former Miami University head football coach Tom Reed.

Thus, it was that my years in college as an undergraduate and graduate student at Miami University, my years in the public-school system in Xenia, my years of growing up in Wilberforce and the Valley, my years of growing up in Springfield, and the time when my first-grade teacher gave me my lesson plans at the hospital established and guided my thoughts and actions about race relations throughout my career and life. These special moments, special places, and special people made a positive impact on me and how I engage with the world today and in the future.

Chapter 1 presents the premise of the book and highlights how national race-relations issues are affecting race-relations issues on college campuses today. We start with the Trayvon Benjamin Martin trial, in which a young African American teenager was shot by a security guard. The incident led former president Barack Obama to share his opinions about this race-relations incident in a national press conference, which in turn started national discussions and debates on college campuses about the status of race relations in America today. The Black Lives Matter movement began in response to the outcries and frustration from the black community due to the ruling in the Trayvon Benjamin Martin trial in which the perpetrator was freed. Our discussion continues with the University of Missouri protests, in which African American students and the entire University of Missouri football team took a stance against university administrators for the lack of diversity initiatives on campus, which caused the chancellor to resign. In the U.S. Supreme Court decision on affirmative action, the court upheld their ruling that race is still one factor that needs to be considered for admissions for college students and is constitutional in the United States. At the University of Maryland, an African American college student was killed at a bus stop by a white Caucasian Euro-American college student who provoked the confrontation. In 2016 five

Dallas police officers were shot and killed by an African American male as payback for the recent shootings of black men by police officers. And finally we look at the election and presidency of Donald Trump—the 45th U.S. president—and his effect on race relations.

Chapter 2 discusses a number of the typical race-relations issues and incidents that normally happen on college campuses today, as well as some of my personal reflections on race-relations issues during my college years some 40 years ago.

Chapter 3 introduces and defines many of the basic concepts associated with race and ethnic relations so that we can not only establish a foundation for these concepts but also get comfortable with discussing these issues ourselves. A cultural-historical approach of race relations is also included in this chapter.

Chapter 4 reviews and highlights the major theories associated with race relations. A cultural-historical review of these theories is presented. Although many typical race-relations theories are highlighted, this chapter introduces a brand-new theory for college students to use when evaluating race-relations issues on their campuses today.

Chapter 5 examines specifically interracial relationships and race relations from a cultural-historical review in the United States. A review of interracial relationships and the types of multiracial, mixed-race populations in the United States is necessary in order for all of us to acknowledge that race-relations issues are different for those who are multiracial in the United States.

Chapter 6 reviews how national politics, in particular our U.S. presidents, have addressed race-relations issues in America. The chapter examines the political strategies and initiatives as they relate to race-relations issues of former presidents Barack Obama and Bill Clinton, as well as our current president Donald Trump.

Chapter 7 examines the negative consequences of poor race relations among college students today. The three major concepts—prejudice, discrimination, and segregation—are elaborated upon in an effort to show how these issues can influence a college student's inability to get along with students who are different from him or her.

Chapter 8 discusses and elaborates upon the positive outcomes of improved race relations for college students. Research studies showing the positive impact that good race relations have on specific racial and ethnic groups, the positive impact that good race relations have on the educational enrichment for the typical college student, and the positive impact that good race relations have on the self-confidence of the typical college student are all highlighted in this chapter.

Chapter 9 shows how typical college students can solve race-relations issues individually and collectively on their particular college campuses.

Excellent solutions from college campuses across the United States and a personal example on how I resolved certain race-relations issues during my college days are presented.

Chapter 10 discusses how any major university or small college can play a significant role in addressing and resolving many of their race- and ethnic-relations issues. A brand-new national initiative titled the Cultural Competency Engagement Initiative (CCEI) is presented to assist all colleges and universities in *rethinking* their approaches to race and ethnic relations on their campuses.

Chapter 11 presents 10 controversial race-relations debate issues in a pro-and-con format so that the typical college student can get a better sense of the opposing viewpoints on these issues. More importantly, this pro-and-con format also presents potential solutions to each of these very controversial topics so that all of us can recognize that there are always potential solutions regardless of how polarizing some of these race-relations issues can be.

Chapter 12 provides my personal and enlightening journey into teaching a race-relations seminar for the first time. This chapter highlights my field-work participant-observation notes as a professor who finally got an opportunity to teach an honors race-relations seminar to a very special set of honor students.

Finally, the appendix highlights a few race-relations class exercises that any instructor can use for their class. The primary purpose of sharing these race-relations class exercises is for students and instructors to realize that discussing, examining, debating, and learning about race-relations issues can also be entertaining and fun.

Acknowledgments

First and foremost, I want to sincerely thank my remarkable, patient, and understanding editor, Debbie Carvalko, for working with me on not only this book project but also several book projects over the years with Praeger/ABC-CLIO Publishing. I am truly grateful for her insight and experience in guiding me in new directions in writing.

In addition, I thank the J. Y. Joyner Library at East Carolina University for their excellent collections of research articles, special archived collections, and superior online services to access their collections at any time of the day.

I also thank my incredible, thought-provoking, engaging, investigative, creative, and hopeful college students throughout all my years of teaching college classes, starting in the fall of 1983 and continuing today. Although at times it was a bumpy ride trying to learn my craft of teaching college classes to all types of college students, at different universities, in different parts of the country, I value this fantastic journey in academic engagement with students who are discovering more about the world and people through my courses and who will be the leaders of tomorrow. I feel blessed to have shared this moment in time with all of you!

In particular, I want to thank the honor students in the Honors College Program at East Carolina University, who were in my most recent race-relations classes. They were Annaliese Gillette, Rachel Grantham, Carly Judd, Lindsey Locklear, Patricia Malcolm, Caroline Morgan, Alexandria Stephens, Angel Chukwu, Michael Denning, Tyler Ebeling, Ariel Fricke, Rachel Heatherly, Noah Lee, Nakaya Melvin, Adrienne Marie Orbita, Brooke Palmer, Mahima Pandoria, Charlotte Pearsall, Stephiya Sabu, Kendall Schunk, Godgive Umozurike, and Claudia Woznichak. These students, with support from the Honors College, the Department of Anthropology, the Department of Public Health, the Thomas Harriot College of Arts and Sciences, the Office of Student Affairs, and the Chancellor's Office at East Carolina University, made it possible for me to venture into new academic territory for my new classes and new areas of research inquiry.

I also thank my family, which includes my wife, Gloria; daughter, Ebony; and sons, Darrien and Marcus. They have been with me throughout a majority of my journey in academia and the writing of my books. I truly appreciate their indulgence, feedback, criticism, and support over the years on each book project and each academic move. It's truly not easy to start, raise, and move a young family around from place to place and institution to institution, so I am most appreciative of my wife, Gloria, who made it all possible during the past 30 years.

I also thank the family in which I grew up, especially my mom, Jean Ethel Ballew Bailey, and my dad, Roger William Bailey Jr., because they were the ones who nurtured, guided, directed, supported, taught, and enculturated me with the types of values, beliefs, and behavior that were reflective of their own families. I am most appreciative of and blessed to have had them in my life. Although both of my parents have passed, they are always with me in spirit. Along with my parents, I also thank my brothers—Dwight, Ronnie, Billy, and Michael—and all my extended family members on the Bailey and Ballew sides of my heritage.

Finally, I thank all my close friends in the neighborhoods where I grew up and all my friends in the primary school, junior high school, high school, and colleges that I attended. Your impact on my life has been very instrumental in how I learned to interact with people, both those who were like me and those who were different from me. I thank each of you for who you are!

PART 1

Overview and Current Issues

CHAPTER ONE

The Impact of National Race-Relations Incidents on College Experience

Our United States of America is a unique and special country when compared to others around the world. From strictly a population perspective, the United States ranks 4th on the list of most populous countries in the world (*The World Factbook* 2017). Globally, the top ten countries are China (1,373,541,278), India (1,266,883,598), European Union (513,949,445), United States (323,995,528), Indonesia (258,316,051), Brazil (205,823,665), Pakistan (201,995,540), Nigeria (186,053,386,), Bangladesh (156,186,882), and Russia (142,355,415) (*The World Factbook* 2016). Japan (126,702,133) and Mexico (123,166,739) are a close 11th and 12th in world ranking. Yet what is so interesting, when we compare the United States with the rest of the world, is that a majority of our citizens, excluding the Native Americans, more than likely descended from one or more of these countries.

The United States of America was founded from people of all racial and ethnic backgrounds who were mostly immigrants seeking a better life. Whether our ancestors were fleeing from political persecution; indentured servants who wanted a better life from their home country; people who wanted to follow a different religious faith than their predecessors; enslaved Africans who were brought here forcibly for over 200 years to North America to help settle, establish, and grow many of the towns, villages, and cities across the United States; or the Native Americans who were first here on this North American continent, all of us respect, honor, and appreciate our individual, familial, group, and collective history. It is this collective history that allows us to call ourselves today the United States of America.

As the saying goes, "We are a nation of immigrants." This is how our country was established, built, and prospered. This basic premise comes from our Founding Fathers when we as a fledgling country declared independence from British authority to establish our new country on this North American continent. As most historians recognize, our key Founding Fathers were John Adams, Benjamin Franklin, Alexander Hamilton, John Jay, Thomas Jefferson, James Madison, and George Washington. All were instrumental in their own way to help establish the United States of America.

Today, the United States of America is very distinctive as a country in comparison to other countries around the world because of our increased racial diversity. According to the 2010 census, 308.7 million people resided in the United States on April 1, 2010—which represented an increase of 27.3 million people, or 9.7 percent, between 2000 and 2010. Furthermore, the U.S. Bureau of Census demographers contended that "the vast majority of the growth in the total population came from increases in those who reported their race(s) as something other than White alone and those who reported their ethnicity as Hispanic or Latino" (U.S. Department of Commerce, United States Census 2000, 2011:3).

The Bureau of Census 2010 reported that "of the 57 racial combinations on the census and those who chose more than one race, most chose one of the four most common combinations: 20.4 percent marked black and white; 19.3 percent chose white and 'some other race'" (U.S. Department of Commerce, United States Census 2000, 2011). The third most prevalent combination was Asian and white, followed by American Indian and white. These four combinations accounted for three-fourths of the total mixed-race population.

Overall, approximately 3 percent (9.9 million) of the total population reported themselves as belonging to more than one race. This equates to an increase of 32 percent from 2000 to 2010, making the two-or-more-races group one of the fastest-growing groups across the decade (U.S. Department of Commerce, United States Census 2000, 2011:5).

By contrast, the two populations that showed the smallest and no percentage growth were the black and white populations. U.S. Bureau of Census demographers noted that "while the Black alone population had the third largest numeric increase in population size over the decade (4.3 million), behind the White alone and Asian alone populations, it grew slower than most other major race groups" (U.S. Department of Commerce, United States Census 2000, 2011). Between 2000 and 2010, the black-alone population group exhibited the smallest growth aside from the white-alone population, increasing 12 percent. Specifically, the black population rose from 34.7 million in 2000 to 38.9 million in 2020, making up 12 percent and 13 percent of the total population (5).

In general, the Bureau of Census 2010 data illustrated that the nation is continuing to change racially and ethnically. During the past 10 years, census data showed that the Hispanic/Latino/Latina and Asian American populations have grown the most when compared to other racial and ethnic populations in the United States (U.S. Department of Commerce, United States Census 2000, 2011:22). The census 2010 data also showed that one of the fastest-growing populations was people reporting more than one race. It is widely believed that "minorities" will be the "majority" in the United States by 2050.

Yet, with all this racial and ethnic diversity that the United States has experienced through the centuries and recent decades, along with proudly promoting our racial and ethnic diversity to countries around the world, we are nonetheless experiencing a monumental and catastrophic crisis as it relates to race and ethnic relations. During the past five years, there have been multiple shootings of black males; multiple shootings of police officers; hate crimes perpetrated against numerous racial, ethnic, religious, socioeconomic, and LGBT groups, along with the accompanying protests related to each local and national race- and ethnic-relations issue, with equal rights and equal treatment at the core. We all recognize the gravity of this once generational historical issue, and now a present-day national problem is a major focus across the country, dividing our country over issues of truth, justice, and human rights.

Without a doubt, there is something disturbing happening in our United States of America regarding race and ethnic relations, which some barely acknowledge and apparently fewer want to take action against. The problem continues to grow from neighborhood to neighborhood, town to town, and state to state. It may be downplayed in local and national media, as authorities do not want heated debates to get out of hand. Yet the so-called authorities have no clue about how to truly address, analyze, confront, and resolve tenuous and confrontational racial incidents that seem to be growing and happening on a much more regular basis in our country in recent years and months.

National Race-Relations Incidents

The Trayvon Benjamin Martin Trial

Perhaps one of the most widely known national race-relations incidents between an African American male and perceived to be white, European American male was the Trayvon Martin shooting and trial. The 2012 shooting of Trayvon Benjamin Martin, a 17-year-old African American male, by George Zimmerman, a white Latino male neighborhood watch volunteer in Sanford, Florida, sparked a nationwide and international debate on racial profiling, self-defense laws, and state laws. Here is a synopsis of the shooting and aftermath of this incident, which became a national, political race-relations issue.

> On the evening of February 26, Trayvon Martin went to a convenience store and purchased candy and a canned drink. As Trayvon Martin returned from the store, he walked through a neighborhood that had been victim-ized by robberies several times that year. George Zimmerman, a member of the community watch, spotted him and called the Sanford Police to report him for suspicious behavior. Moments later, there was an altercation between the two individuals in which Trayvon Martin was shot in the chest and died. George Zimmerman, who was injured in the altercation, was not charged at the time of the shooting by the Sanford Police, who said that there was no evidence to refute his claim of self-defense and that Florida's stand your ground law prohibited law-enforcement officials from arresting or charging him. After national media focused on the tragedy, George Zim-merman was eventually charged and tried in Trayvon Martin's death. On June 10, 2013, Zimmerman's trial began in Sanford and on July 13th, a jury acquitted him of second-degree murder and of manslaughter charges.

Within hours of the acquittal, the case spurred outrage as a national race-relations issue through social media, national television news reporting, pro-test rallies in cities across the United States, protest rallies on college campuses across the nation, and even a personal commentary from then president Barack Obama. Although President Obama attempted to maintain objectivity, he nonetheless shared his opinion by saying, "Trayvon Martin could have been me 35 years ago."

Black Lives Matter

One of the major reactions from the black community regarding the out-come of the Trayvon Benjamin Martin trial was the beginning of Black Lives Matter. According to the #BlackLivesMatter website (http://blacklivesmatter .com), the group was created in 2012 after George Zimmerman was acquitted of the shooting of Trayvon Martin. Founded by Patrisse Cullors, Opal Tometi, and Alicia Garza, Black Lives Matter is a call to action and a response to the antiblack racism that permeates U.S. society. It goes beyond the nationalism that can be prevalent within black communities, which merely call on black people to love black, live black, and buy black (http://blacklivesmatter.com /about) (August 6, 2016).

In addition, Black Lives Matter (2016) states that it affirms the lives of black queer and trans folks, disabled folks, black undocumented people, folks with criminal records, women, and all black lives along the gender spectrum. They focus on those who have been marginalized with the black liberation movement and state that this is a tactic to (re)build the black liberation movement (http://blacklives.matter.com/about) (September 1, 2016).

To highlight further the organization's approach to their movement, they state the following about the ways in which black lives are deprived of basic human rights and dignity:

- Recognizing the impact of black poverty and genocide is a state violence.
- Recognizing the statistical data that 2.8 million black people are jailed is another state violence.
- Recognizing that black women are feeling the impact of a relentless assault on our children and our families is another state violence.
- Recognizing that black queer and transgender people are feeling the impact from a traditional heterosexual society, yet still profits off them, is another state violence.
- Recognizing that the 500,000 black people in the United States are undocumented immigrants and not properly acknowledged in our society is another state violence.
- Recognizing that black girls are being manipulated and used as negotiating entities during tumultuous times of conflict and war is another state violence.
- Recognizing that black folks with disabilities and different abilities are being redefined and standardized in a Westernized model by mainstream white society is another state violence. (https://blacklivesmatter.com/about/) (September 6, 2016)

Finally, the organization explains, at #BlackLivesMatter, that it is striving to create a world in which black lives are not the target of any systematic and intentional agenda by our mainstream society. They will stand firm together to resist oppression on all levels. They have spent their sweat equity and love for black people into creating a forum and place for all black lives striving for liberation (http://blacklivesmatter.com/about) (September 6, 2016).

University of Missouri

Another race-relations incident that quickly became a national news story concerned the student protests at the University of Missouri in the fall of 2015. Apparently, at the University of Missouri, a series of neglected, overlooked discriminatory activities and institutional policies ignored minority student concerns for years (*USA TODAY* 2016).

As documented by CNN reporter Michael Pearson, a number of events from August 9, 2014, to November 9, 2015, eventually led to Missouri university system's president Tim Wolfe's resignation on November 9, 2015: The incident started when a police officer in Ferguson, Missouri, shot and killed an unarmed black teenager, Michael Brown. Protest followed, and the Black Lives Matter movement arrived, bringing more attention to the incident. Racial tension grew each month in the state of Missouri and throughout the United States, seeking answers and justice to this incident.

A little more than a year later, student government president Payton Head (University of Missouri) expressed his frustration through social media concerning discriminatory acts on campus and incidents that directly affected him. Missouri chancellor R. Bowen Loftin responded and issued a statement stating that the recent incidents of bias and discrimination were not acceptable.

Yet, by October 2015, many African American students at the University of Missouri still felt that the top administrators had not taken appropriate actions to counter the growing discriminatory acts on campus. The student group Concerned Student 1950 issued a list of demands:

1. An apology from University System President Wolfe;
2. His removal from office;
3. A more comprehensive racial awareness and inclusion curriculum overseen by minority students.

One month later, black football players on the University of Missouri football team announced they wouldn't practice or play until university president Wolfe was removed. The black football players were supported by their head coach, Gary Pinkel, and many white football players (Pearson 2015; Schmidt 2015).

Then it happened. On November 9, university system president Tim Wolfe resigned. By the end of this confrontational situation between top University of Missouri administrators, Concerned Student 1950, student leaders, and the entire University of Missouri football program (coaches and players), both the University of Missouri system president Tom Wolfe and chancellor of the flagship University of Missouri campus R. Bowen Loftin had resigned. The next changes involved identifying the interim president—Michael Middleton—for the University of Missouri system and the board of curators to order the following diversity initiatives:

- Hire a full-time campus diversity equity and inclusion officer on each of the four campuses.
- Hire a system-level chief diversity equity and inclusion officer.
- Develop a diversity requirement for all incoming students.

The sociocultural and institutional impact of the events at the University of Missouri influenced college campuses (large and small) across the United States to review their diversity initiatives and galvanized student protests at numerous colleges and universities. Such colleges and universities as the University of Alabama, Boston University, Brandeis University (Boston, MA), University of California at Berkeley, Claremont McKenna College (Claremont, CA), Dartmouth College (Hanover, NH), Emory University (Atlanta, GA), Georgetown University (Washington, DC), Ithaca College (Ithaca, NY), University of Kansas, Purdue University (West Lafayette, IN), Princeton University (Princeton, NJ), Vanderbilt University (Nashville, TN), and Yale University (New Haven, CT) reacted to the University of Missouri events, and a majority of these institutions instituted new policies and programs to improve their diversity inclusion initiatives and race relations (*USA TODAY* February 26, 2016).

Supreme Court Decision on Affirmative Action

Ironically with a majority of the race-relations issues focused on so many local, city, and state issues from 2013 to 2016, perhaps the most significant issue that affected race relations on college campuses was the Supreme Court decision on affirmative action during the summer of 2016. On June 23, 2016, in a 4–3 Supreme Court decision, the University of Texas admissions policy taking race into consideration for admissions was found constitutional (CNN June 23, 2016).

This case actually began in 2008 when lead plaintiff Abigail Fisher, a white Caucasian, European American women from Texas, was denied admission to the university. She felt that the university discriminated against her because of her race.

Yet, after much analysis of the continuing admissions obligation to meet the legal test of strict scrutiny by periodically reevaluating the admissions program's constitutionality and by tailoring its approach to ensure that race played no greater role than necessary to meet its compelling interests, the University of Texas was in compliance (Jaschik 2016). Not surprisingly, many leaders of higher education, including college and university presidents, praised the ruling.

For example, Michael V. Drake, president of the Ohio State University, said that Ohio State, like Texas, did consider race and ethnicity but as one factor among many. He further stated: "We are looking for the very best, looking at a variety of factors. This decision affirms the real value of inclusion in a society like ours—particularly in bringing people from traditionally marginalized groups into our system" (Jaschik 2016).

University of Maryland

Of all the varying national race-relations incidents that have happened in recent years, perhaps the University of Maryland tragedy, in which a black

African American male college student visiting University of Maryland was stabbed and killed by a white Caucasian, European American male, will have more of a long-term negative effect on race relations on college campuses than the others. The reason is that it appeared to be a direct hate crime—one college student killing another college student simply because of his race.

According to *Inside Higher Ed* reporter Jeremy Bauer-Wolf (2017), Richard Collins III, a student at Bowie State University and a recently commissioned U.S. Army second lieutenant, was stabbed to death on May 20, 2017, just days before his graduation. The Bowie State senior was visiting the University of Maryland at College Park's campus, waiting outside for an Uber early Saturday morning when a suspect, whom witnesses described as intoxicated, approached Collins and told him to "step left, step left, if you know what's best for you" (Bauer-Wolf 2017). The man then stabbed Collins in the chest, police said.

A University of Maryland student, Sean Christopher Urbanski, was later arrested and charged with first-degree murder. Police and university officials later announced that the slaying may have been racially motivated, as Urbanski was a member of a Facebook group called "Alt-Reich Nation," where people shared racist memes. The Federal Bureau of Investigation (FBI) filed this investigation as a hate crime (Bauer-Wolf 2017).

Responses from the University of Maryland Black Student Union president and a student representative of ProtectUMD, a coalition representing minority groups on campus, were as follows:

> They (University of Maryland's administration) have not been taking this far enough. They may have goals and policies, but those are not clear to students. So I personally I think a lot more needs to be done.
> —Adams, University of Maryland Black Student
> Union president

> Collins' death was the last straw in a series of incidents over the last year. Right now, students are treading carefully considering the campus sensitivity. This wasn't white supremacist posters being hung up, or an email tinged with racism that was forwarded around (both of which have occurred at Maryland)—someone lost his life. But for the future, the students want to plan more town halls with administration and see the hiring of a new chief diversity officer, a vacant position.
> —Ashley Vasquez, student representative of Protect UMD, a
> coalition representing minority groups on campus

(Bauer-Wolf 2017)

This University of Maryland race-relations incident is just in its first phase of investigation at the writing of this book, yet the social and cultural impact of this particular race-relations incident has potentially far-reaching consequences in the future on all college campuses across the United States primarily because it was a one-on-one confrontation between two college students of different racial backgrounds that ended in the death of a high-achieving, prestigious African American male. This tragic outcome should simply not happen particularly now in this day and time in our United States of America.

The Shooting of Dallas Police Officers

On July 7, 2016, five Dallas police officers were shot and killed, nine other officers wounded, and two civilians injured in Downtown Dallas, Texas, in an ambush-style attack in which the assailant, Micah Xavier Johnson, an African American military veteran who served in Afghanistan, told police negotiators that he was upset about the recent police shootings, as well as issues with Black Lives Matter, so that's why he retaliated against the local Dallas police officers. He was also angry at white people and said that he wanted to kill white people, especially white officers. This shooting occurred at the end of peaceful protests by residents in Dallas against the police killings of Alton Sterling in Baton Rouge, Louisiana, and Philando Castile in Falcon Heights, Minnesota—two black men (*New York Times* July 8, 2016).

Following the shooting, Micah Xavier Johnson ran inside a building on the campus of El Centro College. Dallas police followed him there, and a standoff ensued. After some two hours of failed negotiations, Dallas police chief David Brown decided to use their bomb-disposal remote-control vehicle (bomb robot) and place a device on its extension to detonate where Micah Xavier Johnson was located in the building. Once the bomb robot reached its destination, it was detonated, and Micah Xavier Johnson was killed.

Searching Johnson's home the following day, detectives found bomb-making materials, ballistic vests, rifles, ammunition, and a personal journal of combat tactics. Detectives also concluded that the gunman had no direct ties to any protest or political group (Harris and Ladler 2016). Overall, this police shooting was, at that time, the deadliest incident for U.S. law enforcement since the September 11 attacks.

The day after this tragic event, a special interfaith vigil attracted hundreds of people to Thanksgiving Square in downtown Dallas, where Dallas mayor Mike Rawlings and regional faith leaders led prayers for the officers involved in the shooting and for everyone affected by it (WFAA July 11, 2016). A few days later, former president George W. Bush, a Texan, and President Obama spoke at the interfaith memorial and praised the Dallas police as heroes and called the killings "an act not just of demented violence but of racial hatred" (Harris and Landler, 2016).

The Election of Donald Trump as the 45th U.S. President

One of the most unexpected political events of 2016 was the election of Republican candidate Donald Trump as president of the United States. Even during the presidential primaries for each political party, Donald Trump seemed to be a long shot to win the nomination based upon how he presented himself to the media, the general public, and his loyal followers. He openly expressed strong opinions about particular groups of minority people—including Latinos and LGBT community members. He openly expressed unvarnished dislike for certain foreign countries. Most importantly, he voiced his opinion on all types of politically, socially, and racially sensitive topics directly through his social media tweets on Twitter.

Then the unthinkable happened. Donald Trump not only won the Republican nomination for president in the summer of 2016 but also beat the Democratic candidate—Hillary Clinton—for the presidency of the United States in the fall of 2016. Hillary was the favorite and perceived by the majority to be the best person to hold the office. Yet during election night, key votes in key states propelled Donald Trump to victory over Hillary Clinton, not in the popular vote but in the critical Electoral College vote. The country woke up the next day in shock.

Trump, a person widely seen as the most sexist, biased, homophobic, and racist political candidate in the history of the United States by voters nationwide and a vast majority of mainstream media and political experts, throughout the primaries and the months leading to the election, was president. He'd won regardless of all the bad media commentary, protests, debates, and fights across the United States inspired by his campaign comments and "promises" to his largely white rural low-income followers. In the months to come, events organized by his supporters included Nazi rallies and other white supremacist public gatherings—groups that had been for decades forced into remission and hiding by legislation, laws, and public opinion in the United States. Legislation was introduced to reduce or completely remove benefits and programs to assist and laws to protect minorities and the LGBTQ community, as well as women, children, and the elderly. Protests against and clashes with his supporters became regular occurrences, and sometimes violent and even deadly. A dark and shocking new chapter in U.S. history had begun. And it would be a true test of democracy.

Conclusion

In the United States and in a majority of countries around the world, those who go to college find great strength and character in their studies, realizing that educational experience is the best investment that an individual can make for herself or himself or that parents can make for their child. The college experience provides an individual unlimited possibilities not only for a very successful career but also for a lifetime of critical thinking; well-informed, fair, and balanced decision making; and, yes, effective action to make their world—whether that be locally, statewide, nationally, or even more—a better, kinder, more justice-driven place.

The college experience is a time in which students usually discover their direction in life—academically, professionally, personally, and culturally. College students are usually totally immersed in learning about things they might otherwise have never experienced, considered, or ever knew existed. But, today, the average college student is not as uninvolved in society as once was the case. Today, more than ever, national news and events affect the lives of college students in a much more significant way. With all the media outlets (traditional TV, cable, Internet, software apps) and the advent of social media (texting, Facebook, Snapchat, Twitter, and Instagram), college students have become more aware and influenced by national events that relate to them on a personal, social, cultural, racial, and ethnic level than ever before.

Considering my own college experience during the 1970s and 1980s, compared to the college experience of my children today and my students at East Carolina University, there are glaring differences.

Once I was on campus with all the other students, we were isolated and insulated from the outside world. We didn't have any worries other than our studies and college activities. Conversely, college students today are bombarded, at all hours, daily by all types of local and national news. And many are very much aware of and focused on local, regional, national, and international news, especially political and social developments, including those facets very much seen as unjust and threatening to minorities, be they black, Latino, gay, transgender, female, immigrants, or any other marginalized group.

This is one reason why it is important to acknowledge how such national race-relations events as those triggered by the Trayvon Benjamin Martin trial, the Black Lives Matter movement, the University of Missouri protests, the Supreme Court decision on affirmative action, and the University of Maryland stabbing, along with slaying of church members in Charleston, South Carolina, and the taking down of Confederate memorials in New Orleans can have a significant emotional impact on the lives of contemporary college students. College students are more interconnected, informed, and (ideally) open-minded than ever before, so if there is a major race- or ethnic-relations event in one part of the nation, it is felt and reacted to across the country on campuses.

Race- and ethnic-relations issues can no longer just be quietly discussed among students in the hallways and dorms or ignored. Race- and ethnic-relations issues must be discussed and directly confronted in classes, seminars, and debates on campus. These students are the future of the United States. All colleges and universities in the United States must consistently confront race- and ethnic-relations issues and incidents—including those institutions in sheltered and wealthy communities not directly experiencing and scathed by injustice—to significantly empower college students at all mainstream and nonmainstream universities to become better critical thinkers, more understanding, and better able to develop solutions to all types of race- and ethnic-relations incidents, now and in the future.

CHAPTER TWO

Typical Campus Race and Ethnic Relations

When we address race and ethnic relations in the college/university setting, the specifics differ somewhat from how the average U.S. citizen confronts the topic. Basically, race and ethnic relations refer to the ways in which people of different heritages—races and ethnicities—living together in the same community *behave* toward one another. In other words, for us it raises questions of how college students of different racial and ethnic backgrounds

1. get along with each other daily on campus;
2. live together in dorms and apartments as roommates;
3. eat together at the campus cafeterias and local eateries;
4. attend classes together;
5. participate in social events on campus;
6. attend college parties and bars together;
7. get along with each other as teammates on a college athletic team;
8. participate in student-body organizations and fraternity/sorority activities;
9. compete to receive special honors and recognitions throughout their college years;
10. prepare for graduation; and
11. compete for available job and graduate-school opportunities during the next stage of their development.

College students of all racial and ethnic backgrounds live together and must interact with each other in a confined college/university campus. These relational facets are not, overall, so much different from what they are for adults in their neighborhoods, towns, states, and beyond. But the conversations, education, and problem solving best start with our youths, at colleges and universities, in an environment where critical thinking is at the forefront, as are truth, justice, and honest discussion and debate about those ideals.

Increased Diversity on College Campuses

For a majority of universities and colleges, increasing the number of minorities and expanding the percentage of diverse student populations is part of the overall mission of mainstream institutions across the United States. As each year passes, the overall percentage of minority and international students steadily increases. Although some universities and colleges do a better job in recruiting minority and international students than others, the overall trend and projections for public and private universities and colleges is that they are becoming more diverse than ever before, which is a reflection of our "melting pot" nation itself. In some cases, universities and colleges are experiencing a great unexpected growth of minority and international students.

For many, preparing for the increased diversity of their student population continues to be a major institutional challenge. One of the ways to prepare a university and college for increased diversity is to develop new programming and resources for minority- and diversity-related issues. New programming and resources include such activities as developing a minority student center on campus; providing new curriculum focus on minority-related issues; institutionalizing a diversity and inclusive training program for all staff, administrators, and faculty; hiring more minority staff, administrators, and faculty; and highlighting more minority- and diversity-related events regularly on campus throughout the academic year.

Although the increase in minority, international, and diversity initiatives are important for a majority of mainstream public and private universities, it is still one of many priorities in which they are struggling to fully invest resources, time, and commitment. Because universities and colleges across the country have so many new priorities to address, including shrinking operational budgets, mandates to increase extramural funding, increased competition from other institutions for students, and meeting mandates to operate more efficiently, the importance and significance of investing institutional resources to new diversity initiatives have diminished, and they have been pushed back on that list. Some would say that today's diversity and inclusion initiatives are simply "window dressing" or "just for show" for many universities and colleges, because many are barely adhering to the federal guidelines for increasing minority enrollments and lack the commitment to long-term funding for diversity initiatives.

Some of the latest concerns regarding the lack of long-term commitment to minority, diversity, and inclusion initiatives can be seen in a national survey among college and university presidents (Lederman and Jaschik 2016). Some of the results of this national survey are quite startling.

Results of the Gallup poll, featured on the *Inside Higher Ed* website, at https://www.insidehighered.com.news/survey/race-campus-nontradtional-leaders-rising-confidence-survey-presidents, show most university and college leaders praised their own institution but were far less positive about colleges and universities overall:

- At their own institutions in 2016, only 20 percent said race relations were excellent; 64 percent said race relations were good, 16 percent said race relations were fair, and 1 percent called them poor.
- When asked to rate race relations on college and university campuses nationwide, the same respondents rated 0 percent excellent, 24 percent good, 65 percent fair, and 10 percent poor.

Overview

The national survey of college and university presidents (Lederman and Jaschik 2016) found that a majority believed that their institutions are doing and have been doing a great job in minority- and diversity-related initiatives. *Inside Higher Ed*'s sixth annual survey aimed to understand how these leaders perceive and address the challenges facing postsecondary institutions in the United States and explored the following questions:

- How do presidents assess the state of race relations on their own campuses and on campuses nationwide?
- Do presidents believe demands made by those protesting the treatment of racial minorities on college campuses last fall were reasonable? Did some of those protestors' actions violate principles of free speech and academic freedom?
- Should college presidents mainly be selected from those with academic careers, or are business and managerial skills more important in light of the financial challenges colleges are facing?
- How concerned are presidents about legislation that would overturn campus bans on guns?
- How do presidents rate President Obama's treatment of higher education?
- What do presidents think of the new, scaled-down version of the college scorecard?
- Are presidents confident in the sustainability of their institution's financial model in the next 5 to 10 years?

Methodology

The procedure for answering these questions involved conducting a quantitative-survey research study that Gallup completed on behalf of *Inside Higher Ed*. To accomplish this objective, Gallup sent e-mail invitations to 3,046 college and university presidents, with regular reminders sent throughout the January 7–February 2, 2016, field period. Gallup collected 727 completed web interviews, yielding a 24 percent response rate. Additionally, as an incentive for participation, *Inside Higher Ed* offered respondents a chance to win one of ten $100 gift-card prizes (*Inside Higher Ed* 2016, 9).

Gallup education consultants developed the questionnaire in collaboration with *Inside Higher Ed*. The sample did not include specialty colleges, namely Bible colleges and seminaries, or institutions with enrollments under 500. Each institution is represented only once in the sample (*Inside Higher Ed* 2016, 9).

Respondents represented 371 public institutions, 304 private institutions, and 30 institutions from the for-profit sector. Gallup weighted the sample based on institutional control (public or private nonprofit), four-year or two-year degree offerings, student enrollment, and geographical region. Therefore, *Inside Higher Ed* (2016) stated that the weighted sample results represented the views of presidents at colleges and universities nationwide (*Inside Higher Ed* 2016, 9).

Findings

Of all the questions and issues examined from this survey of presidents of colleges and universities, the most intriguing findings were in the area of race relations. In the 2015–2016 academic year, protests about the discriminatory treatment of racial and minority students occurred at a number of college campuses across the United States. These findings bring attention to the significance of race relations on college campuses.

Race-Relations Findings #1

When college/university presidents were asked, "Generally speaking, would you say the state of race relations on your campus is excellent, good, fair or poor?" most presidents described race relations on their campus in positive terms, with 20 percent saying they are "excellent" and 64 percent saying they are "good." *Inside Higher Ed* (2016) stated that this is a far more positive assessment than they give to race relations on campuses throughout the country: only 24 percent said they are good;

most, 65 percent, said they are fair; and 10 percent described them as poor. This pattern of college leaders viewing situations on their own campuses much more positively than in higher education at large has been evident in other *Inside Higher Ed* surveys (*Inside Higher Ed* 2016, 11).

Race-Relations Findings #2

When college/university presidents were asked, "Generally speaking, would you say the state of race relations on college and university campuses in this country is better, about the same, or worse than it was five years ago?" the majority of college presidents, 54 percent, said that they do not believe that race relations have changed on college campuses in this country over the last five years. But twice as many believe race relations have gotten worse (31 percent) versus having gotten better (15 percent) (*Inside Higher Ed* 2016, 11).

Race-Relations Findings #3

When college/university presidents were asked to respond to the statement "I was surprised by the number and intensity of campus protests on racial issues in the fall of 2015," 42 percent indicated they were surprised by the number and intensity of protests, while 27 percent said they were not (*Inside Higher Ed* 2016, 12). Additionally, a slightly higher percentage (45 percent) of college presidents at public universities were surprised by the number and intensity of protests versus college presidents at private nonprofit universities (41 percent) (*Inside Higher Ed* 2016, 13).

Race-Relations Findings #4

When college/university presidents were asked to respond to the statement "The demands made by the student groups in the protests were reasonable," presidents tilted toward being more unsympathetic than sympathetic to the protesters' demands and actions: 22 percent strongly agreed or agreed that the protesters' demands were reasonable while 38 percent strongly disagreed or disagreed; 40 percent were neutral (*Inside Higher Ed* 2016, 13). Moreover, there was a slightly higher percentage (42 percent) of college and university presidents at private nonprofit institutions who were less sympathetic of the demands made by the student groups in their protests versus college/ university presidents at public universities (34 percent) (*Inside Higher Ed* 2016, 13).

Race-Relations Findings #5

When college/university presidents were asked to respond to the statement, "I am concerned that some of the students' demands and actions in the recent protests violated principles of free speech and academic freedom," a majority, 54 percent, strongly agree or agree. They were concerned that some of the students' demands and actions violated principles of free speech and academic freedom; 23 percent strongly disagree or disagree. Concerns about First Amendment violations were exemplified by protestors' attempt to block media photographers from taking pictures of protests (*Inside Higher Ed* 2016, 12).

Race-Relations Findings #6 and #7

When college/university presidents were asked to respond to the statement "I anticipate more protests on racial issues in 2016 in higher education generally," it was not surprising that the majority, 66 percent, strongly agreed or agreed they expected to see more protests on racial issues in higher education this year. Both public (76 percent) and private nonprofit (75 percent) college/university presidents strongly agreed or agreed they expected to see more protests in higher education.

Yet very few college/university presidents expect those protests to occur on their own campus—just 9 percent strongly agreed or agreed they anticipated racial protests at their college in 2016 (*Inside Higher Ed* 2016, 12). There was virtually no difference between public (10 percent) and private nonprofit (9 percent) college/university presidents who strongly agreed or agreed they anticipated racial protests at their college in 2016 (*Inside Higher Ed* 2016, 13).

Race-Relations Findings #8

When college/university presidents were asked to respond to the statement "I believe my campus does a good job of serving minority students," it was also not surprising that a majority, 74 percent, strongly agreed or agreed, while 5 percent strongly disagreed or disagreed. A slightly higher percentage (77 percent) of private nonprofit college/university presidents strongly agreed or agreed versus 72 percent of public college/university presidents (*Inside Higher Ed* 2016, 14).

Race-Relations Findings #9

Finally, when college/university presidents were asked to respond to the statement "I am making an effort to be more visible on my campus in response to what occurred during the racial protests last fall," 50 percent of presidents strongly agreed or agreed they are making more of an effort to be visible on campus in response to what occurred during the protests; 21 percent strongly disagreed or disagreed. A slightly higher percentage (56 percent) of public college/university presidents felt they are making an effort to be more visible on campus than private nonprofit (48 percent) college/university presidents. In fact, *Inside Higher Ed* (2016) stated one outcome of the recent wave of protests is that presidents seem inclined to work harder to interact with students on campus, so they can hear their concerns and engage with them directly (*Inside Higher Ed* 2016, 12).

Race-Relations Findings: Summary

Although this 2016 *Inside Higher Ed* survey of college and university presidents investigated a number of other additional issues as they relate to higher education, the race-relations findings were most significant because they uncovered the disconnect and lack of awareness that many college and university presidents have concerning race relations on college campuses. The key race-relations findings from this survey were as follows:

- College and university presidents took a generally positive view of race relations on their own campuses, with 84 percent describing them as excellent or good.
- Presidents were not inclined to agree that the protesters' demands were reasonable. They also said they were concerned some of the protesters' actions and behaviors violated principles of free speech and academic freedom.
- Campus leaders were much less positive about the state of race relations at colleges nationwide—24 percent said they are excellent or good, down significantly from 2015.
- More presidents were surprised by the number and intensity of protests on racial issues on college campuses in 2015.
- Finally, college and university presidents realize that they have to be more visible and interact more with their diverse student population because it's an effective strategy to show students that the top leadership at their college and university cares for all students.

My Undergraduate College Years (1976–80)

I would be remiss here if I did not include my own personal experiences in college as an undergraduate, mainly because I attended college during the 1970s and this was a period in which race and ethnic relations were highly confrontational, more discriminatory, more visible, and more uncertain, and that affects my teaching for this course. Although a majority of colleges and universities in the United States began to fully implement their affirmative-action recruitment and retention initiatives to ensure a certain small percentage of minority students enrolled each academic year, the student population at mainstream public and private colleges and universities were, in the 1970s, slowly getting used to that new arrangement and the attendant increase of minority and international students on campuses across the country.

During my college years at Miami University in Ohio and Central State University in Ohio, I experienced two completely different types of racial and ethnic relations with college classmates. Miami University is a mid-American, mainstream university consisting of over 20,000 students, with a minority student population of approximately less than 2 percent from 1976 to 1980. I attended Miami University from 1976 through 1980 as an undergraduate.

At the time, it seemed like the total African American student population was less than one percent. I did not regularly see other blacks on campus. Although that did not matter overall to me during my time at Miami University, on occasion, I did wonder why there were so few individuals like myself on campus. It was a rarity to have another African American student in my class. So I was an oddity and sometimes drew stares.

More importantly, throughout my years at MU, I never had a major problem interacting daily with a predominantly white, Caucasian, Euro-American student population. My roommates and best friends were white, and all of us adjusted and learned about our cultural, racial, and ethnic differences. It was that daily interaction and engagement with individuals who were different from me racially, ethnically, economically, politically, and even musically that moved me to adjust my perspectives and opinions about other people and hopefully moved them likewise in a positive way to change their perspective and opinions about African Americans and other people of color.

From the fall of 1977 to spring of 1978, I attended Central State University—a historically black college with a student population of predominately African Americans and Africans. I transferred to Central State University from Miami University primarily because it was located in my hometown of Wilberforce, and I could live with my parents, saving my parents' lots of money, which they were helping pay for my college education. Also, I was able to work a couple of nightly jobs that almost paid for my entire Central State University annual tuition.

Attending Central State University, I was part of the majority student population, and it definitely felt good because I was no longer stared at by other students and I could fit easily into any classroom situation. My relations with other students at Central State University were similar to friends and associates I'd know while growing up in my predominantly black, African American neighborhood of Wilberforce—the Valley—where we all knew each other and we all grew up attending grade school, middle school, and high school together. I shared a lot of common views and interests with my fellow students at Central State University.

Nonetheless, after one year at Central State University, I transferred back to Miami University. Why? After much soul-searching, I really wanted to attend college away from my hometown and experience new things and new people, who most often there happened to be of a different race. Also, I transferred back to Miami University because Central State University did not offer students a major in the field of anthropology—a discipline I instantly fell in love with and wanted to major in.

Once I returned to Miami University, I adjusted back to the racial and ethnic differences and met new classmates and roommates who were of a different racial background. My race relations with white, Caucasian, Euro-American students dramatically improved once I made the MU football team as a walk-on. It seemed sports were the arena where I was most embraced for what I could do, with little to no attention to race.

On the football team, race-relations matters became less of an issue because everyone treated each other with respect, on and off the field. My teammates and I bonded, going through all the practices, drills, sacrifices, and games that all players had to endure to be a true team player and part of a winning team. Along with my teammates, all of my coaches, particularly the head coach, Tom Reed, treated me with respect as a football player and a college student, who happened to be a small, black, African American youth, contributing to the success of Miami University's football team.

I can assure that my race- and ethnic-relations experience at Miami University during the 1970s and 1980s—I also attended graduate school at Miami University from 1981 to 1983—was very positive, enriching, nondiscriminatory, and nonracist. Yes, there were definitely times when white, Euro-American students appeared uncomfortable with my presence at certain fraternity and campus events, but I did not experience blatant discriminatory or racial acts directed at me.

Some of my hometown friends would say that was a rarity. And I do not doubt that some of my peers at the time had a completely different, negative experience in college and other communities.

Race Relations on College Campuses: 1990s

My experiences in college were not met with blatant discrimination and racism, but I heard and knew that some of my African American friends had the exact opposite experience compared to mine. They experienced rejection and denial when trying to join groups and organizations on their campuses. They were disliked by other students, who felt that they had been given a free ride to college just because they were black. They were told that they were "not good enough" to attend their detractors' mainstream, high-level, or elite universities.

Indeed, as more and more students of color started to share their individual college experiences with others, the sheer number of blatant discriminatory and racist actions on college campuses became visibly apparent and no longer undeniable. In the *Journal of Blacks in Higher Education*, an article titled "Race Relations on Campus" (1993) identified more than 35 racial incidents on college campuses. Those included being told to "go home" to Africa, the appearance of Ku Klux Klan flyers on campus, the repeated use of racial slurs, and violence. Here are a few examples at U.S. colleges in the 1990s:

- Central Missouri University: Four black students at Central Missouri University found threatening notes tacked to their dormitory doors. The notes included a warning to refrain from civil rights protests and urged the students to "go home" to Africa.

- Heidelberg College: Racial slurs were found on the dormitory door of a black student at Heildelberg College in Tiffin, Ohio. The incident prompted school administrators to organize a protest march against racism.

- Indiana University: Several racial incidents plagued the campus of Indiana University in Bloomington, which has approximately 1,400 black students or 4 percent of the total student body: (1) A white student was accused of repeatedly telling his black lab partner to "go eat watermelon." (2) Racist fliers recruiting members for the Ku Klux Klan were posted on campus. One flier said, "A brain is a terrible thing to waste, that's why niggers don't have any." (3) White students driving by threw trash at a black student walking on campus while yelling racial slurs at her. (4) The head of the Black Student Advisory Council reported that she had been called "nigger" so many times that "When I first got here, I thought it was my middle name."

- Miami University: A black student at Miami University of Ohio, who was running for the student-government position of vice president of minority affairs, found one of his campaign fliers outside his dormitory room in a puddle of urine. Earlier, he'd found a racial slur scrawled on his dorm door. The student went on to win the election with 75 percent of the vote.

- Texas Tech University: At a fraternity party at Texas Tech University in Lubbock, partygoers darkened their skin, put on Afro wigs, and engaged in derogatory behavior against blacks.

- University of Massachusetts: Three incidents at the Amherst campus of the University of Massachusetts heightened racial tensions at the school. In one incident, black and white students squared off in a fight after a dormitory dance. In a second case, a group of seven or eight black males knocked a white student off his bicycle. Later, another white student was beaten by four blacks as he left his dormitory. Campus police investigated all incidents as possibly racially motivated. ("Race Relations on Campus," 1993)

These racial incidents during the early 1990s reflect the frustrating adjustments and tension among college students at mainstream universities and colleges with the increased number of African American students and students of color. These racial incidents, seen throughout various regions of the United States, indicate that no region of our country was exempt and that race relations among college students still had to mature. These racial incidents may have represented a small number of students overtly against African American students and students of color. But the overall impression was hard-hitting, even where they did not reflect the actions and perspectives of the student body overall.

Race Relations on College Campuses: Present Day

As a college professor for 30 years, I have seen and taught a wide variety of students from one university to another. Throughout these years, I have also seen how students get along—or do not—with each other. When they do get along with each other, it gives me faith that our society has come a long way regarding race relations. When they do not, it saddens me. This is 2018. Race relations should be far better than what I see in my classes, where students of different racial and ethnic backgrounds seldom speak to each other. Why is that?

In an article from *Inside Higher Ed* titled "Campuses See Flurry of Racist Incidents and Protests against Racism," Jaschik (2016) compiled a list of racist incidents on college campuses across the United States. From the University of North Dakota, San Jose University, Ohio University, American University, and Temple University, there were discriminatory and racist incidents directed at particular minority student populations: students posted photographs of themselves in blackface to social media (University of North Dakota); graffiti with swastikas and hateful language was found on dormitory walls (San Jose University); bananas were thrown at black women (American University); the words "Build the Wall" were written in a free-speech area of campus (Ohio University); and resentment was directed at members of the Black Student Union when they declined to stand during the national anthem at the university's football game (Temple University) (Jaschik, 2016; published in *Inside Higher Ed*, 1–8).

These incidents and others like them indicate that even in our present day, our colleges and universities are still struggling with race- and ethnic-relations issues. In Connecticut, in late 2017, a white University of Hartford student was arrested after she boasted on Facebook that she, across weeks, had been wiping bodily fluids and soiled tampons on her black roommate's toothbrush, other personal care items, and accessories in an attempt to sicken and poison her. The roommate had indeed been getting sick, not knowing why.

Whether it is a college or university in the Midwest, on the East coast, in the Southeast, or Northwest, racist incidents—and protests against racism— are increasing, whether we want to recognize and deal with them or not. At some point, we all (students, administrators, faculty, staff, and community members) must collectively confront these issues directly; otherwise, they will continue to escalate.

And the time for that confrontation is now.

Race Relations, Multiracial Students, and Interracial Dating

One of the most overlooked race- and ethnic-relations issues on college campuses today is the significantly increased number of students who classify themselves as multiracial/biracial and interracially dating. Racial groups in the United States have never been absolutely isolated from one another, and once these individual racial groups share the same community, such as a college campus, there is a good chance there will be interracial dating, especially among those who classify themselves as multiracial/biracial.

Data on race have been collected since the first U.S. decennial census in 1790, but it was not until the 2000 census that the census allowed individuals to self-identify with more than one race. The new category, "Two or more races," refers to people who indicate that their heritage is more than one of the six single-race categories. These individuals are referred to as the "Two or more races population" or as persons who reported "more than one race." Today, they are also commonly referred to as "multiracials."

"Multiracial" is also defined as follows:

- Made up of, involving, or acting on behalf of various races
- Having ancestors of several or various races
- People whose ancestries come from multiple races (Root 1996)

Other terms used similarly to "multiracial" are "biracial" and "transracial."

According to the U.S. Department of Commerce's Bureau of Census 2000 report, "the U.S. population was 281.4 million on April 1, 2000 and from that total 6.8 million or 2.4 percent identified themselves as more than one race or multiracial" (U.S. Department of Commerce, United States Census 2000, 2001). This Bureau of Census 2000 report was very unique and the first of its type, primarily because respondents were given the option of selecting one or more categories to indicate their racial identities.

The Bureau of Census 2000 question on race included not only 15 separate response categories but also three areas where respondents could write in a more specific race. The write-in answers and the response categories were combined to create the five standard Office of Management and Budget race categories plus the U.S. Census Bureau category of "some other race." The six categories were as follows:

- White
- Black or African American
- Asian
- American Indian and Alaska Native
- Native Hawaiian or Other Pacific Islander
- Some other race

For example, the U.S. Census Bureau stated that "respondents who reported they were 'White and American Indian and Alaska Native and Asian' or 'White and Black or African American' were included in the Two or more races category" (U.S. Department of Commerce, United States Census 2000, 2001).

When the U.S. Census data on "multiracials" or "Two or more" racial category were further analyzed, an overwhelming majority (93 percent) reported exactly two races, 6 percent reported three races, and 1 percent reported four or more races. Table 2.1 shows the number and percentage of respondents to the 2000 U.S. census by number of races reported.

As the numbers of multiracials have continued to increase in the United States, researchers have also noticed a number of interesting trends among this group. According to Schmitt (2001), "their growth is a reflection of the changing populational patterns within our society and a greater acceptance of the term 'multiracial.'" In the 2000 census, those individuals who preferred to check more than one race on the census form and to embrace multiracialism tended to be younger than 18 (Schmitt 2001).

The new cultural trend of acknowledging and recognizing one's multiracial heritage was also influenced, of course, by the United States' election of its first multiracial president—Barack Obama. Initially, the country became aware of Obama's multiracial heritage when he was a Democratic presidential candidate. In fact, Obama published two best-selling books that highlighted his multiracial background, which not only helped American voters to better understand his background and political perspective, but also enabled the American people to feel comfortable with a potential president with multiracial roots. President Obama's two-term presidency from 2008 to 2016 had another subtle influence on the awareness of multiracials in America, too.

Table 2.1   Total Population by Number of Races Reported, 2000

Number of Races	Number	Percentage of Total Population	Percentage of Total Two or More Races Population
Total Population	281,421,906	100.0	N/A
One race	274,595,678	97.6	N/A
Two or more races	6,826,228	2.4	100.0
Two races	6,368,075	2.3	93.3
Three races	410,285	0.1	6.0
Four races	38,408	---	0.6
Five races	8,637	---	0.1
Six races	823	---	---

Couple the increasing popular cultural trend of embracing a multiracial label with the fact that much of the fast growth in diversity has been driven by an influx of young immigrants, whose birth rates are higher than those of non-Hispanic whites, and increased interracial dating/marriages, we must recognize that the multiracial population is actually driving the U.S. population growth. As stated previously, nationally the multiracial population comprises approximately 6.8 million Americans, or 2.4 percent of the total population.

A closer examination of the geographical distribution of the U.S. multiracial population reveals another interesting pattern. Specifically, the U.S. Bureau of Census reported that "40 percent lived in the West, 27 percent lived in the South, 18 percent lived in the Northeast, and 15 percent lived in the Midwest" (U.S. Department of Commerce, United States Census 2000, 2001). Moreover, nearly two-thirds of all multiracials lived in just 10 states.

The 10 states with the largest percentage of multiracials in 2000 were California, New York, Texas, Florida, Hawaii, Illinois, New Jersey, Washington, Michigan, and Ohio. Combined, these states accounted for 64 percent of the total multiracial population (U.S. Department of Commerce, United States Census 2000, 2001).

The 2000 U.S. Bureau of Census demographers, upon further analysis, stated that "three states had Two or more races population greater than 500,000 and they were California (greater than one million), New York (590,000) and Texas (515,000)" (U.S. Department of Commerce, United States Census 2000, 2001). These three states accounted for 40 percent of the total "Two or more races" population.

The 2000 U.S. Bureau of Census also reported that "states with lower per-centages of Two or more races (1.0 percent or less) were Alabama, Maine, Mississippi, South Carolina and West Virginia" (U.S. Department of Com-merce, United States Census 2000, 2001, 3). These states were expected to have lower numbers of multiracials.

The 2000 U.S. Bureau of Census report showed similar trends for multira-cial populations in counties and cities across the United States. Multiracials were found in higher percentages in the West and Southwest counties and cities of the United States (U.S. Department of Commerce, United States Census 2000, 2001).

Finally, the multiracial population is also younger than other racial popu-lations in the United States. Specifically, the U.S. Bureau of Census reported that "42 percent of the population identified themselves as Two or more races and only 25 percent reported one race" (U.S. Department of Commerce, United States Census 2000, 2001, 9).

Regarding interracial relationships, dating, and marriages, there has been an increase among multiracials and nonmultiracials. What is happening here is that the rates of interracial relationships and intermarriages have increased dramatically, and the strict social boundaries against intermarriage between racial groups are eroding. Intermarriage between members of two given eth-nic groups tends to increase when the degree of social distance (i.e., occupa-tional, educational, and residential) between them declines. Rising rates of intermarriage between groups indicate the acceptance of one another as social equals (DaCosta 2007). Once established, interracial relationships and marriages tend to further erode salient boundaries between groups. When that happens, ethnicity becomes largely a symbolic identification, chosen rather than ascribed, and relatively inconsequential in one's daily life.

For example, Asians and Latinos in the United States have fairly high rates of out-marriage (compared to African Americans). Almost 30 percent of Asians (27.2 percent) and Latinos (28.4 percent) out-marry, while only 10.2 percent of blacks do. Therefore, rising rates of multiracial groupings also indicate the blending and fading of some traditional racial group boundaries, which are also reflective of the college student population throughout the United States.

Race Relations and Diversity Initiatives

Race and ethnic relations, along with diversity initiatives, are part of the foundations of today's colleges and universities. When diversity initiatives are truly enacted at all levels within a college/university system, colleges and university campuses tend to excel in a wide variety of ways—academically, socially, culturally, athletically, and institutionally.

There are three major themes that emerge from all the research studies focused on diversity and higher education. Hurtado et al. (2003) summarize these three major themes as follows:

1. Diverse settings work—college students educated in diverse settings will more than likely live and work in racially and ethnically diverse environments after they graduate.
2. Race and ethnic colleges courses work—college students who took race and ethnic courses and who interacted with diverse peers will more than likely be prepared for life in an increasingly complex and diverse society; and
3. More diverse study body works—college students who go to college with a more diverse student body will improve their learning environment.

Although the data consistently show that educational institutions will greatly benefit from the full implementation of diversity initiatives, there are still a number of colleges/universities that have fallen short in reaching this objective.

According to the Association of American Colleges and Universities (AAC&U) in their initiative "Making Excellence Inclusive" (Milem et al. 2005) and in one of their commissioned reports titled "Making Diversity Work on Campus: A Research-Based Perspective," there are several ways in which presidents and chancellors of universities and colleges can better understand their campus racial climate. Paying attention to the broader issues on college campuses consists of recognizing these six major factors: external forces, compositional diversity, historical legacy of inclusion or exclusion, the psychological climate, the behavioral climate, and organizational/structural diversity.

The six major factors can be explained more specifically as follows:

1. External forces: governmental policy programs and initiatives as well as sociohistorical factors. Examples include state and federal policy regarding affirmative action and events in the larger society that relate to the way in which people view and experience racial diversity.
2. Compositional diversity: numerical and proportional representation of various racial and ethnic groups on a campus.
3. Historical legacy of inclusion or exclusion: historical vestiges of segregated schools and colleges, which continue to affect the climate for racial and ethnic diversity on college campuses.
4. Psychological climate: views held by individuals about intergroup relations as well as institutional responses to diversity, perceptions of discrimination or racial conflict, and attitudes held toward individuals from different racial and ethnic backgrounds.

5. Behavioral climate: status of social interaction on campus, the nature of interactions between and among individuals from different racial and ethnic backgrounds, and the quality of intergroup relations.
6. Organizational/structural diversity: in the curriculum; campus decision-making practices related to budget allocations, reward structures, hiring practices, admissions practices, tenure decisions; and other important structures and processes that guide the day-to-day business of our campuses.

To better illustrate how these six factors influence campus racial climate, figure 2.1 shows their interrelationship.

Perhaps of the six factors highlighted in figure 2.1 regarding a college's/university's racial climate, the behavioral dimension (i.e., social interaction across race/ethnicity) could be the key for developing racial and ethnic harmony on campuses. Thus, the solution to racial and ethnic incidents on college campuses across the United States could be as simple as instituting more social interaction among college students of different racial and ethnic backgrounds.

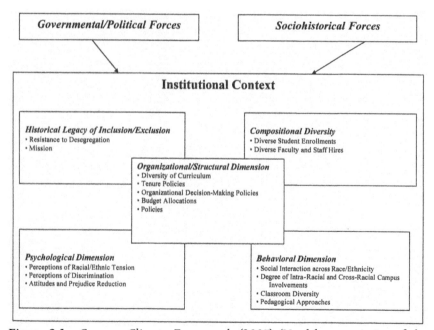

Figure 2.1 Campus Climate Framework (2005) (Used by permission of the Association of American Colleges and Universities)

Conclusion

For a majority of individuals, becoming a college student is a major transition in life and a change of status from high school student to college student. For a majority of individual students, it is the first time in life when he or she is considered an adult, living away from parental authority and making decisions on one's own. Yet with this new lifestyle and extra freedom as a college student, there is also a challenge for many to not only meet new friends and develop new relationships but, perhaps more importantly, interact with individuals who are of a different racial and ethnic backgrounds for the first time. Often, this becomes the starting point and foundation of a student's race- and ethnic-relations pattern.

It is this time period in which many college students start to interact and feel comfortable with peers of other racial and ethnic backgrounds or interact less and feel uncomfortable with students of other racial and ethnic backgrounds. The most critical factor in influencing the typical student's adjustment to college life and his or her interaction with students of other racial and ethnic background is the college or university that the individual student attends (Ancis 2000; Bailey 2000; Bauer-Wolf 2017; Corcoran and Thompson 2004; Dennis 2008; Garam and Brooks 2010; Gonzales 1993; Hurtado, Dey, Gurin and Gurin 2003; Jaschik and Lederman 2016; Kallen 1929; Laird 2005; Lowery et al. 2001; Mark et al. 1997; Martin et al. 2010; McCormack 1995; Pantoja et al. 2014; Pettigrew 1998; Sanday 1970; Santos et al. 2007; Smith et al. 2007; Sydell and Nelson 2000; Torres 2009; Van Laar et al. 1999).

The best college or university experience helps to establish healthy and productive race and ethnic relations on each campus. It is also university policies, the academic curriculum, and the wide variety of social activities on campus for all students that encourage the typical college student to develop a positive pattern for race and ethnic relations. This is why developing a strong, supportive, engaging college experience for all students will dramatically enhance their race and ethnic relations during their years attending college, as well as the rest of their adult lives.

PART 2

Background Issues

CHAPTER THREE

Basic Concepts of Race and Ethnic Relations

Now that we have established that race- and ethnic-relations issues are, and will likely continue to be, at almost every mainstream college and university campus and the fact that many of these issues originate from and reflect national race-relations incidents, let's examine the basic concepts of race and ethnic relations, so all of us are clear about what we are referring to and talking about.

Unfortunately, over the years, society in the United States has purposely avoided speaking of these basic terms and concepts for the purpose of avoiding serious discussion or confrontations among various groups of people. By doing this, however, we—as a society—have further isolated ourselves from the true issues and are filled with misconceptions, misinformation, and misunderstandings of each other.

This chapter aims to highlight the basic terms and concepts associated with race and ethnic relations, as well as to reestablish a new foundation for their importance. The time is now to return these terms and concepts back into our regular discussions and dialogue so that all of us can be a part of the solution rather than continuing the current divisiveness between any and every group in our society.

First, take a step back to review some of the more contemporary cultural-historical issues related to race and ethnic relations in the United States. It was these major national race-relations events involving such renowned civil rights leaders as Dr. Martin Luther King Jr., Johnnie Carr, Barbara Jordan, and Shirley Chisholm that helped pave the way for better justice, voting rights, and opportunity for the underserved, underrepresented, and communities of color throughout the country.

Cultural Historical Review of Race Relations

A Brief Look at the 1950s and 1960s Civil Rights Movement

It was about 10 years ago when the words "civil rights" suddenly returned to national prominence with the election, inauguration, and historical implications of the country's first African American president—Barack Hussein Obama. The jubilation and continuous celebration from the election to the inauguration of the nation's first African American president, along with the first African American First Family, was heartfelt by millions of Americans. Indeed, most political pundits and academic scholars had to admit that the impact of the civil rights movement of the 1950s and 1960s in the United States, particularly for African American communities across the country some 40 years earlier, resulted in one of the most remarkable achievements—the election of Barack Obama as the 44th president of the United States.

Civil Rights

Let us not forget that the words "civil rights" and the "civil rights movement" of the 1950s and 1960s have had a tremendous impact on each and every U.S. citizen. The very term "civil rights" provides every U.S. citizen the protection and privileges of personal power mandated by U.S. laws. Laws guaranteeing civil rights may be written down, derived from custom, or implied. In the United States, civil rights laws are most often written. Examples of civil rights and liberties include the right to privacy, the right to get redress if injured by another, the right of peaceful protest, and the right to a fair investigation or trial if suspected of a crime, as well as more generally based constitutional rights, such as the right to vote, the right to personal freedom, the right to freedom of movement, and the right of equal protection (Bailey 2010, 17). When these civil rights are not granted to a person or an entire group of people, then a civil rights movement can emerge. Such a movement serves to reclaim a groups' civil rights and advocates for new laws to restrict the effects of discrimination. Thus, civil rights and a civil rights movement are terms and actions that apply to every citizen of the United States.

If you ask the average U.S. college student about the civil rights movement, they often refer to the African American civil rights movement of the 1950s and 1960s. Students are surprised when they learn that it was actually begun during the 17th century when blacks and whites protested the institution of slavery. Such individuals as Nat Turner, Sojourner Truth, Frederick Douglass, William Lloyd Garrison, John Brown, and Harriet Tubman became recognized for their pioneering efforts against slavery before the Civil War.

Yet even after the Civil War and the abolishment of slavery, another battle mounted against slavery's legacy—racism and segregation. The landmark Supreme Court decision on May 17, 1954—*Brown v. Board of Education*—outlawing segregation in public schools allowed blacks throughout the United States to attend any public school and receive an equal educational opportunity similar to whites.

The Civil Rights Act of 1964 was passed was passed 10 years later. The Civil Rights Act of 1964 was the most far-reaching and comprehensive law yet ever enacted by Congress in support of racial equality. Here is precisely what the Civil Rights Act of 1964 accomplished:

1. Provided the attorney general additional power to protect citizens against discrimination and segregation in voting, education, and the use of public facilities;
2. Disallowed discrimination in most places of public accommodation;
3. Established a federal community relations service to help individuals and communities solve civil rights problems;
4. Established a federal Equal Employment Opportunity Commission (EEOC);
5. Extended the life of the Commission on Civil Rights; and
6. Eliminated or discontinued funds in the event of a failure to comply with discriminatory practices in federally assisted programs.

Finally, the U.S. Department of Education was authorized to provide technical and financial aid to assist communities in the desegregation of schools. Although some African Americans criticized the act for not going for enough, a vast majority were delighted that a semblance of equality might now be attainable (Bailey 2010).

The primary purpose in highlighting the importance of civil rights and the civil rights movement of the 1950s and 1960s in our discussion of race and ethnic relations for college students today is to show that many of our current programs, policies, concepts, and perceptions still stem from the most recent civil rights years (1950s–1960s) in the United States. Our perceptions related to race and ethnic relations are still framed by and based on a "black and white" comparison.

Yet the civil rights framework of the 1950s and 1960s is not as applicable to the civil rights issues of today—2018 and beyond—for our college student populations, simply because we need to expand its perception, to be inclusive of all types of college students of all various racial, ethnic, religious, spiritual, sexual orientation, physically impaired, mentally impaired, newly immigrant, and military backgrounds. Moreover, the perception of civil rights connects it to legal and judicial issues in accordance with our federal laws thereby forcing academic institutions to adhere to these federally mandated laws, which unfortunately causes more confusion and uncertainty among the average college student regarding what is right or wrong to do when interacting with students of different backgrounds.

Civil rights rulings, laws, and amendments to mandate affirmative action for persons who have not received equal opportunity for higher education are still necessary today. Yet using a civil rights framework to develop and implement diversity programs for mainstream universities does not provide college administrators or faculty with the cultural-competency skills to work with our diverse student body populations; nor does it encourage positive interaction and engagement among our diverse student body populations today. We must find a better framework for evaluating and improving race and ethnic relations on college campuses now and in the future.

Dr. Martin Luther King Jr.

Every year, on the third Monday in January, the United States celebrates the life, achievements, and aims of Dr. Martin Luther King Jr.—a Baptist minister who became one of the most recognized leaders of the African American civil rights movement during the 1950s and 1960s. During his brief life as a civil rights activist, Reverend King led the 1955 bus boycott in Montgomery, Alabama, founded the Southern Christian Leadership conference in 1957, received the Nobel Peace Prize in 1964, and delivered the historic "I Have a Dream" speech on August 28, 1963, on the steps of the Lincoln Memorial, which culminated in the national movement for civil rights for jobs and freedom for all people—not just African Americans.

As John Hope Franklin and Alfred Moss Jr. (1988) explained in *From Slavery to Freedom*, the 1963 demonstrations in which Martin Luther King Jr. and the Southern Christian Leadership joined demonstrators in Birmingham, Alabama, on April 3 to demand fair employment opportunities and desegregation of public facilities were what sparked the national movement and support for their causes. The actions of the Birmingham police in using dogs and high-pressure water hoses on the marchers caused consternation and dismay in many parts of the country where supportive demonstrations were held. During the week of May 18, the Department of Justice noted 43 major and minor demonstrations, 10 of them in northern cities. More such demonstrations were held the following month when Medgar Evers, the leader of the Mississippi chapter of the National Association for the Advancement of Colored People (NAACP), was shot in the back and killed outside his home in Jackson, Mississippi.

There were about as many demonstrations in the North and West as in the South. The emphasis was on increased job opportunities and an end to de facto segregation in housing and education. Neither the president nor Congress could be indifferent to the large-scale demonstrations; nor could

Congress be indifferent to the large-scale demonstrations and the resistance of the white segregationists. In February, before the demonstrations reached their peak, President John F. Kennedy sent a special message to Congress recommending legislation to strengthen voting rights. In June, largely because of events in Birmingham and elsewhere, he submitted a new and broadened civil rights program. In a radio and television speech to the American people during this time, President Kennedy said, "We face ... a moral crisis as a country and as a people. It cannot be met by repressive police action. It cannot be left to increased demonstration in the streets. It cannot be quieted by token moves or talk. It is time to act in the Congress, in your state and local legislative body and, above all, in all of our daily lives" (Franklin and Moses 1988, 445).

As Congress and the nation debated President Kennedy's civil rights program and bill, the March on Washington for Jobs and Freedom occurred. All of the major civil rights groups were joined by many religious, labor, and civil groups in planning and executing the enormous demonstration. The American Jewish Congress, the National Conference of Catholics for Interracial Justice, the National Council of Churches, and the American Federation of Labor-Congress of Industrial Organizations (AFL-CIO) Industrial Union Department were among the strong supporters on the march. On August 28, 1963, more than 250,000 blacks and whites from across the United States staged the largest demonstration in the history of the nation's capital. It was during this demonstration that Dr. Martin Luther King Jr. delivered his "I Have a Dream" speech (Franklin and Moss 1988); numerous other speakers took the stage throughout the day as well.

A few months after that march on Washington and the tragic assassination of President Kennedy, Vice President Lyndon B. Johnson became the 36th president of the United States on November 22, 1963. Johnson was quick to make known his strong support of Kennedy's civil rights program. Five days after he took office, he directed Congress to enact "the earliest possible passage of the civil rights bill" (Franklin and Moss 1988).

The following year, after much debate in Congress and across the nation, the Civil Rights Act of 1964 was passed. The Civil Rights Act of 1964 was the most far-reaching and comprehensive law in support of racial equality ever enacted by Congress. In addition, the U.S. Department of Education was authorized to provide technical and financial aid to assist communities in the desegregation of schools. Although some African Americans criticized the act for not going far enough, a vast majority were delighted that a semblance of equality might now be attainable (Berry and Blassingame 1982).

From April 3, 1963, to June 4, 1965, there were a number of significant political and social events associated with the Civil Rights Act. Bailey (2008) highlights some of the major events during this very critical and tumultuous time period in U.S. history:

1. Dr. Martin Luther King Jr. and the Southern Christian Leadership conference launched a nonviolent protest in Birmingham, Alabama, which was met with much resistance by local authorities and was widely televised.
2. Medgar Evers, an NAACP field secretary, was assassinated on June 12, 1963.
3. President Kennedy introduced civil rights laws to Congress and democrats and republicans worked together from June 19 to November 20, 1963, to finally get committee approval.
4. Dr. Martin Luther King Jr. delivered his "I Have a Dream" speech in front of over 250,000 civil rights demonstrators assembled at the Lincoln Memorial in Washington, DC.
5. Four young African American girls were killed when a bomb went off in the basement of the Sixteenth Street Baptist Church in Birmingham, Alabama.
6. President John F. Kennedy was assassinated in Dallas, Texas (November 22, 1963).
7. Vice President Lyndon B. Johnson then became president of the United States.
8. The House of Representatives approved the civil rights legislation after nine days of debate by a vote of 290–130 on February 10, 1964.
9. President Johnson signed the civil rights bill during a White House ceremony and delivered a nationally televised speech that encouraged the country to abide to the right of freedom for all. Dr. Martin Luther King Jr. and Senator Hubert Humphery were in attendance.
10. Congress passed the Voting Rights Act of 1965, which strengthened voting for the Civil Rights Act from March 17 to August 6, 1965.
11. President Johnson delivered a speech at Howard University (a historically black college in Washington, DC) and phrased the term "equality of results" on June 4, 1965.

So as we continue to celebrate the memory and achievements of Dr. Martin Luther King Jr. every year, we are reminded that Dr. King was one of several million people during this time who believed in and fought for civil rights for all people. When my family and I visited the Martin Luther King Jr. birth home in Atlanta, Georgia, in 1993, we were amazed how "typical" and similar his home was to other African American homes in that area during that time period. The Reverend King was like other Americans. He lived like an average child. He faced the challenges of inequality while growing up. He was not gifted with wealth, power, or any special allowances. But he did have strength and dedication seeking justice and equality for all people. As he matured, there was no doubt that King had a special calling to serve people, speak for justice, and inspire millions to support and defend his cause. In that process, he became the cultural icon for the civil rights movement of the 1950s and 1960s.

Johnnie Carr

Another person who played a significant part in the civil rights movement and worked alongside Dr. Martin Luther King yet is often overlooked by historians, media, and the general public is Mrs. Johnnie Carr. A childhood friend of Rosa Parks, she participated in the Montgomery, Alabama, bus boycott and helped end school segregation and voting discrimination in Alabama. Carr succeeded Dr. Martin Luther King Jr. as president of the Montgomery Improvement Association in 1967 and held the post until her death at the age of 97. It was that newly formed association that spearheaded the boycott of city buses in the Alabama capital in 1955, after Rosa Parks was arrested for refusing to give up her seat to a white person on a crowded bus (Hunter 2008).

Arlam Carr, the son of Johnnie Carr, discussed his mother in an interview with an Associated Press reporter: "One of the things I respect her for is she did not have the rancor and anger that so many local African Americans had in the civil rights movement...She was very willing to build bridges. Montgomery's always been very divisive, and she showed an example of reaching across racial lines (Hunter 2008).

In another interview about Johnnie Carr, Mayor Bobby Bright of Montgomery, Alabama, had this to say: "She was always an encourager and not a divider. She was just a loving person. She was truly the mother figure that we all so desperately needed in Montgomery during a very trying period of our history. She would always say, 'It was tough, but we made it and we made it better—and we're going to continue to make it better'" (Hunter 2008).

As the years went by, more and more members of the African American community, including media folks like Tavis Smiley, a PBS television host, became aware of Johnnie Carr and what she meant to the civil rights movement. Recognizing Johnnie Carr's accomplishments provides us with a better understanding and appreciation of what the average individual African American had to endure, sacrifice, and adjust to during the civil rights era. Thus, Johnnie Carr became a significant person who sacrificed her time, effort, and soul to the civil rights movement and race relations.

Barbara Jordan

One of the first African American women who championed the cause of civil rights in her political career was Barbara Charline Jordan. A dynamic orator, legislator, and educator, Jordan left an indelible mark in American history. Her journey—from the segregated Fifth Ward of Houston of her childhood to her status as a legendary public figure on the international stage—was filled with a series of "firsts" (Parham 1999).

Here are a few of Barbara Jordan's amazing accomplishments in civil rights, politics, and race relations:

- started in Houston's Fifth Ward inner-city district;
- became a well-known lawyer in the state of Texas;
- recognized as the first African American woman to be elected and to serve in the Texas senate;
- became the first African American woman from the South to serve in the U.S. House of Representatives;
- sponsored bills in the U.S. Congress that targeted the poor, disadvantaged, and people of color;
- participated in the 1974 Watergate hearings in which her speech stood out among all the rest;
- gave the keynote address at the 1976 Democratic National Convention, being the first woman and African American to achieve this accomplishment.

Once her days in the U.S. Congress were over, Barbara Jordan took a professor position at the University of Texas in Austin in the School of Public Affairs, where she taught law courses for 17 years (Scarborough 2003).

Of all her memorable speeches throughout her groundbreaking civil rights, higher education, and political career, one in particular directly relates to civil rights and the civil rights movement of the 1950s and 1960s, as well as to civil rights issues today. The following is an excerpt from her speech at Northwestern University in 1993: "Does the American experience of segregation and integration have any lessons to teach us? My proposition is that we have learned from our past. Our experience with race, slavery, civil rights, and the rule of the law is unlike that of any other nation on earth. One distinction is that, notwithstanding our differences, there is homogeneity. We speak of race more than we speak of ethnicity. We don't have deep cultural differences that exist in other parts of the world. In a sense, we are all immigrants" (Scaraborough 2003, 63–69).

This particular speech, along with Jordan's achievements, illustrates how one African American woman utilized her skills in politics, academia, and civil rights to provide a foundation in public policy and civil discourse for rights that this nation is still discussing, fighting for, and lobbying—civil rights for everyone.

Shirley Chisholm

Although this country has had its very first African American president in Barack Obama, it may be surprising for some to learn that he was not the first African American to run for president. Indeed, Reverend Jesse Jackson sought the nomination from the Democratic Party to run for president in 1984 and 1988. But there was another pioneer even before Jackson and Obama, and this person was not a man. This person was Shirley Anita St. Hill Chisholm, better known as Shirley Chisholm, or "Ms. Chis."

On January 25, 1972, Shirley Chisholm announced here run for U.S. president. Here is a small portion of her speech:

> I stand before you today as a candidate for the Democratic nomination for the Presidency of the United States of America. I am not the candidate of black America, although I am black and proud. I am not the candidate of the women's movement of this country, although I am a woman, and I am equally proud of that. I am not the candidate of any political bosses or fat cats or special interests. I stand here now without endorsements from any big name politicians or celebrities or any other kind of prop. I do not intend to offer to you the tired and glib clichés, which for too long have been an accepted part of our political life. I am the candidate of the people of America. And my presence before you now symbolizes a new era in American political history. I have always earnestly believed in the great potential of America. Our constitutional democracy will soon celebrate its 200th anniversary, effective testimony to the longevity to our cherished constitution and its unique bill of rights, which continues to give to the world an inspirational message of freedom and liberty. (Gutgold 2006)

Shirley Chisholm's speech showed the political establishment that she was running for president of the United States not only because of who she was as a person but also, and more importantly, because her campaign messages connected to young and diverse voters. In the book *Paving the Way for Madam President*, author Nichola Gutgold states that Chisholm challenged the status quo and asserted her right to run for U.S. president. Although she met tremendous campaign challenges in New Hampshire, Florida, and New York, Shirley Chisholm continued.

Civil rights for blacks, women, and the poor; reforms in the U.S. judicial system and in prisons; reducing police brutality, increasing gun control, and tolerance of political dissent; and new approaches to drug abuse prevention and treatment—these were issues that Chisholm consistently addressed during her campaign. After six months of campaigning in 11 primaries, she had 28 delegates committed to vote for her at the Democratic convention (Freeman 2009).

The 1972 Democratic National Convention in July in Miami was the first major convention in which an African American woman was considered for the presidential nomination. Although she did not win the nomination, she received 151 of the delegates' votes. She stuck it out until the end, and she did go into the convention with delegates. She wanted to affect political change with the power of her delegates, and she did so. At two different events (the women's caucus and black caucus) at the 1972 Democratic National Convention, Chisholm made the following comments:

> I am just so thankful that in spite of the differences in opinions, the differences of ideology, and even sometimes within the women's movement the differences of approaches, that here we are today at a glorious gathering of women in Miami.
>
> My brothers and sisters let me tell it to you this afternoon like it really is. There's only one thing that you my brothers and sisters have going—the only thing you have going is your one vote. DON'T sell that vote out!! The black people of America are watching us. Find out what these candidates who need our votes to get across the top are going to do for us concretely. (Chisholm 2010)

After her presidential campaign, Chisholm continued to serve in the U.S. House of Representatives until 1982. As a member of the black caucus, she saw representation grow in Congress and welcomed other black women as U.S. representatives. In 1984, she cofounded the National Political Congress of Black Women and worked vigorously for Rev. Jesse Jackson's presidential campaigns in both 1984 and 1988 (Cosby and Pouissant 2004). Several years later, President Bill Clinton nominated her to be ambassador to Jamaica.

When a producer and director of a film about her life asked her how she would like to be remembered, Chisholm said, "When I die, I want to be remembered as a woman who lived in the 20th century and who dared to be a catalyst of change. I don't want to be remembered as the first black woman who went to Congress. And I don't even want to be remembered as the first woman who happened to be black to make a bid for the presidency. I want to be remembered as a woman who fought for change in the 20th century. That's what I want" (Cosby and Pouissant 2004).

Contemporary Race-Relations Issues

It can be heartening to see how race relations have improved between blacks and whites in the United States since the civil rights movements and my childhood years. Many of the issues that caused racial confrontations and tensions in the past—interracial friendships, interracial dating and marrying, primary and secondary school choice, college choice, job selections, voting, and even just sitting in the front portion of a bus—are things of the past. So whether one is young, middle-aged, or elderly, a vast majority of Americans most likely would say that race relations have improved, right?

Interestingly, a Gallup poll conducted during the summer of 2008, right before Barack Obama's nomination as Democratic presidential candidate, found a very positive trend for race relations, particularly among African Americans, with most respondents having a more optimistic view than a pessimistic one. About 58 percent of Americans felt that race relations would be worked out versus 38 percent stating that race relations would always be a problem (Page and Risser 2008).

This Gallup poll included 702 non-Hispanic whites, 608 non-Hispanic blacks, and 502 Hispanics and was conducted between June 5 and July 6, 2008. Sample comments from participants were as follows:

> "I don't believe we've totally overcome everything that's necessary for equality, but I do believe things are getting better," said Ricardo Russell, a 30-year-old African American retail sales manager from Oak Park, Michigan.

> "They're better than they used to be, that's for sure. It's the younger people who are doing this," said Susann Matarese, a 52-year-old medical receptionist from Port Charlotte, Florida who is Caucasian and who is not entirely comfortable with the interracial dating she increasingly sees.

Additional findings included:

1. Blacks and whites continue to see different worlds when it comes to race.
2. Most blacks identified racial discrimination as a major factor in a list of problems that the African American community faces.
3. Blacks' views have improved a bit when it comes to equality in employment and housing, though a wide gap with whites' views remains.
4. The gap between blacks and whites in assessing race relations seems to be narrowing.
5. Most Americans said race relations are getting better. (Page and Risser 2008)

Four months after this Gallup poll, Americans elected their first African American as president of the United States. Not surprisingly, another Gallup poll was conducted immediately following the presidential election in November 2008. Apparently, Barack Obama's election inspired a wave of optimism about the future of race relations in the United States.

Confidence that the nation would resolve its racial problems rose to a historic level. Two-thirds of Americans predicted that relations between blacks and whites "will eventually be worked out" in the United States, by far the highest number since Gallup first asked the question in the midst of the civil rights struggle in 1963. In this 2008 poll of 1,036 adults, optimism jumped most among blacks. Five months earlier, half of African Americans predicted the nation eventually would solve its racial problems. Now, two-thirds saw this as a possibility.

Additional major findings from this postelection Gallup poll were as follows:

- Those surveyed saw Obama's election as a seminal moment in African American history.
- One in three respondents called it the most important advance for blacks in the past 100 years.
- Thirty-eight percent of respondents described the election as one of the two or three most important advances in race relations.
- Ten percent of respondents described the election as not important on race relations.
- Twenty-eight percent said race relations in the country will get a lot better; and 42 percent said that race relations will get a little better. (Page and Riser 2008)

Perhaps one way to illustrate the significance of Barack Obama's election to African Americans as the first African American president of the United States comes from commentary written by Robert Robinson, an African American deputy managing editor at *USA TODAY*. To summarize his feelings, which can be said from many black Americans at the time, Robinson (2008) thought about:

1. the discriminatory history of the United States toward blacks;
2. his personal battles of racial discrimination in his neighborhood; and
3. the overriding joy he felt to be alive in America!

In general, that is how a vast majority of African Americans felt after the presidential election. Not only were we going to get our first African American president, but we also were able to release all of the pent-up frustration from past discriminatory and racist acts against us. Thus, the newly elected president, Barack Obama, symbolized a change of status and a new day in race relations for all Americans, particularly African Americans.

Not surprisingly, candidate Barack Obama received a consistent high number of votes from blacks (95 percent) and other communities of color (Latino, Asian, Pacific Islanders, and Native Americans) throughout the primaries and general election. The fact that no other African American democratic candidate had been considered seriously to run for president since

Jesse Jackson (1984 and 1988) and Shirley Chisholm (2010) tells us that our U.S. society still has an issue about race and politics.

It took only one simple press conference during President Barack Obama's early days in the White House to make him and the rest of the country realize that the country still had a long way to go before we really are a "postracial society." The incident occurred at the end of President Obama's press conference on July 22, when he responded to the final question regarding the arrest of African American Harvard professor Henry Louis Gates by a Caucasian Cambridge, Massachusetts, police officer. The key phrase that got President Obama in political trouble with the country was when he made an "acted stupidly" remark about the Cambridge police officer.

Although the incident had started a national debate about racial profiling, the president's remarks heightened the race-relations issue to a fully new level. Two days later, the Cambridge police defended their officer's arrest of Professor Gates in a press conference, and President Obama held his own press conference stating that he regretted saying those words to describe the incident. By the end of this race-relations nightmare, President Obama invited both individuals—Professor Henry Louis Gates and Cambridge Police Sgt. James Crowly—to the White House. Unfortunately, this issue was never truly resolved, thereby causing blacks and whites to further hold onto their misperceptions and stereotypes of each other (Bailey 2010).

Major Concepts and Definitions

Race and Ethnic Relations

The phrase "race and ethnic relations" refers to the ways in which people of different races and ethnic backgrounds living together in the same community *behave* toward one another. This is one of the simplest concepts and definitions in this field of study yet the most overlooked issue by many scholars, researchers, teachers, administrators, and students. The reason why is that it causes all of us to assess how we "behave" to one another. In other words, how do we truly *treat* each other—not just living together in the same community, but "interacting," "intermingling," "talking," "understanding," "appreciating," and "respecting" each other every day, not just during a special social, cultural, or ceremonial event, but each and every day of the week, particularly for college students who must interact with various racial and ethnic groups daily simply because they share the same living space, share the same classrooms, share the same social events, share the same student groups, share the same sporting events, and share the same party settings, on and off campus.

Therefore, the definition of race and ethnic relations covers multiple levels of significance to average college students because they must ask of themselves these significant questions:

- How well do I interact with students of different racial and ethnic backgrounds?
- How many friends do I really have who are of a different racial and ethnic background?
- How well do I intermingle with students of different racial and ethnic backgrounds?
- How well do I talk with students of different racial and ethnic backgrounds?
- How well do I understand students of different racial and ethnic backgrounds?
- How well do I appreciate students of different racial and ethnic backgrounds?
- How well do I respect students of different racial and ethnic backgrounds?
- How do I feel when I am around lots of students of different racial and ethnic backgrounds?

Answers to these questions for the individual college student are the starting point for better understanding some hidden issues connected to race and ethnic relations. That's why it's important to define and clarify the significance of this first major concept—race and ethnic relations.

Answering these questions also reveals the sensitive nature of this topic, not only to the individual college student but also the entire college/university community, which includes administrators, faculty, staff, and local community residents. What would be the response from college administrators, faculty, staff, and local community residents to these very same questions? More than likely, the responses would be different, yet they would reveal a number of sensitive, hidden issues that we all have about an individual or group that is different from us.

These are the hidden issues that most folks do not talk about yet assume that everyone knows about. We assume that all college students know how to get along with other students of different racial and ethnic backgrounds, and we assume that all college students have a deep knowledge base about each other. Yet the fact is that a majority of college students do not know how to get along with other students of different racial and ethnic backgrounds, and a majority do not have a deep knowledge base about each. The same is true of college administrators, faculty, staff, and local community residents.

Thus, we must make the college experience for all college students, administrators, faculty, staff, and local community residents a *teachable* moment in time. This is the moment to learn about the basic issues of race and ethnic relations. This is the moment to better understand the major divisive issues connected to each racial and ethnic group. This is the moment to empower oneself with understanding of race and ethnic relations. Most importantly, this is the moment where all of us can come together to create new solutions for better race and ethnic relations on all college/university campuses, as well as communities and neighborhoods all across our United States of America.

Race

Race is our next major concept and definition to discuss. If there is one concept in our U.S. society and globally that is the most controversial and politically charged issue to discuss, it is race. Race is an issue that many people want to avoid discussing because it tends to pit one group against another—no matter what subtopic you discuss. Yet the plain fact is our society is very much race-based with a long history of racial segregation and racial conflict.

From an anthropological perspective, race is considered a social-political concept solely to stratify society into specific groupings. It is not a concept being used in its truest capacity to highlight similarities between various populations. It is used more to highlight the differences between various populations.

With that said, here is one definition of race:

- Race refers to differential concentrations of gene frequencies responsible for internal genetic traits and external physical traits. (Kitano 1997)

This definition of race does not infer or mean that one race has exclusive possession of any particular genetic or physical trait or that there is a predetermined amount of genetic or physical traits that categorizes an individual either "this race" or "that race." It infers that all human populations are made up of a wide variety of genetic and physical traits, which are the result of our adaptation to a specific ecological environmental setting. We also know many types of environmental stressors influence our human diversity, such as

- temperature and humidity,
- solar radiation,
- altitude,
- nutrition, and
- disease. (Molnar 1975: 118)

All these environmental stressors or factors greatly influenced our outward physical traits (i.e., skin color, body type, facial features, hair texture, height, and weight) as well as our inside genetic traits (i.e., sickle cell trait, lactase gene, blood glucose intolerance). Therefore, our definition of race reflects the wonderful, amazing, surprising, and most importantly *adaptive* nature of our species to the environment. It is as simple as that! We—the human species—are a reflection of our environment, past and present.

In this context, race is a positive outcome that should be celebrated at all times. Each day, we see the amazing, beautiful diversity of our human species. All of us are unique in our physical and genetic characteristics. In fact, between our so-called racial populations, we are genetically more similar than different, whereas within so-called racial populations, we tend to show more genetic variation. Thus we are more *similar* than different—another reason to celebrate the positive outcome of the concept of race as opposed to the negative.

Ethnic Groups

Anthropologically, ethnic groups are defined as "those that share a sense of cultural and historical uniqueness, and to act as a member of an ethnic group is to express feelings or call attention to their uniqueness" (Mindel and Habenstein 1981). There is a degree of conformity and commonality between all who share this social and cultural heritage. It is expressed in a variety of ways: physical appearance, kinship organization, food traditions, long-standing rituals, health beliefs, religious belief systems, and language.

In other words, within each racial population, there are a wide variety and number of ethnic groups, which distinguish themselves physically, religiously, in language, clothing, and food traditions. For example, let's identify some ethnic groups within each racial population here in the United States. Tables 3.1 through 3.6 highlight the major ethnic groups affiliated with each racial population identified in the United States. The major racial populations include American Indian and Alaska Natives, Asian, black or African Americans, Hispanic or Latino, Native Hawaiian or other Pacific Islander, and white or Caucasian or Euro-American.

By reviewing all these ethnic groups affiliated with the major racial populations in the United States, it becomes apparent that all of us have a very rich, diverse ethnic history. Whether each individual is aware of his or her ethnic connection and history or not today, each of us has our generations of family members who fought for their uniqueness and freedom at some point in time. It is this ethnic history and uniqueness affiliated with each racial group in the United States that makes our country so unique.

Table 3.1 American Indian or Alaska Native

Alaskan Athabaskans	Lumbee
Aleut	Menominee
Apache	Navajo
Blackfeet	Osage
Cherokee	Ottawa
Chickasaw	Paiute
Chippewa	Pima
Choctaw	Potawatomi
Colville	Pueblo
Comanche	Puget Sound Salish
Cree	Seminole
Creek	Shoshone
Crow	Sioux
Delaware	Tlingit-Haida
Eskimo	Tohono O'odhan
Houma	Ute
Iroquois	Yakama
Kiowa	Yuma
Latin American Indian	

Table 3.2 Asian

Chinese	Japanese
Filipino	Korean
Hmong	Vietnamese
Indian	

Table 3.3 Black or African American

African (ex. Nigerian, Ethiopian)	Caribbean
Afro-Latin American	Haitian
Black Hispanic	

Table 3.4 Hispanic or Latino

Central America (ex. Costa Rican, Guatemalan, Honduran, Nicaraguan, Panamanian, Salvadoran, Other Central American)	Puerto Rican
Cuban	South America (ex. Argentinean, Bolivian, Chilean, Columbian, Ecuadorian, Paraguayan, Peruvian, Uruguayan, Venezuelan, Other South American)
Dominican Republican	Spanish
Mexican	

Table 3.5 Native Hawaiians or Other Pacific Islanders

Chamarros	Samoans
Guamanians	Others
Hawaiian	

Table 3.6 White, Caucasian, or Euroamerican

Albanian	English
Armenian	Estonian
Austrian	Finnish
Azerbaijani	French
Basque	Georgian
Belarusian	German
Belgian	Greek
Bosnian	Hungarian
British	Icelandia
Bulgarian	Irish
Catalan	Italian
Croatian	Latvian
Cypriot	Liechtenstein
Czech	Lithuanian
Danish	Luxemburg
Dutch	Macedonia
	Maltese

(continued)

Table 3.6 (*continued*)

Moldovan	Scottish
Monegasque	Serbian
Montenegrin	Slovak
Norwegian	Slovene
Pennsylvania Dutch	Spanish
Polish	Swedish
Portuguese	Swiss
Romanian	Turkish
Russian	Ukrainian
Sammarinese	Welsh
Scandinavian	Yugoslavian
Scots-Irish	Other European

U.S. Department of Commerce. Ancestry 2000: Census 2000 Brief. Bureau of Census. Washington, DC: U.S. Government Printing Office, Issued June 2004.

U.S. Racial Populations: The Framework

The U.S. Department of Commerce's Bureau of Census annually collects data on the U.S. population. It is the federal agency that collects this data, analyzes the data, and projects certain population trends for our country every 5 to 10 years. Yet it is the Office of Management and Budget (specifically its Directive No. 15) that determines and categorizes the racial populations in the United States. This office and directive provide the framework for how each individual in the United States of America is categorized and placed into his or her individual racial category. Ironically, this framework was an agreed upon collective process by our federal government administrators to find a way to manage the diverse and ever-growing U.S. population.

According to the Office of Management and Budget Directive No. 15, these classifications have been "developed in response to needs expressed by both the executive branch and the Congress to provide for the collection and use of compatible, nonduplicated, exchangeable racial and ethnic data by Federal agencies" (https://wonder.cdc.gov/wonder/help/populations/bridged -race/directive15.html).

Furthermore, the Office of Management and Budget (OMB) states that the categories that were developed represent a political-social construct designed to be used in the collection of data on the race and ethnicity of major broad population groups in this country and are not anthropologically or scientifically based. They are used for census taking, household surveys, mortgage lending applications, school registration, and in medical/social research studies (https://wonder.cdc.gov/wonder/help/populations/bridged-race/directive15.html).

Thus, even the OMB admits that their U.S. racial categories are not scientifically based but strictly a political-social construct to be used in a wide variety of ways, whether in the education field, business, housing, or medical/social research. Therefore, the general public needs to be better informed on how race and ethnicity data are utilized at their institutions. In other words, the question is, does the race and ethnicity data at your college/university accurately and truly reflect the diversity of your student population?

U.S. Racial Populations: The Categories

Now that we have a better understanding on the framework for the U.S. racial populations and the why/how it was developed in the manner in which it was, we can identify the categories. In accordance to our federal government's Office of Management and Budget, the U.S. population is categorized racially and ethnically in the five major categories as follows:

1. American Indian or Alaska Native
2. Asian
3. Black or African American
4. Native Hawaiian or Other Pacific Islander
5. White

There are two categories for data on ethnicity: "Hispanic or Latino" and "Not Hispanic or Latino."

According to the OMB Directive No. 15 for Race and Ethnic Standards for Federal Statistics and Administrative Reporting, here are the descriptions for each major racial and ethnic population in the United States:

*   American Indian or Alaska Native: A person having origins in any of the original peoples of North and South America (including Central America) and who maintains tribal affiliation or community attachment.
*   Asian: A person having origins in any of the original peoples of the Far East, Southeast Asia, or the Indian subcontinent, including, for example, Cambodia, China, India, Japan, Korea, Malaysia, Pakistan, the Philippine Islands, Thailand, and Vietnam.
*   Black or African American: A person having origins in any of the black racial groups of Africa. Terms such as "Haitian" or "Negro" can be used in addition to "Black or African American."

- Hispanic or Latino: A person of Cuban, Mexican, Puerto Rican, South or Central American, or other Spanish culture or origin, regardless of race. The term "Spanish origin" can be used in addition to "Hispanic or Latino." Hispanic origin can be viewed as the heritage, nationality group, lineage, or country of birth of the person or person's parents or ancestors before the arrival in the United States. People who identify their origin as Hispanic, Latino, or Spanish may be any race (U.S. Bureau of Census 2011).

- Native Hawaiian or Other Pacific Islander: A person having origins in any of the original peoples of Hawaii, Guam, Samoa, or other Pacific Islands.

- White: A person having origins in any of the original people of Europe, the Middle East, or North Africa. (https://wonder.cdc.gov/wonder/help/populations /bridged-race/directive15.html)

To provide a deeper understanding and appreciation for OMB's racial and ethnic groupings, we need to highlight some of the major sociodemographics and cultural patterns often associated with these populations. As a reminder, these sociodemographics and cultural patterns are not stagnant or exclusive to each population and are only used to provide more specificity to each group.

American Indian and Alaska Native

According to the 2000 U.S. census, approximately 2.9 million Americans self-identify as American Indian or Alaska Native alone or in conjunction with another race. Approximately, 16 percent of all Indians reported themselves as Cherokee, 12 percent as Navajo, and 6 percent each as Chippewa and Sioux (U.S. Department of Commerce 1993). The Choctaw, Pueblo, and Apache had populations of at least 50,000 persons. The Choctaw accounted for 4 percent of the Native American population. The Iroquois Confederacy, Lumbee, and Creek all had 43,000 or more persons (U.S. Department of Commerce 1993; www.ncai.org [accessed June 14, 2017]).

Presently, there are approximately over 562 federally recognized Indian tribes, bands, nations, pueblos, *rancherias*, communities, and Native villages in the United States. Approximately 229 of these are located in Alaska; the rest are located in 33 other states (www.ncai.org [accessed June 14, 2017]).

American Indian and Alaska Natives live predominantly in 26 states, with most residing in the western part of the country as a result of forced westward migration. Although many Indians remain on reservations and in rural areas, just as many of them live in cities, especially those on the West Coast. Oklahoma, Arizona, California, New Mexico, and Alaska traditionally have the highest numbers and concentration of American Indians.

Additional sociodemographics of importance are migration patterns and the percentages of elders. Approximately 54 percent of American Indians and Alaskan Natives have migrated from reservations to urban areas, primarily for economic opportunity. Moreover, the American Indian and Alaskan Native elders make up approximately 6 percent of the American Indian and Alaskan Native population and are the fastest growing ethnic population (Rousseau 1995, 83).

Asians

Asians are defined as the federally designated population whose origins are the Far East, Asia, and Southeast and Southwest Asia. According to the Bureau of Census (2011), approximately 14.7 million (about 5 percent of all respondents) identified their race as Asian alone (U.S. Bureau of Census 2011). Between 2000 and 2010, the Asian alone population experienced the fastest rate of growth—increasing 43 percent, more than any other major race group. The Asian alone population had the second-largest numeric change (4.4 million), growing from 10.2 million in 2000 to 14.7 million in 2010. Additionally, the Asian alone population gained the most in share of the total population, moving up from about 4 percent in 2000 to about 5 percent in 2010 (U.S. Bureau of Census 2011).

Black or African American

According to the Bureau of Census (2011), the black or African American alone population was 38.9 million and represented 13 percent of the total population. While the black alone population had the third-largest numeric increase in population size over the decade (4.3 million), behind the white alone and Asian alone populations, it grew slower than most other major race groups. In fact, the black alone population exhibited the smallest percentage growth outside of the white alone population, increasing 12 percent between 2000 and 2010. This population rose from 34.7 million in 2000 to 38.9 million in 2010, making up 12 percent and 13 percent of the total population respectively (U.S. Bureau of Census 2011).

Hispanic/Latino

According to the Bureau of Census (2011), the Hispanic/Latino population was 50.5 million, comprising 16 percent of the total population. Between 2000 and 2010, the Hispanic/Latino population grew by 43 percent—rising from 35.3 million in 2000, when this group made up 13 percent of the total population. The Hispanic/Latino population increased by 15.2 million between 2000 and 2010, accounting for over half of the 27.3 million increase in the total population of the United States (U.S. Bureau of Census 2011).

Native Hawaiian or Other Pacific Islander

According to the Bureau of Census (2011), the smallest major race group was Native American and other Pacific Islander alone (0.5 million) and represented 0.2 percent of the total population. The Native Hawaiian and other Pacific Islander alone population grew substantially between 2000 and 2010, increasing by more than one-third. This population numbered 398,835 in 2000, rising to 540,013 in 2010 with its proportion of the total population changing from 0.1 percent to 0.2 percent respectively (U.S. Bureau of Census 2011).

White

Finally, according to the Bureau of Census (2011), the white alone group (223.6 million) accounted for 72 percent of all people living in the United States. From 2000 to 2010, the white alone population experienced the slowest rate of growth among race alone populations. The white alone population made up just under half of the growth—increasing 12.1 million. Within the white alone population, the vast majority of the growth was propelled by the Hispanic/Latino population (U.S. Bureau of Census 2011).

The only major race group to experience a decrease in its proportion of the total population was the white alone population. While this group increased the most numerically between decennial censuses (211.5 million to 223.6 million), its share of the total population fell from 75 percent in 2000 to 72 percent in 2010 (U.S. Bureau of Census 2011).

Multiracials

In addition, according to the Bureau of Census (2011), approximately 3 percent (9.9 million) of the total U.S. population reported themselves as multiracial—belonging to more than one race. Among people who reported more than one race in 2010, the vast majority (about 92 percent) reported exactly two races. An additional 8 percent of the "Two or more races" population reported three races, and less than 1 percent reported four or more races (U.S. Bureau of Census 2011).

In 2010, four groups were, by far, the largest multiple-race combinations in the United States: white *and* black (1.8 million), white *and* some other race (1.7 million), white *and* Asian (1.6 million), and white *and* American Indian and Alaska Native (1.4 million). Together, these four combinations composed nearly three-fourths of the multiple-race population in the 2010 census (U.S. Bureau of Census 2011).

Negative Concepts with Race and Ethnic Relations

As we are very much aware, race and ethnic relations invoke a wide array of reactions, emotions, and opinions from those who are a part of any racial and ethnic group. Yet the reality is that no matter which group an individual is associated with, he or she tends to view the world from that group's perspective. In other words, all of us have varying degrees of bias that favor the racial and ethnic group that we are associated with. This is an issue that most people would not want to admit, but it is a reality, a product of the vast majority of us living, being raised, and educated exclusively or very largely only in one racial/ethnic group.

Ethnocentrism

Ethnocentrism refers to the tendency to apply one's own values and belief system in judging the behavior, actions, and patterns of other groups. When people judge another person or group based upon their own value system and believe that their value system and beliefs are superior to the other individual and/or group, it leads to misunderstanding, misinformation, and a biased opinion about that individual and/or group (Kottak 2011, 39).

In Conrad Kottak's (2011) *Cultural Anthropology: Appreciating Cultural Diversity*, he reminds us that we witness ethnocentrism when people consider their own cultural beliefs to be truer, more proper, or more moral than those of other groups. However, fundamental to anthropology, as the study of human diversity, is the fact that what is alien (even disgusting) to us may be normal, proper, and prized elsewhere (Kottak 2011, 39).

For example, consider a general scenario of a race and ethnic relations issue on a college campus, where there is a confrontation and fight between two males (one white and one black) that results in punishment for both parties, and when observers of the event are asked by authorities who started and who caused the fight, there are conflicting opinions. A majority of the Caucasian, Euro-American students felt that the black student started and caused the fight. On the other hand, a majority of the African American students felt that the white student started and caused the fight. Both sets of student observers (white, Caucasian, Euro-American and black, African American) had opposing views and opinions based upon what they saw, how they interpreted what they saw, and who they felt would be the culprit even if they didn't see all of the confrontation and fight.

This scenario is an example of ethnocentrism at work. All of us are influenced every day by our individual biases, values, beliefs, opinions, and perspectives. We are often not aware of our individual biases on a daily basis. Yet when we are placed in a setting in which there are opposing individuals and/or groups, and when we have to arrive at a decision as to what actually happened, we often fall prey to our ethnocentric perspectives.

That's why it is critical for all of us to try our best to see and evaluate race- and ethnic-relations issues from the other person's or groups' perspective. Thereby, we increase our understanding of their issues and actions while reducing our ethnocentric perspective on everything we see or hear.

Discrimination

Another negative concept associated with race and ethnic relations, which is closely connected to ethnocentrism, is the concept of discrimination. Discrimination refers to policies and practices that harm a group and its members. Kottak (2011) elaborates by stating the following: "discrimination may be *de facto* (practiced, but not legally sanctioned) or *de jure* (part of the law). An example of de facto discrimination is the harsher treatment that American minorities (compared with other Americans) tend to get from the police and the judicial system. This unequal treatment isn't legal but it happens anyway" (Kottack 2011, 145).

In general, discrimination is the next level of ethnocentrism, in which those who judge others based upon their own value system actually take action against the other individual or group in a manner that is harmful or showing preferential treatment to another individual or group. When discrimination occurs against an individual or group and it is discovered, it not only has an immediate harmful effect, but it also has a long-lasting detrimental psychological effect. That's what is often overlooked when discriminatory practices are implemented against another group—it is the psychological and mental impact that stay with the individual/group well beyond the discriminatory act itself.

For example, if a college student who is a person of color gets highly scrutinized or denied access on a regular basis when he or she wants to attend a college bar or nightclub just like any other college student, that is a discriminatory act by the college bar or nightclub—no question about it. Another example is when a fraternity or sorority makes it extremely difficult on a regular basis to join or denies the addition of a person of color to their fraternity/sorority, or when a white person attempts to join a person-of-color fraternity/sorority and that fraternity or sorority makes it extremely difficult on a regular basis or denies the addition of this person to the fraternity/ sorority; this is a discriminatory act.

These previous examples of discriminatory practices highlight the general type of discriminatory practices often experienced at colleges and university campuses. The four major types of discriminatory practices are

- isolate discrimination,
- small-group discrimination,
- direct institutionalized discrimination, and
- indirect institutionalized discrimination.

They are defined as follows:

1. Isolate discrimination refers to harmful actions intentionally taken by a member of the dominant group against members of the minority (Kitano 1997, 73).
2. Small-group discrimination refers to harmful actions taken intentionally by a small number of dominant group individuals acting in concert against members of a subordinate group (Kitano 1997, 73).
3. Direct institutionalized discrimination refers to organizationally prescribed actions that are intentional and have been in practice continuously so that they have become institutionalized (Kitano 1997, 73).
4. Indirect institutionalized discrimination refers to discrimination by organizations that is not directly motivated by prejudice or intent to harm (Kitano 1997, 73).

Although these four types of discriminatory practices are not as widely experienced in today's college and university settings, they still do exist and occur in more subtle ways on campuses across the United States.

Prejudice

Another negative concept associated with racial and ethnic relations, which is closely related to the concept of discrimination, is prejudice. Prejudice means devaluing (looking down on) a group because of it assumed behavior, values, capabilities, or attributes (Kottak 2011). People are prejudiced when they hold stereotypes about groups and apply them to individuals.

Kottak (2011) emphasizes that prejudiced people assume that members of the group will act as they are "supposed to act" (according to the stereotype) and interpret a wide range of individual behaviors as evidence of the stereotype. They use this behavior to confirm their stereotype (and low opinion) about the group (Kottak 2011, 145).

When the word "prejudice" is used in a conversation, it usually evokes strong emotions and a reaction because it pits one individual or group versus another based on a set of stereotypical beliefs and attitudes. Thus having "prejudicial views" or a "prejudicial perspective" automatically sets individuals and groups a part. This usually causes a negative outcome to race and ethnic relations.

Yet what is even more interesting about the concept of prejudice is that most people would claim they are not prejudiced or do not have prejudicial views. That is the usual response, yet all of us must recognize that a vast majority of us do have varying degrees of prejudicial views about other groups of people. Unfortunately, that's a reality in today's world.

Racial Prejudice

Racial prejudice is exactly the same as prejudice yet obviously it is a prejudice targeted at a particular racial individual and/or group. Racial prejudice refers to an irrationally based negative attitude toward a racial or ethnic group, and it is maintained through stereotypes (Kitano 1997).

For example, here are a few racial-prejudice comments about various racial and ethnic groups in the United States:

> "They all are thugs."
>
> "They lower property value."
>
> "They don't know how to take care of themselves."
>
> "They all are illiterate."
>
> "They all smell bad."
>
> "They all in gangs."
>
> "They all just kill themselves."
>
> "They all don't have any values."
>
> "They breed like rabbits."

Each one of these comments is based on an exaggerated belief and generalization associated with a group of people. As stated earlier, these prejudiced remarks are based on stereotypes, which help to further create an emotional distance from another group. If these racial comments and opinions are not challenged by others, then they become further reinforced as "truths" about a particular racial and ethnic group by the prejudiced individual or group.

Racism

The final concept and the most negative concept associated with race and ethnic relations is racism. Although most people do not want to admit that racism is still much a part of our U.S. society, many people are surprised when they learn about a racist act in their own community, in their state, or at their college or university. It's as if racism is an issue of the past and does not really exist in the present. Let me be very clear: racism and racial prejudice are very much alive and well in 2018. Why? Let's examine the definition.

Racism refers to the ideology that considers the unchangeable physical characteristics of groups to be linked in a direct, casual way to their psychological and intellectual functioning and, on that basis, distinguishes between superior and inferior races. In other words, it means that one group believes that it is superior in every way to another and has power to reinforce this perspective (Kitano 1997, 12).

Just by reviewing the concept and definition of racism, we recognize that practically all present-day societies still have portions of their citizens believing that they are superior to others. These groups/individuals also hold certain levels of power to enact their racist beliefs upon others. Unfortunately, this has occurred in practically every society of the past. It is still occurring in the present and more than likely will continue in the future.

Racism today is in some ways different from the past. Indeed, our society has experienced blatant racism on all levels affecting almost every immigrant and enslaved group of people coming to this country. We do not have to go far back in our past to see the remnants of racism and racist acts that shaped our country.

Yet racism today is definitely different. There are three major types of racism: (1) direct racism, (2) indirect racism; and (3) internalized racism. Here are the definitions:

- Direct racism occurs when a person is confronted and placed at a disadvantage because of his/her race.
- Indirect racism racism is a side effect of other concerns, such as unemployment, poverty status, lack of diversity programs, and higher incarceration rates for minorities.
- Internalized racism acceptance by members of stigmatized races of negative messages about their own abilities and believing these misconceptions from others. (Kitano 1997, 8)

Today, indirect racism and internalized racism are the two most common forms of racism. Although we still experience some direct racist acts of confrontation, a majority of racism is subtle. For example, individuals and groups who are living in poverty, underserved, and in areas of the country with high unemployment rates would more than likely say that their living conditions and economic situations are an indirect result of racist policies and programs targeting their communities. Indirect racism is very troubling because it justifies the inequities and the disparity in our societies in that they are the result of past racist policies or programs targeted at certain groups, which created a permanent underclass of underserved, uneducated, underemployed, and poverty-stricken communities.

Yet some would say that internalized racism is even more troubling, simply because affected members of the stigmatized group believe they are not deserving of fair treatment or opportunities similar to nonstigmatized groups. They hold themselves back or put themselves down. This becomes an even more powerful, psychologically damaging form of racism.

Positive Concepts with Race and Ethnic Relations

It is truly unfortunate that whenever our society focuses upon race and ethnic relations, the dialogue and issues tend to be negative or problematic. As previously highlighted in the earlier sections, there are more negative concepts and terms associated with race and ethnic relations than positive ones. Why is that, and does our American culture influence our perspective on this issue?

To contrast such negativity associated with race and ethnic relations, we are going to highlight two major positive concepts in concluding this chapter: cultural relativism and enculturation.

Cultural Relativism

Anthropologists employ cultural relativism not as a moral belief but as a methodological position. In order to understand another culture fully, we must try to understand how the people in that culture see things. What motivates them—what are they thinking—when they do those things? Kottak (2011) states that such an approach does not preclude making more moral judgments. Thus, cultural relativism refers to an individual's attempt to understand the values, beliefs, and behaviors of another individual or group from their own internal logic (Kottak 2011, 39).

The key to this concept is that the individual sincerely "attempts" to view the world from the other individual's or group's perspective—not judging them based upon some moral values. Once individual's embrace more of a cultural-relativistic perspective of other racial and ethnic groups, then it will have a chain-reaction effect on eliminating ethnocentrism, discrimination, prejudice, racial prejudice, and racism.

This powerful concept of cultural relativism is actually the key to getting racial and ethnic groups to come together on the most basic and serious issues of life. It is just that simple and powerful if all of us embrace a cultural-relativistic approach to racial and ethnic relations.

Enculturation

Another positive concept associated with race and ethnic relations is enculturation. Enculturation refers to the process by which culture is learned and transmitted across generations (Kottak 2011, 27). It begins when we are children and we slowly learn and become enculturated into the values, beliefs, and behaviors of our immediate familial, ethnic, and community group.

This process also begins when we embrace more of a cultural-relativistic perspective on life so that we can immerse ourselves slowly into another person's culture. Once we are totally immersed into another person's culture, we are said to be enculturated.

What is more fascinating about the enculturation process is that once the individual is totally enculturated, he or she is accepted by members within the new ethnic or racial group as one of them. The key here is *acceptance* by members of this ethnic or racial group, because they recognize the process by which the individual immersed himself or herself into their culture and now sees the world from "their" perspective. Thus enculturation and cultural relativism are interconnected concepts that lead all of us to a better understanding and appreciation of race and ethnic relations.

Conclusion

One of the challenges when addressing race- and ethnic-relations issues is establishing a foundation and basic understanding of the terminology and concepts often used in this field of study. As is in any field of study, certain concepts and terms are regularly used, and most people assume that the general public understands these concepts. This is exactly what has happened in the field of race- and ethnic-relations studies.

Although experts and the general public may know these basic concepts associated with race and ethnic relations, there are many—particularly younger—college students who are unfamiliar with the cultural history of race relations, along with the specificity of these terms and the true sociocultural impact that these terms may have on particular racial and ethnic groups. We must invest quality time to reexamine these basic concepts and reframe our thinking about these issues, to help improve race and ethnic relations not only on college campuses but also in communities across the United States.

CHAPTER FOUR

Race- and Ethnic-Relations Theories

Now that we have a deeper understanding and appreciation of the basic positive and negative concepts associated with race and ethnic relations, we examine, discuss, and challenge the major theories that are often used to explain the problems with race and ethnic relations. One reason why we should challenge the major theories is that they are overutilized and outdated.

These theories are actually reflective of racial and ethnic relations of the 1960s, 1970s, and 1980s. In fact, these theories are often not applicable to today's racial and ethnic student populations; therefore, it is vital to propose new theory that better frames out or explains the positive impact of good race and ethnic relations on college campuses today and in the future.

Race- and Ethnic-Relations Research Studies on College Students

In general, for the average college student, college life is supposed to be filled with a new sense of independence and an opportunity to learn about life in a whole new, academic way. Most students who attend a two- or four-year college/university have expectations of graduating in a particular field of study, developing higher levels of critical thinking about life, and networking with students from all walks of life.

Yet for most students, college life is filled with much more than that: daily challenges of academic rigor, extracurricular activities, varying living arrangements, self-discovery, group affiliation, and race relations. To better understand these challenging issues, there has been a wide array of research studies investigating each one. But a most frequent research area investigated among college students, particularly among racial- and ethnic-minority college students, has included studies related to discrimination, racial attitudes, prejudicial acts, and race relations.

There are two research studies that need to be highlighted in this section in order to show how race and ethnic relations has changed significantly because of the increase of racial diversity on college campuses today. First, Smith, Bowman, and Hsu (2007) conducted a study among 575 Caucasian/ Euro-American and 122 international college students from Asia (China, Japan, Korea, and Taiwan) attending a public university in the Rocky Mountain region of the United States. They found the following:

1. Caucasian/Euro-American college students were least comfortable interacting with Hispanic/Latino students and most comfortable interacting with African American/black students.
2. Asian students were most comfortable interacting with Caucasian/ Euro-American students and least comfortable interacting with black students.

These two general findings indicate that racial attitudes differ moderately across race and that college students of all various backgrounds would greatly benefit from programs that enhance interracial understanding and relations (Smith, Bowman, and Hsu 2007). These findings are similar to those found in other related studies (Lowery, Hardin, and Sinclair 2001; Mack et al. 1997; McCormack 1995).

In another related study, Ancis, Sedlacek, and Mohr (2000) conducted a study on race relations among 578 African American, Asian American, Latino/a, and Caucasian/Euro-American undergraduate students at a large mid-Atlantic university. They found the following:

1. African American college students consistently reported more negative experiences compared with Asian American, Latino, and Caucasian/ Euro-American students.
2. Asian American and Latino/a students reported experiences of stereotyping and prejudice in the form of limited respect and unfair treatment by faculty, teaching assistants, and students and pressure to conform to stereotypes.
3. Caucasian/Euro-American students reported less racial tension, fewer expectations to conform to stereotypic behavior, an experience of being treated fairly, a climate characterized by respect for diversity, and immunity from interracial tension on campus.

In summary, Ancis, Sedlacek, and Mohr (2000) contend that their findings should encourage counselors on college campuses across the United States to provide university programming that focuses on creating an accepting and comfortable campus climate while also sending a message to all students that exposure to differences is enriching for all.

These two previous research studies, along with many others (Martin, Trego, and Nakayama 2010; Torres 2009; Garam and Brooks 2010; Laird 2005; Gonzales 1993), highlight the significant impact of campus diversity on students' personal and social development. Experiencing an ethnically diverse campus community creates a healthy and positive community in which all students regardless of racial, ethnic, and social backgrounds could greatly benefit throughout their college years. As a result, each student becomes more well rounded, experienced, and compassionate toward others.

Theoretical Framework

One of the major challenges to better understanding the major and minor issues related to race and ethnic relations is determining what or which type of theory best explains this field of study. Since there are a number of fields that have a history of evaluating and conceptualizing the concept of race (e.g., sociology, biology, ethnic studies), for the sake of this discussion, I am going to use my own field of study—anthropology. Indeed, it was the field of anthropology in all of its glorious beginnings, with scholars coming from other disciplines during the late 1800s and 1900s, that helped to frame our thinking about the concept of race in all its good, as well as all its negative, aspects.

Anthropology

Ironically, this field of study often gets overlooked and has received years of scrutiny from scholars outside the discipline and the general public for its lack of commitment to seriously addressing race and ethnicity. Anthropology is still a discipline that is viewed by many as one that teaches and promotes only a certain viewpoint about the beginnings of the human species and only concentrates on the biological and physical attributes of the human species. Yet the field of anthropology is far more encompassing than that. It is a discipline that studies the biological and cultural aspects of human populations— past and present.

When I had decided to make anthropology my major while a junior at Miami University in Ohio, my parents, friends, and relatives thought I was throwing my college education away by majoring in a discipline that was not perceived to have relevance to the "real world" and "present-day issues," along with being a discipline that conflicted with their religious point of view. Yet as I immersed myself fully into the field of anthropology, I realized then that anthropology has far-reaching implications and possibilities, if used and approached correctly.

Now, as a professor who has been teaching anthropology for more than 30 years, I still see students surprised by the breadth of anthropology. It is a uniquely comparative and holistic science. Holism refers to the study of the whole of human condition: past, present, and future, biology, society, language, and culture. Anthropology also offers a unique cross-cultural perspective by constantly comparing the customs of one society with those of others (Kottak 2014, 5). Thus, with its approach, anthropology is actually a discipline well suited to address issues of race and ethnicity in all countries— not just the United States.

Since the field of anthropology—and in particular the professional association within the field, the American Anthropological Association—had not sufficiently addressed publicly what its actual stance on and definition of race was for decades, it was not until the late 1990s that the association clarified its stance on and definition of race for the general population. This occurred when the association's executive board commissioned a position paper on race authored by American Anthropological Association (1998) and Smedley and Smedley (2012) and had it reviewed by a working group of prominent anthropologists: George Armelegos, Michael Blakey, C. Loring Brace, Alan Goodman, Faye Harrison, Jonathan Marks, Yolanda Moss, and Carol Mukhopadhayay. This paper covered a wide array of controversial issues related to race.

Here are some key points from the American Anthropology Association's paper (1999) on race:

1. From its inception, race was a classification linked specifically to peoples in the colonial situation.

2. To rationalize European attitudes and treatment of enslaved populations, race was used to retain the institution of slavery.

3. As the ideology of racial differences grew among Europeans, Africans, and Indians, it established a rigid hierarchy of socially exclusive categories and rankings that contributed to the inequality associated with certain populations. Highlighting the physical differences between populations became a symbol and marker for inequality among the races.

4. This ideology of race spread globally, which caused further division, ranking, and inequality among other populations around the world.

5. Eventually, race became a world view—one in which misconceptions, stereotypes, and myths were used by the colonial populations to control the colonized population along with providing a philosophical belief that their strategy was a natural and God-given strategy.

6. Once each society established certain racial categories, it allowed the elite, the powerful, and the wealthy to assign some groups to perpetual low status

and unequal opportunity. Additionally, each society established certain policies and practices to maintain the strict stratification and demarcation between the various racial groupings.

7. It is a basic tenet of anthropological knowledge that all healthy human beings have the capacity to learn any cultural behavior. Regardless of any physical differences that we may have or differences in upbringing or cultural history, we all are human.

This publicly available academic position paper on race by the American Anthropological Association was overdue in the eyes of many anthropologists and scholars, who appreciated the theoretical approach and strategies that the field brings to the topic. It helped to reframe the discussion on race and ethnicity and provided evidence that anthropology has had a long-standing history in addressing, investigating, and conducting fieldwork among all types of racial and ethnic populations, with the topic undertaken at the very beginnings of this discipline.

Major Subdisciplines of Anthropology

Now that we've highlighted how anthropology addressed the issue of race, let's get a deeper understanding of the field itself. As stated earlier, anthropology is a holistic discipline in which scholars examine the physical and cultural characteristics of a human population. But anthropology is so much more than that, too.

There are four major subdisciplines of anthropology. They are physical anthropology, archeology, linguistics, and cultural anthropology. Although each subdiscipline is uniquely focused on some aspect of human populations, they are nonetheless supportive of the overall approach in investigating human populations from a holistic perspective.

First, physical anthropology investigates and analyzes the physical, biological, and genetic characteristics of human populations. Second, archeology examines the material remains of human populations—past and present. Third, linguistics examines the language patterns of human populations—in particular, the descriptive elements of each language system, the historical aspects of each language system, and the sociocultural aspects of each language system. Finally, cultural anthropology examines the cultural beliefs, values, behaviors, and patterns associated with various human populations. In summary, these four subdisciplines help scientists to view and examine human populations from a much broader perspective than many other academic disciplines.

Although there were a number of distinguished scholars (Lewis Henry Morgan, Sir Edward Tylor, Brownislaw Malinowski, Ruth Benedict, and Margaret Mead) who contributed to the beginnings of American anthropology, it is Franz Boas (1858–1942)—a German immigrant to the United States—who is considered the father of American four-field anthropology. His book *Race, Language and Culture* (1940) is a collection of essays specifically on the topics of race, language, and culture.

Franz Boas—Father of American Anthropology

Recognized as the father of American anthropology, Franz Boas was a German immigrant to the United States fascinated primarily by the biological, linguistic, and cultural aspects of human populations throughout the world. In his early studies, Boas studied European immigrants as they became acculturated and assimilated to American culture. His biological studies revealed interesting biological adaptations and changes. The children of immigrants differed physically from their parents not because of genetic change but because they had grown up and adapted to a different environment. Thus Boas showed that human biology was "plastic," or, in other words, could change or be altered by environments, including cultural forces (Kottak 2011).

Yet if there was one major distinguishing attribute of Franz Boas that separated him from his professional peers at the time, it was his emphasis and commitment to fieldwork. Boas felt that in order for any scholar to truly learn about another culture or race, he or she needed to commit to time in the field—learning the values, traditions, history, and rituals of that particular group. His fieldwork among such Native American populations as the Kwakiutl Indians in British Columbia has become a classic example of his commitment to fieldwork, and it also helped establish fieldwork as a true scientific strategy in the field of anthropology.

His emphasis on fieldwork helped to further establish and connect the field of anthropology with such other fields of study as psychology, biology, race, and ethnicity. In addition, Boas mentored several famous students who conducted their own classic fieldwork activities, including Margaret Mead (Coming of Age in Samoa 1929), Ruth Benedict (*Race, Science and Politics* 1940), and Zora Neal Hurston (*Mules and Men*, 1935).

One of the issues that Franz Boas perhaps does not get enough credit for was his analysis and statements on race, particularly during a time in which the prevailing thought regarding race was very ethnocentric and biased. In *Race, Language and Culture* (1940), which originated in an address he gave as president of the American Association for the Advancement of Science in 1931, Boas (1940) stated the following: "Permit me to call your attention to the scientific aspects of a problem that has been a long time agitating our country and which, on account of its social and economic implications, has given rise to strong emotional reactions and has led to varied types of legislation. I refer to the problems due to the intermingling of racial types" (Boas 1940, 3).

The address—titled "Race and Progress"—further states: "The first point in regard to which we need clarification refers to the significance of the term race. In common parlance when we speak of a race we mean a group of people that have certain bodily and perhaps also mental characteristics in common" (Boas 1940, 4).

These two quotes highlight the significance of his presentation and his statement on race in the United States at the time. He actually challenged the major philosophy on race and the impact of interracial relations on the human species. In effect, Boas stated that all racial populations differ among themselves and one's environment plays an important factor in the variability of each racial population (Boas 1940, 5). This was a major statement on race in this country and helped to solidify scholars who were of a different mind-set and sympathetic to all the racial, ethnic, and immigrant groups dealing with discriminatory and racist situations throughout the United States.

Zora Neale Hurston—Anthropologist and Writer

One of Franz Boas's renowned students, Zora Neale Hurston (1891–1960), was an African American anthropologist, folklorist, short story writer, and novelist who became well known for her novels *Jonah's Gourd Vine* (1934), *Their Eyes Were Watching God* (1937), and *Moses, Man of the Mountain* (1939) years after her death. Growing up in Eatonville, Florida, Hurston began her high school and college academic career at Morgan Academy (later Morgan State University in Baltimore). She then attended Howard University in 1924 and completed her studies at Barnard College of Columbia University in 1928, where she studied as a graduate student under Franz Boas.

Zora Neale Hurston published seven books—four novels, two books of folklore, and an autobiography—and more than 50 shorter works between the middle of the Harlem Renaissance (1920s) and the end of the Korean War (1953), when she was the dominant African American writer in the United States. Yet it was her ethnographic fieldwork in the South and the Caribbean that helped not only to document the sharp racial divide between blacks and whites in various communities of the South, but also, and more importantly, provided some of the first African American anthropological analyses and perspectives on the issues of race in the United States during this period.

Providing an introduction to Hurston's book *Mules and Men* (1935), Franz Boas stated the following about her ethnographic fieldwork:

It is the great merit of Miss Hurston's work that she entered into the life of the southern Negro as one of them and was fully accepted as such by the companions of her childhood. Thus she has been able to penetrate through that affected demeanor by which the Negro excludes the White observer effectively from participating in his true inner life.

To the student of cultural history the material presented is valuable not only by giving the Negro's reaction to everyday events, to his emotional life, his humor and passions, but it throws into relief also the peculiar amalgamation of African and European tradition which is so important for understanding historically the character of the American Negro life, with its strong African background in the West Indies, the importance of which diminishes with increasing distance from the south. (Hurston 1935, xiii–xiv)

Zora Neale Hurston was delighted to get the opportunity to conduct field-work in the South and particularly beginning in her home town of Eaton-ville, Florida. She writes in the introduction to *Mules and Men*, "I was glad when somebody told me you can go and collect Negro folklore" (1).

Hurston further states why she returned to her hometown to start her eth-nographic fieldwork and study on African American folklore: "Dr. Boas asked me where I wanted to work and I said Florida. Florida is a place that draws people—white people from all over the world, and Negroes from every Southern state surely and some from the North and West. So I knew that it was possible for me to get a cross section of the Negro South in the one state. And then I realized that I was new myself, so it looked sensible for me to choose familiar ground" (Hurston 1935, 1).

Interestingly, Hurston recognized her unique opportunity to gather field-work data on a people (African Americans) and topic (folklore) that no other anthropologist, scholar, or fieldworker was able to collect at the time, simply because no others were from that community or of the same racial back-ground as she was. Hurston also recognized that folklore was a way in which a people (African Americans) expressed their beliefs, values, and traditions in a way that was metaphorical and theatrical in telling stories without revealing their true personality and thoughts—very similar to the agreed upon definition of folklore, which is, as defined by Kottak (2011, 318), "the art, music and lore of ordinary people."

This is explicitly highlighted in Hurston's comments on folklore:

Folkore is not as easy to collect as it sounds. The best source is where there are the least outside influences and these people, being usually under-privileged, are the shyest. They are most reluctant at times to reveal that which the soul lives by. And the Negro, in spite of his open-faced laughter, his seeming acquiescence, is particularly evasive. You see we are a polite people and we do not say to our questioner, "Get out of here!" We smile and tell him or her something that satisfies the white person because, knowing so little about us, he doesn't know what he is missing. The Indian resists curiosity by a stony silence. The Negro offers a feather-bed resistance. That is, we let the probe enter, but it never comes out. It gets smothered under a lot of laughter and pleasantries. (Hurston 1935, 2)

In essence, there is a twoness or double experience that many of her African American informants had to live with in a white-dominated society. Ironically, Zora Neale Hurston had to do the same during this time period—"live a double experience"—as a woman in a male-dominated world and as a black person in a nonblack world (Gates and Appiah 1993).

W. E. B. Du Bois—Social Scientist, Father of Race and Ethnic Relations

Without a doubt, the most influential African American intellectual during the late 1800s and early 1900s was William Edward Burghardt (W. E. B.) Du Bois. Du Bois (1868–1963) was an established scholar, social scientist, political activist, historian, civil rights activist, pan-Africanist, author, writer, editor, leader, and spokesperson for addressing race and ethnic relations in the United States and globally during the early 1900s. His extraordinary life spanned the century between Reconstruction and the modern civil rights ears. His many pioneering books of sociology, history, politics, and race relations include *The Suppression of the African Slave Trade* (Harvard doctoral dissertation), *The Philadelphia Negro: A Social Study* (the first case study of a black community in the United States), *The Souls of Black Folk: Black Reconstruction in America*, and *Dusk of Dawn*. Du Bois was also the founder of the Niagara Movement, a forerunner of the NAACP; the editor of the NAACP's *Crisis* magazine; a leader of pan-African movement; and a founder of the World Peace Council (Bailey 2000). Although W. E. B. Du Bois was always challenged on his thoughts, interpretations, experiences, and political stances among his African American and white colleagues, he nonetheless helped to bring to light the multiple layers of social, economic, historical, political, and cultural issues that were all interconnected with the discriminatory and racist policies associated with race and ethnic relations during this period.

Born in Great Barrington, Massachusetts in 1868, Du Bois described his birthplace in his autobiography, *The Autobiography of W. E. B. Du Bois: A Soliloquy on Viewing My Life from the Last Decade of Its First Century* (1968), in the following manner:

I was born by a golden river and in the shadow of two great hills, five years after the Emancipation Proclamation, which began the freeing of American Negro slaves. The valley was wreathed in grass and trees and crowned to the eastward by the huge bulk of East Mountain, with crag and cave and dark forests. Westward the hill was gentler, rolling up to gorgeous sunsets and cloud-swept storms. The town of Great Barrington, which lay between these mountains in Berkshire County, Western Massachusetts, had a broad Main Street, lined with maples and elms, with white picket fences before the home. The climate was to our thought quite perfect. (Du Bois 1968, 61)

Du Bois's mother, Mary Burghardt, and father, Alfred Du Bois, came to live temporarily after their marriage ceremony in the village of Housatonic, which adjoined Great Barrington on the north. Then after a few years, Du Bois's father went east into Connecticut to build a life and home for his mother and him. W. E. B. Du Bois and his mother went to live on the lands of his mother's clan on South Egremont Plain in the southern part of their town (Du Bois 1968, 62).

Du Bois described some elders in his immediate family as follows: "My immediate family, which I remember as a young child, included a very dark grandfather, Othello Burghardt. I dimly remember him, 'Uncle Tallow,' strong-voiced and redolent with tobacco, who sat stiffly in a great high chair beside the open fire, because his hip was broken. He was good-natured, but not energetic. The energy was in my grandmother, Sally, a thin, tall, yellow and hawk-faced woman, certainly beautiful in her youth, and efficient and managing in her age. She had Dutch and perhaps Indian blood, but the rest of the family were black" (Du Bois 1968, 64).

According to Du Bois, his family and the town of his upbringing (Great Barrington) played a significant role in his early perspectives of life. In fact, he described his early education in Great Barrington in the following manner: "The schools of Great Barrington were simple but good, well-taught; and truant laws were enforced. I started on one school ground, and continued there until I was graduated from high school. I was seldom absent or tardy. The curriculum was simple: reading, writing, spelling and arithmetic; grammar, geography and history. We learned the alphabet; we were drilled vigorously on the multiplication tables and we drew accurate maps. We could spell correctly and read with understanding" (Du Bois 1968, 77).

He also describes the town of Great Barrington as follows:

Great Barrington was a town of middle-class people, most native white Americans of English and Dutch descent. There were differences of property and income and yet all the men worked and seemed at least to be earning their living. Naturally the income was not proportioned to the effort; some men worked three hours a day and earned several thousands dollar a year; carpenters worked 12 hours a day for a dollar, and servants toiled day and night for two dollars a week. But we did not dream of a day when a man doing nothing could be a millionaire at 35, while his fellow broke back and heart and starved. The women were housekeepers, with a few exceptions, like teachers, the postmistress, and a clerk now and then in stores like Fassett's shop for women's apparel. (Du Bois 1968, 78)

Upon graduating high school, W. E. B. Du Bois attended Fisk University, a historically black college in Nashville, Tennessee, from 1885 to 1888 for his undergraduate college experience and degree and then later attended Harvard University from 1888 to 1890. Another interesting note from Du Bois's autobiography is his description of Harvard College: "To make my own attitude toward the Harvard of that day clear, it must be remembered that I went to Harvard as a Negro, not simply by birth, but recognizing myself as a member of a segregated caste whose situation I accepted but was determined to work from within that caste to find my way out" (p. 132).

Du Bois went on from Fisk University and Harvard College to the University of Berlin. After returning from Europe and completing his graduate studies, he earned his doctorate from Harvard University and became the first African American to earn a PhD from this very prestigious Ivy League university. A select number of professional job offers came his way. He chose a job at Wilberforce University—a "colored" church school in Ohio.

Du Bois's description of Wilberforce University, a university I grew up around in the 1960s and 1970s, is as follows:

Wilberforce was a small colored denominational college married to a State normal school. The church was too poor to run the college; the State tolerated the normal school so as to keep Negroes out of other State schools. Consequently, there were enormous difficulties in both church and State politics. This I soon realized. I had been hired to teach "Latin and Greek." They were not my specialty and despite years spent in their study I really knew far too little to teach them. But I had assumed that I was to assist Professor William Scarborough, a well-known Negro scholar long working at Wilberforce. To my amazement, I found that I was to replace him, since in quarrel between him and the President, he had been ousted and I had been advertised as a learned professor just from Germany. This was my introduction to church politics. I did not like it but the name of Wilberforce lured me. (Du Bois 1968, 185–86)

Most of Du Bois's spare time at Wilberforce University was devoted to the revision of his doctoral dissertation. "The Suppression of the African Slave-Trade to the United States of America, 1638–1870" was accepted by Harvard, and Du Bois obtained his PhD in 1895. In October 1896, the dissertation was published as the initial volume in the Harvard Historical Studies Series (Marable 1986, 22). The bulk of the text examined the political and legal dimensions of the growing attempt to abolish the slave trade and condemned the moral and political hypocrisy of American democracy—its inability to check this existent, growing evil that paved the way that led straight to the Civil War.

By the spring of 1896, Du Bois was ready to conduct more research and accepted an offer from the University of Pennsylvania to conduct an extensive study on the "social condition of the Colored People of the Seventh Ward of Philadelphia." From August 1, 1896, until the end of 1897, with the exception of two months in the summer of 1897, Du Bois worked on the project. Du Bois studied published volumes on Philadelphia's historical and socioeconomic conditions and reviewed archival materials. He developed comprehensive questionnaires on family units, individuals, and domestic workers. He personally interviewed 5,000 people. The result of his intense research project was the book *The Philadelphia Negro*, the first sociological text on an African American community (Marable 1986, 24–25).

In *The Philadelphia Negro*, Du Bois emphasized history in the analysis of any particular group. Du Bois was especially convinced that careful sociological measurement, combined with a proper cultural and historical understanding of a social group, could lead to the construction of a social agenda for reform (Marable 1986, 25). In this groundbreaking book, Du Bois also recognized the class stratification in black America—the black poor, the Negro middle class, and the Negro elite.

According to Marable (1986), Du Bois's scholarly activities assumed three major forms:

1. Drawing upon his experiences in Philadelphia, Du Bois initiated a series of sociological studies of various African American communities, which established the foundations for the field of black sociology.
2. Du Bois's research focused on the Atlanta University conferences—a plan of social study by means of recurring decennial inquiries into the same general set of human problems.
3. Du Bois's scholarly activity proposed a scientific, national study of the African American condition that would be the focus of all careful historical and statistical research on African Americans.

Not surprisingly, a few years later, in 1903, a small Chicago publishing house, A. C. McClurg, had contacted Du Bois concerning the possible publication of a collection of essays. The outcome of the publication of these 14 essays resulted in Du Bois's most famous book—*The Souls of Black Folk* (1903)—which presented the three major areas of his research: political history, sociology, and cultural criticism.

In the title of the book, "souls" refers to the twoness of the black American, and with the use of "folk," Du Bois was making a strong claim for the recognition of the dignity and separate identity of African Americans. Taken together, the text blends the main themes that comprised Du Bois's emerging social theory: "double consciousness," the beauty and originality of Negroes' "sorrow songs" and black religion, the unique spirituality of the Negro people, the necessity to develop black educational institutions, and the general division of the modern world along the "color line" (Marable 1986: 47–48).

With this brief overview of W. E. B. Du Bois's life, academic career, and scholarly works, it is clear why he is considered the father of race and ethnic relations in the United States. Despite years having passed since Du Bois's death, many of the same issues regarding race and ethnic relations are still relevant decades later.

Another interesting historical fact is that even Dr. Martin Luther King Jr. recognized the major accomplishments of Du Bois in a speech delivered during an International Cultural Evening at Carnegie Hall on February 23, 1968, in New York City, honoring Du Bois's life and works. Here are some of the key points that King made concerning Du Bois:

- He was an extremely talented teacher.
- He believed that black people have been kept in oppression by lies of inferiority.
- He believed that both blacks and whites believed in this inferior mentality.
- He dedicated his life to challenging this "inferiority" ideology that many Americans believed. (King 1970)

Race and Ethnic Relations

Historically, from one society to another, race and ethnic relations continued to be a growing issue and problem as more differing racial and ethnic groups lived in closer proximity to one another, particularly in the United States. As each metropolitan and suburban area expanded through the 19th, 20th, and 21st centuries, different racial and ethnic groups had to live closer together simply because of the limited space within a confined residential area, as well as more racial and ethnic groups being in the same socioeconomic status. Thus, understanding how various racial and ethnic groups can get along with each became a higher priority in each century for scholars, city planners, and politicians.

To analyze race and ethnic relations within a single nation, the concept of the plural society was elaborated by the anthropologist M. G. Smith. In *Pluralism in Africa* (1969) edited by Leo Kuper and Smith, he described a plural society as one in which different groups are internally distinguished from each other by institutional and cultural differences. Instead of one overarching homogenous identical system of institutions shared within a society, a plural society consists of ethnic groups that differ in social organization, beliefs, norms, and ideals. Building on this framework, anthropologists have utilized the phrase "cultural pluralism" to describe how various ethnic groups maintain diverse cultures within one society (Scupin 2012, 70). These ethnic groups may share the same language and dietary practices and subscribe to the same values and beliefs, but they have minimal social interactions with other ethnic groups. Although the concept of cultural pluralism became more popular in the field of anthropology, it was also used in other disciplines to describe what was really happening among racial and ethnic populations throughout the United States and elsewhere.

Cultural Pluralism

Actually, the concept of cultural pluralism has been with us for over 100 years, and it has been used in the scholarly world as a key concept in understanding the complexity of our ever-changing society from one decade to the next. The first scholar to use the term, the philosopher Horace M. Kallen (1929), envisioned a nation of European multiethnic nations within an "American civilization" and utilizing the English language as a common language. Decades later in 1970, Sanday (1970) described cultural pluralism as existing in any society where there is more than one style dimension, where there is more than one set of cultural themes, information components, and behavior styles sanctioned in a society. Because of the mechanism of intra-cultural diffusion, the members of these systems are in differing degrees articulated to the mainstream culture and hence can share elements in the culture. Yet, more than often, the subcultural groupings of which we are all a part of do not share particular elements of their culture with others. This is debatable, yet more recent evidence supports this pattern.

For example, Pantoja, Perry, and Blourock (2014) stated that the cultural-pluralism movement is based on a group's positive affirmation of its differences and its values in a multicultural society. This position rejects traditional stances of integration, assimilation, and acculturation. The goal of the new movement is to change the group's status and its circumstances while working toward promoting a socially just society. The cultural-pluralism movement recognizes and embraces other cultural groups identifiable through their adoption of alternative lifestyles because these new groups, along with people of color, are now viewing themselves as members of oppressed communities. Separation is now accepted by these groups as a necessary step as well as an objective for the development of a cultural-pluralistic society (Pantoja, Perry, and Blourock 2014, 14).

In general, cultural pluralism today refers to the maintenance of ethnic subcultures with their traditions, values, attitudes, styles, behaviors, and patterns. A person who adheres to more of a cultural-pluralism approach to life tends to have a stronger connection with his or her particular social, regional, rural, and ethnic subculture than other subcultural groups. This cultural-pluralism approach to life promotes more of a separatism adaptation in which all groups coexist with one another yet *none* truly interacts with each other on a consistent basis; therefore, these subcultural groups and other populations know *less* of each other's traditions, values, attitudes, styles, behaviors, and patterns than ever before.

In applying the cultural-pluralism approach to race relations among college students, we would have students of all various racial and ethnic backgrounds experiencing the same activities yet not truly interacting with one another. Examples include attending a football, basketball, or baseball game and rooting for the college's team yet not interacting after the event in any substantial way. Therefore, these student groupings *coexist* with one another yet do not truly interact or engage with each other on a deeper level.

Perhaps the most apparent example of cultural pluralism that is practiced nationwide by most U.S. colleges/universities is the daily classroom lectures given by professors and instructors in which students of all varying racial and ethnic backgrounds sit for an hour or two in their lecture hall, taking notes, interacting, and asking questions of the professor/instructor, as well as interacting with their fellow classmates for an entire semester/quarter. Although untapped in this way for the most part, the classroom lecture hall is a greatly available and very appropriate site in which to get college students interacting on a deeper level.

Yet many colleges/universities and professors/instructors do not take advantage of this ideal setting for this because of the misperception that just bringing students of varying racial and ethnic backgrounds together will generate a more enriching learning environment. Again, that is a fallacy.

Cultural pluralism does not promote group or subgroup interactions. It merely allows individuals/groups to share the same event together. Unfortunately, when students share the same experiences together, they still remain in their own secluded world, aided by their own values and beliefs about other groups of people and today aided by our new technology (laptops, smartphones, and so on). In fact, if you go to any college/university campus today, you will more than likely see a very high percentage of students talking, typing, viewing, engaging, or scrolling on their smartphones regularly, as opposed to interacting with another college student. Thus the outcome of a cultural-pluralistic college campus does not fulfill its intended expectations—providing a well-rounded, engaging, and inclusive higher educational learning experience for all.

Biculturalism

The third major approach to help all of us better understand race and ethnic relations is the concept of biculturalism. The concept of biculturalism has also been with us for years, and it has been used in the scholarly world as a key concept in understanding the complexity of our ever-changing society from one decade to the next. The idea of biculturalism has come into sharper focus due to changing intranational and international demographic shifts, expanding global economic markets, and persistent ethnic and religious warfare across many continents (Dennis 2008).

There are individuals who contend that it is best to live in two cultural worlds and believe themselves to be culturally and socially enriched by the differing institutions, customs, and social networks made available by this opportunity. Biculturalism exists among individuals who simply choose to move from one cultural group to another or because two groups live in close proximity and engage in trade and sociocultural activities. Over time, a degree of cultural exchange may occur, and a subordinate group may be forced to adopt some of the cultural attributes of a more dominant group for sheer individual and group survival. In the process, a degree of biculturalism emerges (Dennis 2008).

In reality, one seldom encounters those who believe themselves to be insiders in both cultures, especially during youth, for it is during these years that biculturalism may be viewed as more "oppositional and contradictory" (Dennis 2008). Many bicultural individuals seem to arrive at a state of cultural peace in which they are more likely to see themselves as having the right to "lay full claim to both identities." It is important to note here that being at ease in both cultures does not mean, or suggest, that one is assured of having been accepted in both cultures. It simply means that the person is familiar with the cultural nuances and subtleties of both cultures and is unafraid of moving within and between the cultures, and less intimidated by the possibilities of rejection (Dennis 2008, 17).

Biculturalism represents an unfreezing of cultures and a recognition of the cultural validity of another group. The difficulty of establishing its legitimacy can be attributed to the cultural hegemony of certain groups and the cultural suppression of others. The reality is that humans are perfectly capable of biculturality. Indeed, most of the world exists in bicultural or multicultural spheres, and it is this cultural adaptability that makes one society progress faster than others.

In general, biculturalism is based on the interaction and engagement of the individual with several cultures throughout one's life. An individual with a bicultural orientation would have friends in several cultures, enjoy various ethnic traditions, appreciate various languages, and be able to interact with various groups while maintaining an appropriate sensitivity to the different cultures. Therefore, biculturating individuals' broader cultural knowledge and higher integrative complexity may allow them to act as intermediaries, alleviating the difficulties associated with cross-cultural communications or race-relations issues.

Yet the reality and the implementation of biculturalism's approach for a majority of students simply does not happen at any significant level on most college/university campuses. Although there may be many sponsored college/university events celebrating various cultural and ethnic aspects throughout the academic year, the average college student has no incentive or motivation to participate in such events. Thus, a missed opportunity to interact and engage with students from different racial and ethnic backgrounds happens each and every day on college/university campuses nationwide.

This is why biculturalism and cultural pluralism are two models that appear to be ideal for the college/university environment yet both are ineffective in actually creating constructive dialogue and actions to improve race and ethnic relations among college students of all walks of life. For a majority of administrators and academicians, this may be difficult to read and accept because these concepts, models, and frameworks have been widely accepted as status quo for decades. Nonetheless, they have been mostly ineffective in changing the culture of race and ethnic relations among average college students across America.

Biopsychosocioculturalinguistics (BPSCL)

The fourth and final approach to better understand race and ethnic relations is a brand-new concept referred to as biopsychosocioculturalinguistics. Biopsychosocioculturalinguistics, or BPSCL, is a concept based in the field of anthropology that is directly applicable for investigating and developing new strategies in race and ethnic relations. This concept and framework goes far beyond the previous concepts (bicultural, cultural pluralism, and civil rights) primarily because it addresses race and ethnic relations in the following areas:

- biological
- psychological
- sociological
- cultural
- linguistics

In other words, a holistic, well-rounded, in-depth, and personal approach in understanding, evaluating, and working with people of different racial and ethnic backgrounds is an approach no other concept, model, or framework has even come close to. So how does this BPSCL model actually help us to better understand and appreciate race and ethnic relations? Here is the step-by-step approach:

1. Biological: In race and ethnic relations, we often judge individuals, groups, and populations based upon their physical, visual, outward appearances or other phenotypic physical expression. Moreover, in our westernized society, we are taught and enculturated to categorize individuals based upon their skin color, their hair texture, their facial features, and their physique. Whether it's right or wrong, all of us make these biased judgments on others based upon these biological features. Unfortunately, it's a fact and reality of the world in which we live. In order for all of us to eliminate prejudgment and misperceptions that we have of other groups, individuals, and populations based upon our individual biology, we must clearly and directly correct individuals about our racial and ethnic backgrounds so that a better and more accurate understanding of various racial and ethnic populations can be appreciated. Thus, biology must be a key component of our new model as it relates to race and ethnic relations.

2. Psychological: In race and ethnic relations, we are often self-evaluating who we are racially and ethnically, particularly among those who are multiracial, biracial, or mixed. Not only are these individuals psychologically self-evaluating themselves, but society is psychologically evaluating them simply because a majority of our U.S. population does not know how to approach or what to say to a multiracial, biracial, or mixed person when discussing race and ethnicity. Race and ethnicity therefore gets overlooked, avoided, misunderstood, and dismissed as a nonfactor when evaluating a racial and/or ethnic incident. A more appropriate and effective method in evaluating an incident of racial and ethnic relations is to investigate the psychological issues, whether it is between two individuals who are of different racial and ethnic backgrounds or whether it is between an individual or group of the same racial and ethnic background. Investigating the psychology—the mental health and culturally based values and beliefs—of a racial- and ethnic-relations issue may provide a deeper understanding and appreciation as to why a racial- and ethnic-relations issues occurred. Thus, psychology must be a key component of our new model as it relates to race and ethnic relations.

3. Social: In race and ethnic relations, we often pay attention to all the social issues that are associated with a particular racial and ethnic group. Usually when a problem occurs with the individual and/or racial and ethnic group, such social issues as social-economic standing (SES), educational level, employment status, and income are major contributing factors to an individual's and/or racial and ethnic group's problems. Yet this is too simplistic of a connection—social factors with racial- and ethnic-relations

problems. Without a doubt, social factors do provide academicians and administrators a clue as to which major factors could have greatly contributed to a person's inability to get along with a person from a different racial and ethnic background. Whether the student comes from a lower or higher social-economic standing, or whether the student has a lower or higher educational level than the other student, social factors oftentimes influence the student's perspective about other students. In general, social factors must be kept in their proper context. They can be used as general markers or indicators related to a student's behavior yet not used as absolute and specific determining factors to account for a student's behavior. That's why in this new model, I recognized social factors as one of the key components to our new model as it relates to racial and ethnic relations.

4. Cultural: In race and ethnic relations, we often overlook the cultural factors associated with specific individuals and/or groups when attempting to resolve a racial- and/or ethnic-relations issue. A major reason why scholars, administrators, and the general public have not paid attention to the cultural factors is that many do not believe that culture is a significant factor in race and ethnic relations, and many do not know the cultural factors affiliated with certain groups and populations. The fact of the matter is that culture is the key component to our new model. Culture has been and will continue to be the driving force for better understanding each other and better understanding our world. Yet how do you actually examine and use culture in improving race and ethnic relations?

Culture is defined as a system of shared beliefs, values, traditions, and customs that are transmitted from generation to generation by learning (Bailey 2010). The concept of culture can be used in six major ways to improve race and ethnic relations: (1) culture is learned; (2) culture adds meaning to reality; (3) culture is transmitted by symbols; (4) culture is integrated; (5) culture is differently shared; and (6) culture is adaptive.

First, with respect to the fact that culture is learned, the same can be said of race and ethnic relations. Race and ethnic relations are learned processes—that is, each of us has learned positive and negative approaches and/or good or bad experiences with people of different racial and ethnic backgrounds. Overall, these approaches and experiences, whether positive or negative, set a learned pattern when all of us are attempting to better understand racial and ethnic groups.

Second, with respect to the fact that culture is transmitted by symbols, the same can be said for race and ethnic relations. Race and ethnic relations are transmitted symbolically—verbally and nonverbally. Nonverbally refers to our body language, gestures, or postures that an individual conveys when interacting with another person. For example, if a person is uncomfortable around another person of a different racial or ethnic background, it will more than likely show in his or her body language, gestures, or postures. Yet if a person is comfortable around another racial or ethnic person, then more than likely his or her body language, gestures, and postures will show it by being very relaxed and interacting with that other person. In general, a person shows how he or she feels about a person of a different racial or ethnic group, whether comfortable or not comfortable through body language, gestures, and postures.

Third, with respect to the fact culture adds meaning to reality, the same can be said for race and ethnic relations. Race and ethnic relations are practical issues based in real-world, day-to-day reality in which individuals have to learn skills in getting along with those who are different from you. This is an issue that is often overlooked because individuals do not realize that it takes a certain set of skills or experiences to interact successfully with individuals of different racial and ethnic backgrounds. If individuals have not developed these skills or had previous experiences interacting with other groups, then racial and ethnic relations will remain difficult and uncertain. Thus, the reality of race and ethnic relations is that it needs to be nurtured, experienced, and appreciated in order for better racial and ethnic relations to occur on college campuses.

Fourth, with respect to the fact culture is integrated, the same can be said for race and ethnic relations. That is, race and ethnic relations are highly integrated into the total fabric of our society because our U.S. and global societies are made up of all different racial and ethnic groups in all different facets of our society—political, educational, health and medical care, economic, entertainment, and sports. We, as a global society, must accept that we are no longer isolated within our own communities or our own racial and ethnic groupings, and we are regularly going to interact with so many individuals of various racial and ethnic groups on a daily and weekly basis. That is a reality and a reality that our communities, neighborhoods, and particularly our college campuses need to clearly realize.

Fifth, with respect to the fact that culture is differently shared, the same can be said of race and ethnic relations. Race and ethnic relations are typically different for everyone depending on one's exposure, experience, and ability to get along with others. For a majority of college students, understanding the various racial- and ethnic-relations issues, whether on campus or from national events, tends to be a challenging endeavor. Yet there are ways in which every college campus could make it easier for each college student to better understand and relate to various racial and ethnic populations simply by offering courses or campus programs that get the average student to interact throughout his or her academic career. Finding ways to regularly reward students for their interaction and engagement with one another will greatly benefit not only the college/university but most importantly the individual college student. Thus, a college student's experience with other racial and ethnic groups on campus can result in more positive experiences than negative ones.

Finally, with respect to culture being adaptive, the same can be said of race and ethnic relations. Race and ethnic relations have dramatically changed over the decades in which the focus has traditionally been black-versus-white race-relations comparisons. Whether African Americans were discriminated against by whites or whites were unfairly treated by African Americans, this was the regular conflict.

Yet times have dramatically changed, and race relations have adapted to our changing times, where presently there are race- and ethnic-relations issues between all major racial and ethnic groups in our society. None are left out, and all groups have had their confrontations and issues with others. Thus, race relations today are a multiracial and multiethnic issue—no longer just a black-and-white issue.

5. Linguistic: Finally, in race and ethnic relations, we fail to recognize that language is a key factor in how individuals interact with each other. Using the appropriate language or dialect or slang term is often the key to better interrelationships among different racial, ethnic, and social groups. When a person speaks the language of a particular group and sounds like the group, he or she will more than likely connect with that particular group on a deeper cultural level. Conversely, that particular group will more than likely respect and reach out to the individual who learns their language, specific dialect, or slang terms. Therefore, language is the final key factor and component of my brand-new model and framework for evaluating, understanding, and improving race and ethnic relations on college campuses.

Conclusion

One of the most challenging aspects related to race and ethnic relations is to find a way to understand this very complex, politically and socially sensitive societal issue. As highlighted in this chapter, there have been a wide variety of models and frameworks that have been developed, used, and followed by numerous scholars and administrators for several decades. It is my contention that these earlier models have been used and followed again and again by others simply because they were a convenient and safe way to approach race and ethnic relations.

Yet this book offers a new approach and model in framing our discussion and assessment associated with race and ethnic relations. In fact, this is exactly what is needed in the field of race and ethnic relations and for all those who are in search of a new theory and framework to tackle the most challenging issue of our times on college campuses across the United States.

It is time for a new narrative on all the issues related to race and ethnic relations. No longer can we continue with the same theories, analyses, and interpretations of why we as human beings have difficulty getting along with one another. If we do not attempt to examine race and ethnic relations from a new perspective or framework, then all of the groundbreaking efforts of a number of renowned, passionate, insightful, and thought-provoking scholars of the past will continue to be overlooked, and attempts to improve race and ethnic relations will continue to fail.

Interracial Relationships and Race Relations: A Cultural-Historical Review in America

With the increased diversity on college campuses today, interracial relationships among college students has also increased. As mentioned in chapter 2, interracial dating has become a part of the college experience, and there is not the same cultural taboo that there was several decades ago on college campuses.

Yet the concepts of race and race relations still evoke all types of sensitive personal, social, familial, and cultural emotions. These issues become particularly heightened when individuals of different races develop interracial relationships that may result in offspring between the two. When this occurs, there is usually some type of reaction, whether positive or negative, from close family members, friends, associates, community members, and society in general.

Since 1967, when the U.S. Supreme Court ruled bans on interracial cohabitation and marriage are unconstitutional, interracial relationships in the country have increased sharply. As of 2005, rates of interracial marriage were 10 times greater among whites, blacks, and Hispanics than in the 1960s. Even among Asian Americans, 12 percent of the men and 25 percent of the women married non-Asians (Alderman 2007, 12).

In spite of these increases, interracial marriage occurs less frequently than same-race unions. In 2002, interracial marriages accounted for only

2.9 percent of all marriages in the United States, and only 5.7 percent of Americans involved in serious romantic relationships were dating or living with partners of a different race. In a study conducted by Cornell University, researchers found that while youths were more likely than their elders to be involved in interracial relationships overall, they nevertheless remained relatively secretive about them, apparently fearing the disapproval of their families or their peers. Young women were also reportedly more likely to hide pregnancies resulting from intercourse with a partner of a different race. Thus, the relative infrequency of mixed-race unions and the need for secrecy or discretion described by many who date interracially suggest that while attitudes may be changing, a cultural stigma is still associated with such relationships (Alderman 2007, 12).

Why do members of our society feel this way in 2018? Why are we still amazed when people, and particularly college students, of all types of racial and ethnic backgrounds decide to have interracial relationships? The answer lies in U.S. history—a history that many would love to forget.

The Beginnings of Interracial Relationships in America

From an anthropological perspective, human populations have always been successful in interbreeding and reproducing offspring who can in turn interbreed. From one continent to another, and from one earlier time period to another, human populations have been very successful in increasing their numbers despite the uncertainty of their immediate natural environments and other populations. Whether interbreeding takes place among a population similar in physical attributes or among people with different physical attributes, human populations have been a highly adaptable species (Molnar 1975).

Unfortunately, over time, as human populations interacted with other types of human populations that may have had different physical attributes, categories used for typing different human populations became popular. Thus, we can see the term "race" is a historical artifact from an archaic biology. These categories of typing human populations also became the beginnings of racial categorizations.

As Europeans fanned out across the globe during the age of exploration, the elites of the societies found unparalleled opportunities for the accumulation of wealth and power (Murphy 2001). In many cases, however, these opportunities were only available through the destruction of local societies in North and South America, the Caribbean, Africa, Asia, and the Pacific Islands. In other cases, local indigenous populations were subjugated and recruited into social, economic, and political systems that placed them in the lowest and least privileged classes of the newly emerging colonial social structures (Murphy 2011).

As Murphy (2001, 3) explains, "By the time the American colonies traversed the road of separation from English rule, the concept of race with its implications of institutionalized superiority and inferiority was well embedded in the consciousness and the economy of the emerging body politic." The nation's founders struggled to reconcile the concepts of liberty, equality, slavery, and their own economic self-interest. Perhaps they were torn, and perhaps they agonized over the issues, but the union they formed retained slavery for several more generations and culminated in the most costly, tragic, and divisive crisis in American history (Murphy 2001, 3).

Murphy states, "Although the Civil War freed slaves in the United States, it could not eradicate racial divisions nor the attitudes and beliefs that they engendered. Nor was racial discrimination in America confined to the African American population" (3). Native Americans suffered terribly as the country engaged in the westward expansion that many white Americans considered the United States' "manifest destiny." Chinese and other Asian people were the target of many discriminatory laws. Even immigrants of European backgrounds commonly suffered discriminatory practices based on their racial backgrounds (Murphy 2001, 3).

With time and the passing of generations, speech accents disappeared, and European immigrants gradually became more acceptable to the established white Anglo-Saxon Protestant majority. As American-born offspring of formerly despised European immigrant groups replaced their parents in the population, discrimination against them decreased, and many experienced upward social mobility (Murphy 2001, 3–4).

Many researchers believe that the African American population experienced a similar pattern of discrimination and gradual acceptance; even so, because of their skin color and other physical attributes (e.g., hair, eyes, nose, lips, and body type), their discrimination was far more severe and pervasive. For example, an African American who was darker complected was often perceived as less intelligent, less attractive, and less desired than African Americans with lighter skin. Therefore, these darker-complected African Americans received fewer opportunities throughout their lives, ensuring that they maintained at a lower social-economic standing than their lighter-complected counterparts.

Mixed-Race Children

Mulattoes

Historically, the term "mulatto" was used to refer to a person with one white parent and one black parent or, more broadly, a person of mixed black and white ancestry (Winters and DeBose 2003). As Winters and DeBose note, "the term 'mulatto' was also used to refer to the offspring of whites who intermarried with South Asian indentured servants brought over to the British American colonies by the East India Company" (43). In 1680, a typical person referred to as mulatto was a Eurasian daughter born to a South Asian father and Irish mother in Maryland and later sold into slavery. Although still in use in the last half of the 20th century, the term "mulatto" was not used as often and was considered culturally insensitive by some in the United States.

With the concept and the sociopolitical system firmly established around the rules of race and racial discrimination at the early beginnings of the United States, interracial relationships had to adhere to the nation's law of the land at this point in U.S. history. That law of the land stipulated that people of different races—particularly whites and blacks—were not to have any intimate relations that might potentially result in offspring. Although in the pre–Civil War South, sexual liaisons between white men and African American women were not uncommon, the opposite was true for black men and white women. Sexual intimacy and interracial relationship between a black man and a white woman was unthinkable and forbidden both before and after the Civil War. Black men were targets of some of the cruelest torture and murder ever known in American history in the period between the 1870s and the 1940s, and their abuse was often triggered by accusations of sexual interest in white women (Murphy 2001, 40).

"Amalgamation" was the initial term used to describe sexual reproduction—within or outside the context of marriage—involving individuals who were presumed to belong to distinct races, especially those sociologically and biologically designated as black or white. As explained by Ifekwunigwe (2004), with the publication of *Miscegenation: The Theory of the Blending of the Races Applied to the American White and Negro* in 1864, David Goodman Croly introduced the work "miscegenation," which he thought sounded more scientific than "amalgamation." He combined two Latin words, *miscere* ("to mix") and *genus* ("race"), to create "miscegenation" (10).

Black and white miscegenation dates back to the 16th century and the beginning of the trans-Atlantic slave trade, wherein West Africans were forcibly removed their homeland and sold as chattel slaves to work on plantations in the southern United States, the Caribbean, and Brazil. In societies whose economies were originally dependent on the exploitation of nonwhite slaves, miscegenation between slave women and their slave masters contributed to the viability of the labor force (Ifekwunigwe 2004, 10).

In 1619, 20 African slaves were purchased in Virginia and used to cultivate the tobacco crop. These early slaves were set to work side by side with white European indentured servants. Children of mixed race were born soon thereafter. The fathers of some these children were white slave traders in Africa and seamen from the Middle East, but miscegenation also occurred frequently within the combined slave and indentured-slave laboring class (Zack 1993, 78).

In 1662, Virginia enacted the first law prohibiting interracial marriage, in an attempt to reduce the number of mixed-race children. Although the most frequent interracial sex was between white men and black women, the children of these unions were not regulated to their fathers in the tradition of British patriarchy but rather were given the status of their mothers. The mixed-race children of white women were not slaves, but they were often bound to indentured servitude well into their adult years. The white mothers of such children, who had their own periods of servitude extended, were subject to fines and other legal penalties. For example, in 1691, Virginia enacted a law requiring that any free white woman bearing a mulatto child had to pay a fine within 30 days of race indentured servitude for 5 years for herself and 30 years for her child. The child was to be sold as a servant (Zack 1993, 79).

In 1705, the Virginia assembly decreed that any minister who married a racially mixed couple had to pay a fine of 10,000 pounds of tobacco. Eventually it became illegal for mulattoes to marry blacks in Virginia. The states of Maryland and Pennsylvania had stricter penalties against interracial unions and the resulting mulatto children (Zack 1993, 79).

During the period from 1705 to 1725, most of the colonies passed laws similar to those in Virginia, Maryland, and Pennsylvania. However, despite this proscriptive legislation, it has been estimated that by the time of the American Revolution there were between 60,000 and 120,000 people of mixed black and white race in the American colonies. The official U.S. census counted the total black population as 757,000 in 1790, although there was no official count of mixed-race individuals until 1850, when it was estimated that they represented approximately 3 percent of the minority population.

By the 1850s, the mixed-race population dramatically increased in numbers in all the states, but their treatment and acceptance varied from state to state. Zack (1993) states in her book *Race and Mixed Race* that in the upper South approximately 37 percent of all mulattoes were free and made up 35 percent of the total free Negro population. In Georgia, for example, free mulattoes had all the rights of whites, except for voting and sitting in the assembly. Throughout the lower South, free mulattoes tended to be recognized by whites as an intermediate caste between whites and blacks, perhaps because there were fewer whites in proportion to black slaves in the lower South.

In Louisiana and South Carolina, many free mulattoes were prosperous: they owned both land and slaves, accumulated wealth, and were successful artisans, tradespeople, professionals, and artists. During the entire period of slavery in South Carolina, there was no law against racial intermarriage. In the upper South, free mulattoes were associated with their lower-class white colonial forebears, and they tended to be marginalized both economically and legally (Zack 1993, 81).

Between 1850 and 1915, race relations changed significantly in the United States. As Williamson (1980) notes in *New People: Miscegenation and Mulattoes in the United States*, this was a period in which the country's definition of race evolved from a stringent slave paradigm of race relations. The transformation in race relations was tied to the emergence of the Industrial Revolution. In the 17th and 18th centuries, the American South had developed plantation slavery to contribute significant quantities of tobacco, rice, and sugar to world commerce. Early in the 19th century, it turned the vast productive power of plantation slavery to supply most of the world's cotton (Williamson 1980, 61).

In 1850, African Americans were integral to the Industrial Revolution through the institution of slavery. In 1915, they were excluded from direct and organized participation in the Industrial Revolution by institutions of segregation, disfranchisement, and proscription. Thus, in both slavery and freedom, African Americans were steadily and firmly excluded from enjoying an appreciable share of the benefits of industrialization (Williamson 1980, 62).

During this same period, the position of mulattoes and the attitudes held by and about mulattoes were an index to the changeover in race relations. In essence, particularly in the lower South, the dominant white society moved from semiacceptance of free mulattoes to outright rejection of these individuals. Williamson (1980, 62) states that "as mulatto communities continued to grow, they experienced more stringent rules against them in the form of laws of social pressures." Eventually, more and more of the mulatto elite class gave up white alliances and picked up black alliances. This transformation increased in the Civil War, took firm hold during the critical year 1865, and continued throughout Reconstruction, the post-Reconstruction period, and into the 20th century. By the two decades between 1905 and 1925, mulattoes and the mulatto elite had allied themselves totally with the black world (Williamson 1980, 62).

Williamson (1980) also notes that the mulatto elite were strikingly effective in uniting themselves with the black masses and black leadership. Southern-bred black leaders, naturally enough, tended to be ex-slaves from the "black belts," and they represented the interests of ex-slaves. What their constituents most wanted was economic opportunity. In an agrarian society, this desire translated primarily into access to the land and its produce. Mulattoes, in contrast, were more interested in full admission to American society. Thus, they stressed integration in all public facilities, from the schools through the common carriers to libraries, the theater, and even the opera. Mulatto and black leaders exhibited a ready ability to mediate their differences and join together in the pursuit of their goals. In terms of legislation, they quickly proved successful in achieving their collective goals (Williamson 1980, 81).

During this changeover of race relations, the number of mulattoes had grown in both absolute and relative terms. The 1850 census counted 406,000 mulattoes among 3,639,000 Negroes. In 1910, it counted 2,051,000 mulattoes in a total Negro population of 9,828,000. In 1850, mulattoes accounted for 11.2 percent of the total Negro population; in 1910, they represented 20.9 percent of the total. According to Williamson (1980), these figures represented only mulattoes whose mixed ancestry was visible to the census takers. Officials of the census estimated that actually some three-fourths of the Negro population in America were mixed race in some degree at this time (63).

In general, although mulattoes were identified, acknowledged, and categorized as a distinguishable racial population separate from the black population by the U.S. census, they were still treated by many Americans as though they were black. Thus, in the white world as well as in the mulattoes' world, they were considered black.

The One-Drop Rule

The so-called one-drop rule is a societal and cultural rule that significantly changed racial categories and the way in which Americans thought about race, particularly as it related to African Americans. The basic premise behind the one-drop rule is just that: one drop of blood from a particular ancestor (black) will cause a person to be a part of that group. Thus, most supporters of this rule contended that a person with one drop of black blood was, in fact, black.

The one-drop rule is similar to the term "hypodescent," meaning that Americans of African physical appearance are considered black, even if their African admixture is less than 50 percent of their total genetic heritage (Harris 1964). Developed by anthropologist Marvin Harris (1964), the concept of hypodescent contends that there are always some physical signs of an individual's blackness regardless of his or her admixture. Some scholars and researchers say that such heritage is revealed in the color of the half-moons at the base of the thumbnails or in the shape of the heel or in blue or purple marks at specific locations on the body. To them, the one-drop rule is the belief that no matter how diluted African blood may be, a residue of visible evidence will always remain as a legacy, generation after generation (Harris 1964).

The one-drop rule can also closely align with the notion of "invisible blackness." Sweet (2005, 268) states that "this means that someone who appears European is considered Black anyway, presumably due to having some distant intangible Black ancestry." Furthermore, the one-drop rule's contention of invisible blackness happens only in the United States (Sweet 2005, 269).

In Sweet's (2005) *Legal History of the Color Line: The Notion of Invisible Darkness*, five major areas of data are cited to illustrate why the one-drop rule of invisible blackness developed in the North between 1830 and 1840: (1) a bidirectional strategy, (2) journals and diaries, (3) literature and drama, (4) court cases, and (5) graphs and charts. In general, Sweet suggests that "the origin of the one-drop rule in the 1830s helped to ensure that blacks could not enter the white world and that whites would be ostracized if they claimed to have any African American heritage since the races lived in parallel, but unequal social statuses" (11). At the same time, the one-drop rule was reinforced and encouraged by African American ethnic leaders seeking to strengthen group loyalties and to maintain their numbers.

Mixed Bloods

As early as the 1500s, the terms "mixed blood," "half-breed," and "breed" appeared in historical records to describe the descendants of Indians and the newcomers to the American continent (Baird-Olson 2003). The label "mixed blood" is used most often, given its widespread lay usage. Yet a number of other labels have been used at times as synonyms for all of the various ethnic/national combinations of the descendants of European American "sanctified" unions with American Indians, "nonsanctified" relationships between Indians and non-Indians, and sexual assaults against Indian women by non-Indian males (Baird-Olson 2003, 196).

The fate of the offspring of widespread First Nations miscegenation has been a matter of concern since the colonizers of the 1400s and 1500s came into the lands of the indigenous peoples of the Northeast, Southeast, and Southwest. As Baird-Olson (2003) states in her book's chapter "Colonization, Cultural Imperialism, and the Social Construction of American Indian Mixed-Blood Identity," initially, "although both First Nations and Europeans sought political marriages to protect economic and political interests, the invaders and colonizers racialized ideologies created a social issue: What would be the fate of 'mixed-blood' offspring?" (195).

By the 1860s, American Indians were actually recorded independently on the general U.S. census. According to the U.S. Census Bureau, the average degree of mixed blood among American Indians fell between 35 percent and 45 percent. In 1880, "Indian Division" schedules recorded whether respondents were "of full-blood" or whether they embodied "mixture" with whites, blacks, mulattoes, or another tribe (U.S. Census Bureau 1973). In 1910, fractions of Indian, white, and Negro blood were recorded. The U.S. Census Bureau (1973) reported that while "census takers changed to a simple full-blooded/mixed blood dichotomy in 1930, the 1950 census reintroduced the blood quantum construct with the category 'degree of Indian blood' and its response options: 'full blood,' 'half to full,' 'quarter to half,' and 'less than quarter.'"

According to U.S. census data from 1910 to 1950, mixed bloods totaled approximately 94,000 (35 percent of the total Indian population) in 1910, and their number increased to approximately 137,000 (40 percent of the total Indian population) in 1950. It is obvious from the census numbers and criteria for mixed bloods that the percentage of mixed bloods dramatically increased during the 40-year period.

Morning (2003) notes that the census officials' definitions of mixed-race people of American Indian origin differed from their definitions concerning mulattoes. The differences are as follows:

1. Although Indian blood percentage would be evaluated, the social status of the individual in question remained salient.
2. People of mixed-race ancestry could be assigned to the higher status rather than the lower status of the two racial groups with which they were identified.
3. Individuals of white and Indian origin could be identified as white if their communities recognized them as such.
4. Those of Indian and black origin could be recorded as Indian.

Yet those who were designated as mulatto were given no such option; no amount of community recognition could legitimate the transformation from black to white (Morning 2003, 46).

Mestizo

"Mestizo" is a term traditionally used in Latin America and Spain for people of mixed European and Native American heritage or descent (Winters and DeBose 2003). In the early colonial period, a mestizo ("mestiza" for a female) was a child born to Indian and Spanish or Portuguese parents. Typically, the father was Spanish or Portuguese and the mother was Indian, reflecting both the demographics of the early colonial period, where there were far fewer European women in the Americas, and the socially accepted patterns of marriage, concubinage, and sexual relations between members of different racial groups (Sanabria 2007, 111).

In his book *The Anthropology of Latin America and the Caribbean*, Harry Sanabria (2007, 111) states that "as unions between Spanish/Portuguese men and Indian or African women produced large numbers of children of mixed ancestry, the categories of *Mestizo* and Mulatto, respectively, came to reflect the emerging racial diversity." Over time, however, racial classification became increasingly complex, as generations of mixing led to multiple intermediate categories in such places as Brazil, Mexico, and Cuba.

As the years passed and intermixing continued, it became more difficult to readily distinguish members of different categories based on physical appearance alone. In Brazil, for example, researchers have compiled a list of

134 physical types based on skin color and other physical characteristics (Sanabria 2007, 112). Sanabria (2007) emphasizes not only that these different categories highlight the remarkable complexity of racial classifications in Brazil, but also that these categories are cultural and not biological classifications. This is true for the following several reasons:

1. The simple recognition that systems of racial classifications differ from society to society points to the social construction of racial difference.
2. The means by which racial categories are recognized and the meanings attached to these categories change over time and in different contexts.
3. Racial classification and identities are rational, emerge, and show themselves through social interactions among people.
4. The markers of racial difference after the early colonial period are as much cultural as they are physical.

Therefore, one's identification as a mestizo, for example, is as much a recognition of differences in dress, language, and occupation as it is a comment on the phenotypic characteristics of that individual (Sanabria 2007, 113).

Over time, as mestizos moved into mainstream American society, they became doubly mixed, doubly mestizo. Velazco Y Trianosky explains: "We are mixed for the second time by culture, through our encounter with the dominant culture in this new land. We are mixed for the second time by race, as we intermingle with our new Anglo-European cousins. Thus, we become Puerto Rican Americans, Mexican Americans and Cuban Americans" (Velazco Y Trianosky 2003, 177).

Amerasians

The term "Amerasian" refers to a person born in Asia to a U.S. military father and an Asian mother. According to the Amerasian Foundation (AF) and Amerasian Family Finder (AFF), "Amerasian" is defined as any person who was fathered by a citizen of the United States (an American serviceman), American expatriate, or U.S. government employee (regular or contract) and whose mother is, or was, an Asian national (2011).

The term "Amerasian" is also applied to half-Japanese children fathered by U.S. servicemen in Japan on the island of Okinawa, to children of Filipinos and American rulers during the U.S. colonial period of the Philippines, and to the children of Thais and U.S. soldiers during World War II and the Vietnam War. Since 1898, when the United States first colonized the Philippines, there have been Amerasians (Nimmons 2011).

Hapa Haole

In the Hawaiian language, *hapa* is defined as follows: "portion, fragment, part, faction, installment; to be partial, less" (Winters and DeBose 2003). The term *hapa haole*, meaning "half-Caucasian," is used to describe those persons who are half-Asian of Chinese, Japanese, Korean, or Filipino ancestry and half-Caucasian. On the islands, those individuals mixed with Asian, Polynesian, and European heritage are most often described as cosmopolitan or local (Nimmons 2011, 48).

Moreover, the term *hapa* can be used in conjunction with other Hawaiian racial and ethnic descriptors to specify a particular racial or ethnic mixture. Some examples follow:

- *Hapa haole* (part Caucasian/white)
- *Hapa kanaka* (part Native Hawaiian)
- *Hapa popolo* (part African/black)
- *Hapa kepani* (part Japanese); the term "hapanese" is also used
- *Hapa pilipino* (part Filipino)
- *Hapa pake* (part Chinese)
- *Hapa kolea* (part Korean)
- *Hapa kamoa* (part Samoan)
- *Hapa sepania* (part Spanish)
- *Hapa pukiki* (part Portuguese/white)

Historically, it is believed that the Hawaiian Islands were first populated by the Polynesians from the Marquesas and Tahiti somewhere between 300 and 500 CE (Nimmons 2011, 47). Centuries later, Europeans arrived to the islands around 1778, with the voyages of British explorer James Cook. The Hawaiian Islands soon became a convenient location for ships to stop and a source of supplies for traders and whalers.

The next major groups to migrate significantly to Hawaii were the Chinese and Japanese. Nimmons (2011, 47) notes that "Chinese workers settled upon Hawaiian shores in 1789 followed by the first legal Japanese immigrants arriving in 1885 also as contract laborers for the pineapple and sugarcane plantations." Shortly afterward, Puerto Rican immigrants entered Hawaii after a natural catastrophe wiped out the fertile lands of Puerto Rico. Next, two waves of Korean immigration occurred, first between 1903 and 1924 and again around 1965.

Other groups of ethnicities also immigrated to the Hawaiian Islands, such as Samoans, Mormons, Fijians, Gilbert Islanders, Norwegians, Spaniards,

Germans, and Russians (Nimmons 2011). Filipino immigrants also traveled to Hawaii during the 1840s during the push for plantation labor. Although the Portuguese and Japanese frequently migrated as entire families, most of the laborers who were imported to work in the fields were young men who oftentimes married within the local community of women (Nimmons 2011, 47).

Conclusion

America was, and continues to be, a land of opportunity for many native, indigenous populations, as well as immigrants. Whether due to political persecution, indentured servitude, forced slavery, familial customs, or individual decision, all types of racial and ethnic populations came to North America to establish their own new cultural history. Their adaptation to the new world and new living situations brought various communities together, resulting in a wide array of interracial relationships and marriages.

Regardless of the laws and endogamous rules (encouraging individuals of certain racial and ethnic backgrounds to marry within their race or ethnic group) that most populations adhered to, interracial relationship and marriages occurred and eventually increased. As each decade and century passed, more and more interracial relationships and marriages occurred. Their offspring, in turn, were categorized as what we now refer to as "multiracial populations." This self-identification as "multiracial" is still a new racial concept.

CHAPTER SIX

National Politics and Race Relations

One of the most critical issues that has divided and brought together people of all ethnic and racial backgrounds in this nation is politics and race relations. As we have already defined earlier in this book, race relations refers to the ability of two distinctly different populations to get along with each other, whether it is living in the same or adjoining neighborhoods, sharing job situations, attending the same college setting, dating, or even socializing in public venues. Throughout our melting-pot history, Americans of all racial and ethnic backgrounds have had to endure varying types of race relations with each other. As we all know, some race relations went smoothly, whereas others have included major confrontations—physical, verbal, social, cultural, and political.

When we speak of politics, however, we are referring to the art or science concerned with guiding governmental policy. Those who guide government policy are individuals who are either elected, appointed, or born into a position of authority by members of their society. They are representatives of their societies, or, as commonly termed, politicians.

Anthropologists and political scientists share an interest in political systems and organizations, but the anthropological approach is global and comparative and includes nonstates as well as the state and nation-states usually studied by political scientists. Kottak (2014) emphasizes that anthropological studies have revealed substantial variation in power (formal and informal), authority, and legal systems in different societies and communities.

In fact, these two concepts—power and authority—and how they are used in one society versus another determine whether there are good race relations or poor race relations within that society. Power is the ability to exercise one's will over others. Authority is the socially approved use of power.

Members of a society who feel that those who use their power and authority the wrong way oftentimes have more problems with relating to certain segments of their society—racial and ethnic groups. Members of a society who feel that those who use their power and authority the right way oftentimes have fewer problems with relating to certain segments of their society—racial and ethnic groups. How an individual and/or group utilize their power and authority, particularly in the context of politics, greatly influences whether a politician will have good race-relations experience with various segments of the population or struggle with various segments of the population. This is the very reason why politics and race relations are such sensitive, highly-charged, and highly-divisive elements among a majority of all societies of the world today.

This chapter examines the role in which national politics affects race relations in the United States. In particular, this chapter focuses on how our current and recent U.S. presidents have had to deal with race-relation issues during their presidencies. The primary purpose of examining how our national leader—the president of the United States—addresses race-relations issues during his presidency shines a light on the seriousness of this issue on a national scale and also provides insight into how our country continues to struggle in developing any significant strategies that will improve or resolve this matter.

Contemporary Race-Relations Issues

It is truly amazing to see how race relations have improved between blacks and whites in our country since the civil rights movement years. Many of the issues that caused racial confrontations and tensions in the past, such as interracial friendships, interracial dating and marrying, primary- and secondary-school choice, college choice, job selections, voting, and even just sitting in the front portion of a bus are things of the past. So whether one is young, middle-aged, or elderly, a vast majority of Americans most likely would say that race relations have improved, right?

Interestingly, the day after Donald Trump won the presidential election against Hillary Clinton in 2016, a unique wave of despair, anger, fear, and depression washed over much of black America (Washington 2016). The columnist Jesse Washington, reporting for the online magazine the *Undefeated*, stated that after learning that Donald Trump had been elected president, some folks cried, sought refuge in the Bible, comforted frightened children, and prepared themselves for a life under a president who had used social media—Twitter—to express his opinion on a wide array of issues: support for white supremacists, intentions to increase stop-and-frisk policing in poor black neighborhoods, alleged connections of Mexican immigrants to crime, and attacks on the legitimacy of the first black president's birth certificate.

Washington (2016) highlighted that according to exit polls, Trump won the votes of 67 percent of whites without a college degree, overall capturing 58 percent of the total white vote; he beat Clinton 49 to 45 percent among college graduates and won 54 percent of the vote among white, male college graduates.

Among black voters, Trump garnered 8 percent of the vote, better than GOP presidential nominee Mitt Romney, who received 7 percent against President Barack Obama in 2012; and among Latinos, 29 percent backed Trump, more than Romney's 27 percent (Washington 2016, 4).

Washington (2016) stated that one sentiment rang loudest from many African Americans: "The election shows where we really stand. Now the truth is plain to see, many said—the truth about how an uncomfortable percentage of white people view the concerns and lives of their black fellow citizens" (Washington 2016, 2).

To examine further how blacks and whites feel about race-relations issues in America today, a number of polls were conducted months after Trump's presidential election, and they found the following:

- An overwhelming 87 percent of black Americans say black people face a lot of discrimination in the United States, but only 49 percent of white Americans say the same thing.
- Sixty-six (66 percent) of nonwhites label prejudice a "very serious" problem, while only 39 percent of whites felt the same way.
- More than 6 in 10 Americans (63 percent) say the level of hatred and prejudice has increased since Trump was elected president and higher (70 percent) among nonwhites (7 in 10).
- More than 4 in 10 Americans (42 percent) now worry "a great deal" about race relations in the United States—more than doubling since 2014. (Struyk 2017)

Yet just a decade ago, the African American population felt completely different about race relations in the United States and the presidency. Interestingly, a Gallup poll conducted during the summer of 2008, right before Barack Obama's nomination as Democratic presidential candidate, found that blacks and whites continued to have profoundly different perspectives on the prevalence of racism in the United States and a modest narrowing in some of those gaps, along with a jump in optimism about the future. A record 58 percent of Americans said that race relations "eventually will be worked out," while 38 percent said there will "always be a problem." For the first time since the Gallup poll began regularly asking that question in 1993, slightly more African Americans took the optimistic view over the pessimistic one (Page and Risser 2008).

This Gallup poll included 702 non-Hispanic whites, 608 non-Hispanic blacks, and 502 Hispanics and was conducted between June 5 and July 6, 2008. Sample comments from participants were as follows:

> "I don't believe we've totally overcome everything that's necessary for equality, but I do believe things are getting better," said Ricardo Russell, a 30-year-old African American retail sales manager from Oak Park, Michigan.

> "They're better than they used to be, that's for sure. It's the younger people who are doing this," said Susann Matarese, a 52-year-old medical receptionist from Port Charlotte, Florida, who is Caucasian and who is not entirely comfortable with the interracial dating she increasingly sees.

> "There was a time when people couldn't live in certain places, but now it seems as long as you have the money you can live anywhere. There are a lot more disadvantaged black people than there are white," said Angela Ross, a 44-year-old African American stay-at-home mom from Houston, Texas. (Page and Risser 2008)

In general, that is how a vast majority of African Americans felt after the presidential election. Not only were we going to get our first African American president, but we also were able to release all of the pent-up frustration from past discriminatory and racist acts against us. Thus, the newly elected Barack Obama as president symbolized a change of status and a new day in race relations for all Americans, particularly African Americans.

The Obama Administration

Not surprisingly, presidential candidate Barack Obama received a consistent high number of votes from blacks (95 percent) and other communities of color (Latino, Asian, Pacific Islanders, and Native Americans) throughout the primaries and general election. The fact that no other African American democratic candidate has been considered seriously to run for president since Jesse Jackson (1984 and 1988) and Shirley Chisholm (1972) tell us that our U.S. society still has an issue with race and politics.

There are two major visible areas in which the Obama administration supported race-relations issues in 2009:

1.   Appointed cabinet positions
2.   Civil rights White House issues

The most visible signs in which President Obama addressed race-relations issues were through his nomination and confirmation of political appointees to his cabinet. Those who were selected and confirmed to a cabinet post with the administration not only helped to support Obama's major political agenda but also helped to symbolize a new beginning for the new administration. That was exactly what Obama attempted to do in his political appointments to his cabinet.

Overall, Obama picked five women, four blacks, three Hispanics, and two Asians as cabinet-level appointments. Although two of his nominations had to resign (Bill Richardson and Tom Daschle) because of their failure to pay taxes, Obama's cabinet was one of the most diverse in history. By comparison, President's Trump's cabinet in 2016 had four women, one Indian American, one Asian American, and one African American. Additionally, President's Bush first cabinet in 2001 had four women, two African Americans, one Hispanic/Latino American and two Asian Americans. Finally, President Clinton's first cabinet in 1993 had four women, four African Americans, and two Hispanic/Latino Americans.

President Obama's cabinet was as follows:

- Hillary Rodham Clinton, Secretary of State
- Eric Holder, Attorney General and Justice (African American)
- Gary Locke, Secretary of Commerce
- Tom Vilsack, Secretary of Agriculture
- Arne Duncan, Secretary of Education
- Steven Chu, Secretary of Energy (Asian American)
- Kathleen Sebelius, Secretary of Health and Human Services
- Janet Napolitano, Secretary of Homeland Security (Hispanic/Latina)
- Shaun Donovan, Secretary of Housing and Urban Development
- Ken Salazar, Secretary of Interior (Hispanic/Latino)
- Hilda Solis, Secretary of Labor (Hispanic/Latina)
- Ray LaHood, Secretary of Transportation
- Timothy Geithner, Secretary of Treasury
- Eric Shinseki, Secretary of Veterans Affairs (Asian American)

Finally in one of President Obama's most controversial nominations, Sonia Sotomayor became the first Supreme Court justice whose heritage is Puerto Rican. Her nomination and confirmation hearings provoked more debate about the issues of race than the administration anticipated. There was also lively discussion on how one's race or individual life experiences give an individual a certain "empathy" to see and feel how other people live. Although this word "empathy" and some of her comments caused much controversy, by the end of the hearings this was apparently a good thing for everyone—even Supreme Court justices.

The second most visible area in which the Obama administration addressed race-relations issues is civil rights in the White House agenda. Although the word "race" is not included in any of the White House agenda issues, reexamining their two major programs for civil rights shows a connection.

For example, the two civil rights issues that the White House lists were antidiscrimination laws and criminal justice reform (Bailey 2010, 143). In terms of antidiscrimination laws, President Obama signed the Lilly Ledbetter Fair Pay Restoration Act on January 29, 2009. The Lilly Ledbetter Fair Pay Restoration Act ensured that all Americans received equal pay for equal work. The Civil Rights Division of the Justice Department was to ensure that voting rights are protected and Americans do not suffer from increased discrimination during a time of economic distress. President Obama continued to support the Employment Non-Discrimination Act and believed that U.S. antidiscrimination employment laws should be expanded to include sexual orientation and gender identity. He supported full civil unions and federal rights for lesbian, gay, bisexual, and transgendered (LGBT) couples and opposed a constitutional ban on same-sex marriage (Bailey 2010, 143).

As for criminal justice reform, the Obama White House led the fight to build a more fair and equitable criminal justice system. He also sought to strengthen federal hate-crime legislation and worked to ensure that federal law-enforcement agencies did not resort to racial profiling (Bailey 2010, 143).

First and foremost, no one can possibly completely evaluate the trials and tribulations that Barack Obama has had to endure throughout his lifetime, particularly as it relates to his racial and ethnic identity. In his book *Dreams from My Father: A Story of Race and Inheritance*, Obama passionately traces his family's unique history and gives the reader a psychological and cultural insight into what it is like to be raised and to grow up as a biracial individual (Obama 2004). Nonetheless, he admits that his personal history is not representative of the black American experience that most people think of when they think of the typical African American (Bailey 2010).

Obama's public acknowledgment of the importance of race-relations issues in his life as a private citizen, as a U.S. senator, and later as a presidential candidate came full circle when he had to make his now famous "race speech" in Philadelphia. On March 18, 2008, presidential candidate Obama delivered a speech titled "A More Perfect Union" and addressed the controversy surrounding the comments made by his former pastor Rev. Jeremiah Wright, as well as race-relations issues associated with his presidential campaign. The massive media coverage of Obama's race speech not only elevated his presidential candidacy, but also enamored him with the mainstream media (including NBC, CBS, ABC, MSNBC, and CNN). The fact that mainstream media had a difficult time addressing the issues of race and race relations without coming off as "racist," particularly when talking about Obama as a serious political candidate, gave candidate Obama the upper hand. He became the one and only political figure who could talk about race and racism. From that point forward, whatever presidential candidate Obama said became "gold" in the eyes of the mainstream media, mainstream America, and the African American community (Bailey 2010, 146).

This speech that presidential candidate Obama delivered was exactly the type of race speech that the country needed to hear. In his speech, Obama even said the following about the legacy of slavery: "But race is an issue that I believe this nation cannot afford to ignore right now...We do not need to recite here the history of racial injustice in this country. But we do need to remind ourselves that so many of the disparities that exist in the African American community today can be directly traced to inequalities passed on from an earlier generation that suffered under the brutal legacy of slavery and Jim Crow" (Obama 2008).

The Clinton Administration

Another U.S. president who strongly addressed race relations in our country during his presidency was William Jefferson Clinton—our 42nd president (January 20, 1993–January 20, 2001). Coming from the state of Arkansas as a state governor, Bill Clinton always had a way to relate to all types of people regardless of their racial, ethnic, economic, political, social, and cultural backgrounds. Clinton prided himself in reaching out to all types of folks as a state governor and continued the same charismatic approach as a presidential political candidate and of course as a two-term president.

During his second term, President Bill Clinton and his administration developed and implemented a race initiative for the entire country: "One America in the 21st Century: The President's Initiative on Race" (Clinton 2009). The plan was announced on June 14, 1997, and although this race initiative did not fulfill its overall objectives and was highly criticized by political parties, ethnic groups, and scholars in various academic fields, Clinton nonetheless used his position as president of the United States and his own childhood experiences growing up in segregated Arkansas to engage the nation in a dialogue about race and race relations. The president recognized that, even as America had rapidly become more of a multiracial democracy, race relations remained an issue that divided the nation.

Clinton's race initiative had five major goals:

1. To articulate the president's vision of racial reconciliation and a just, unified America
2. To help educate the nation about the facts surrounding the issue of race

3. To promote a constructive dialogue, to confront and work through the difficult and controversial issues surrounding race

4. To recruit and encourage leadership at all levels to help bridge racial divides

5. To find, develop, and implement solutions in critical areas such as education, economic opportunity, housing, health care, crime, and the administration of justice—for individuals, communities, corporations, and governments at all levels. (Clinton 2009)

The president also convened an advisory board of seven distinguished Americans. Led by respected African American scholar John Hope Franklin, the advisory board worked with the president to engage the many diverse groups, communities, regions, and various industries in the country. The board consisted of Dr. John Hope Franklin, Angela E. Oh (lawyer), Lina Chavez-Thompson (AFL-CIO), Gov. Thomas Kean (New Jersey), William Winter (former governor of Mississippi), Robert Thomas (businessman), and Rev. Suzan Johnson Cook (Bronx, New York). The advisory board was asked to join President Clinton in reaching out to local communities and to listen to Americans from all different races and backgrounds so that the country could better understand the causes of racial tensions.

After yearlong community forums about race across the country, President Clinton presented the race initiative report to the American people and coordinated the efforts through a new White House office headed by Ben Johnson (Clinton 2004). Although Clinton's race-initiative report received much criticism from all types of scholars and especially politicians on both sides of the debate, it provided policy suggestions on such national race-relations issues as education, affirmative action, health, the criminal justice system, and immigration—all of which are very significant issues today in 2018.

For some reason, no other presidential administration (Bush, Obama, and Trump) has followed up on Clinton's race initiative. Why have past and current administrations avoided the issues of race and race relations in America?

By now, you know the answer—politics (Bailey 2010).

The Trump Administration

Finally, let's look at the Trump administration's current initiatives as they relate to race relations in the United States. As indicated at the beginning of this chapter, a large percentage of U.S. citizens were stunned with the election of Donald Trump in 2016. Beating all odds and going against all political strategists' suggestions, Donald Trump managed to beat Hilary Clinton in one of the most polarizing presidential campaign in U.S. history. The manner in which Donald Trump campaigned instigated major protests against his campaign themes and also ignited major resentment concerning how he addressed race-relations issues in America.

Once in office, President Trump stated that more jobs would help race relations in the United States. In another one of his contentious news conferences in August 2017, President Trump emphasized that his administration would create millions of jobs and stronger growth in wages, thus having a tremendous positive impact on race relations. President Trump stated, "What people want now, they want jobs. They want great jobs with good pay. And when they have that, you watch how race relations will be" (Irwin 2017).

Certainly jobs and wages influence Americans' sense of well-being and their worldview. But attitudes about race relations seem to be overwhelmingly shaped by developments unrelated to things like the unemployment rate or growth in household incomes (Irwin 2017).

Supporting President Trump's commitment to improve race relations, particularly for African Americans, Katrina Pierson—a spokeswoman for America First, a conservative organization that supports Trump's legislative agenda—urged African Americans to give Trump a chance, saying that Trump would help improve the quality of life for African Americans through education, jobs, health care, and building the border wall to crack down on crime, drugs, and human trafficking (Cottman 2017). Pierson further stated, "Illegal immigration impacts the black community. When illegal immigrants settle in the United States, they don't settle in gated communities, they settle in black communities and poor communities. You can't have an honest discussion about illegal immigration without talking about the cost of illegal immigration, financially, socially and culturally" (Cottman 2017).

Yet civil rights organizations took issue with Pierson and her conservative views. They believed Trump's policies would be detrimental to the prosperity of African Americans and were distrustful of black conservatives.

In particular, Marc Morial, the president of the National Urban League, said that the Trump administration would cut social programs that benefit black Americans instead of making good on his campaign promise to rebuild urban communities (Cottman 2017). Furthermore, Morial said, "People—blacks, whites, Latinos—are all dealing with wage stagnation and a jobs initiative could unite America. It's a challenge for urban America. It's a challenge for rural America."

When all the rhetoric had subsided between the White House and civil rights organizations regarding what the Trump administration would actually do to improve race relations in the United States, President Trump released his budget for the fiscal year 2018. Here are the major budget priorities as proposed by the Trump administration's "A New Foundation for American Greatness" (Office of Management and Budget 2018):

- A new foundation that solidifies our commitment to the border's security.
- A new foundation of policies to produce new American jobs.
- A new foundation for immigration policy that serves the national interest and the American taxpayer.
- A new foundation of federalism that trusts States to help manage America's health care.
- A new foundation that creates a pathway to welfare reform that is focused on promoting work and lifting people out of poverty.
- A new foundation that places America first by returning more American dollars home and ensuring foreign aid supports American interests and values.
- A new foundation that spurs innovation and enables the American worker and family to thrive.
- A new foundation of restraint that limits Government regulation and intrusion.
- A new foundation of discipline that puts our budget on a path to balance.
- And, a new foundation of focus on the forgotten American worker who now has an advocate in the Oval Office.

In addition to the president's 2018 fiscal budget for the country, let's review President Trump's cabinet leaders as we did with President Obama. Here are his political appointees:

- Rex W. Tillerson, Secretary of State
- Steven Mnuchin, Treasury Secretary
- James N. Mattis, Defense Secretary
- Jeff Sessions, Attorney General
- Ryan Zinke, Interior Secretary
- Sonny Perdue, Agriculture Secretary
- Wilbur Ross, Commerce Secretary
- R. Alexander Acosta, Labor Secretary
- Tom Price, Health and Human Services Secretary
- Ben Carson, Secretary of Housing and Urban Development
- Elaine L. Chao, Transportation Secretary
- Rick Perry, Energy Secretary
- Betsy DeVos, Education Secretary

- David J. Shulkin, Secretary of Veterans Affairs
- John F. Kelly, Homeland Security Secretary
- Mike Pompeo, CIA Director
- Nikki R. Haley, UN Ambassador
- Scott Pruitt, EPA Administrator
- Linda McMahon, Small Business Administration
- Mick Mulvaney, Director of the Office of Management and Budget
- Dan Coats, Director of National Intelligence
- Robert Lighthizer, U.S. Trade Representative
- Kevin Hassett, Chairman of the Council of Economic Advisors

As stated earlier in this chapter, President's Trump's cabinet has four women, one Indian American, one Asian American, and one African American. As the *New York Times* (2017) stated in May 2017, President's Trump's cabinet is more white and male than any cabinet since Ronald Reagan's. Although a president's cabinet does not necessarily reflect how he views or connects to race-relations issues in America, it may indicate that the issues of race and race relations are not a high priority symbolically or actually to address during the administration.

Furthermore, when a national race-relations incident occurred in August 2017 as a white-supremacist and neo-Nazi rally converged in Charlottesville, Virginia, to protest the removal of a Confederate statue, causing the death of a counterprotester when a car plowed into a crowd, and two Virginia troopers died in a helicopter crash as they aided in the response, Senator Tom Scott, the Senate's only black Republican, questioned President's Trump moral authority. Following a meeting that Senator Scott had with President Trump after Trump's initial comments about the incident, Senator Scott said the following: "He simply was trying to convey...that there was an antagonist on the other side. My response was, while that's true—if you look at it from a sterile perspective, there was an antagonist on the other side—however, the real picture has nothing to do with who's on the other side. It has to do with the affirmation of hate groups who over three centuries in this country's history have made it their mission to create upheaval in minority communities as the reason for their existence" (Dumain and Kumar 2017).

Senator Scott also said: "One of the things that I was very clear to do was not to have a racial conversation with the president as if that somehow will solve problems or change minds. My goals was to have a conversation about fairness, access to opportunities and remedies that will help people who are impoverished today, people who feel hopeless today. That encompasses black folks and white folks" (Dumain and Kumar 2017).

Yet before any national initiative focused on fairness, access to opportunities, and remedies that will help people who are impoverished—black and
white—a serious conversation about race and race relations, starting with
the president of the United States, is a necessity in this country, particularly
in 2018 and beyond. Without such conversations and the inclusion of folks
who represent the totality and diversity of the United States, then much of
the same rhetoric and race-relations problems will persist.

Conclusion

This chapter examined the interrelationship between national politics and
race relations in the United States. In particular, this chapter reviewed how
past presidents Barack Obama and Bill Clinton, along with current president
Donald Trump, have addressed race-relations issues during their presidencies. As indicated, Presidents Obama and Clinton dealt with race-relations
issues in a more direct approach through initiatives, cabinet appointments,
and life experience. On the other hand, our current president is still struggling through—or perhaps ignoring—a wide array of race-relations issues,
which need proper attention and priority.

Race relations continue to be a national issue each and every day whether
we like it or not. Our country's foundation is based upon immigrants and
people of all different racial and ethnic backgrounds coming to America to
start and find a new life. The bottom line is we were a nation of immigrants,
are a nation of immigrants, and will always be a nation of immigrants. Our
population will continue to grow, in its diversity, colors, and cultures, and
must continue to adapt to all the various new immigrants that will come to
our country in the future.

As a nation, we must face all the issues related to our diverse world—head on.

PART 3

Practical Outcomes of Race Relations

CHAPTER SEVEN

Negative Consequences of Poor Race and Ethnic Relations among College Students

In our politically correct world, whether it's outside or inside academia, we tend to discuss only the perceived positive outcomes or "good things" that happen when we adhere to a given agenda, policy, or law established by a society or institution. It is a way, or subtle subliminal strategy, to get all citizens—or, in the case of academia, students—to follow the rules. So in order to get more students to follow the rules, institutions or society in general will primarily promote the perceived good or positive outcomes of a program.

In this book, however, we are not taking this approach. In this chapter, we are going to do the opposite and focus on the negative consequences of poor race relations among college students. That's correct—the negative consequences of having no or poor relations with a person of a different racial and ethnic background.

What are those negative consequences? Here are a few concepts and issues associated with negative consequences of poor race relations:

1. Misconceptions
2. Ethnocentrism
3. Prejudice
4. Racial Prejudice
5. Racial Attitudes
6. Discrimination

7. Reverse Discrimination
8. Racism
9. Discrimination and Power
10. Segregation

Although this short list is not nearly exhaustive of all the negative consequences related to poor race relations—and there are obvious consequences
of poor race relations—it does highlight (as in chapter 3) some of the most
significant issues as they relate to the average college student. In general, this
chapter will focus on three major negative consequences of poor race relations: prejudice, discrimination, and segregation.

Unsurprisingly, these three thought patterns and behaviors are ones that
a majority of colleges and institutions do not often admit happen at their
institution, but they do. These three lay the foundation for poor race relations among college students and on college campuses across the United
States. That's why it is so important to confront, discuss, debate, and elaborate on them.

This chapter and the remaining chapters of this book will specifically
focus on the practical implications of these concepts to the average college
student. Often, many students are not aware of the impact of these concepts
and issues in their lives or their friends' lives. The first negative consequence
of poor race relations among college students that we will discuss is
prejudice.

Consequences of Prejudice

In reality, each and every one of us are prejudiced. There is not one person
on this earth who is not prejudiced in some form and to some degree. It's
almost a natural response among humans that we prejudge others based
upon our individual perspectives, how we are raised by our family, friends,
and communities, and even influenced by mass media. If a person claims
that to not be prejudiced, he or she is not being self-aware or sincere, or is
trying to be as politically correct as possible.

Basically, prejudice is a preconceived opinion that is often based on misconceptions and stereotypes, as we highlighted in chapter 3. Most of us have
a wide array of misconceptions and stereotypes about other persons or other
racial/ethnic populations. It is very understandable that a vast majority of us
know very little about the culture, history, values, beliefs, and behavioral
patterns of other racial and ethnic groups.

What we do know, however, are certain misconceptions and stereotypes
of other racial and ethnic groups, which only reflects a certain percentage of
that population under certain conditions (e.g., economic level, educational

level, region of the country, and history). Unfortunately, most people make their judgments or preconceived opinions about other racial and ethnic groups based upon these misconceptions, stereotypes, and limited exposure to these other groups. These misconceptions and stereotypes lead to our prejudicial views about other groups.

It is not until we gather more accurate information about another group—whether it is gathered through daily interaction, living with, socializing with, playing sports with, partying with, working with others, or educating oneself through research—that we can reduce and eliminate our prejudiced views of other groups.

For example, in my race-relations and cultural-anthropology classes, I present to students a class exercise on describing the cultural traits, traditions, and patterns associated with the major racial populations in the United States—African Americans, Hispanics/Latinos, Asian Americans and Pacific Islanders, American Indians and Alaska Natives, and Caucasians. Here are the steps to my class exercise:

1. I divide the class into six groups and assign each group to one of the racial groups.
2. After 10–15 minutes, I ask the group leader to write the group's results on the board so that the whole class can see their list.
3. Next, each group leader comes to the board in the lecture hall and reads the group's responses to the rest of the class.
4. As each group leader describes the list of cultural traits, traditions, and patterns for the particular racial group, the class reacts in mostly a startled way.
5. Once every group leader is completed, I then ask the entire class, "What do you notice about these lists from each group?"

That's when class members notice and state that their views and knowledge about each group have often been based on stereotypes and misconceptions, which led to prejudicial views of various racial and ethnic groups.

Therefore, this class exercise for describing the cultural traits, traditions, and patterns associated with the major racial populations in the United States shows that the average college student today still has a number of preconceived ideas about other racial groups. This is truly unfortunate because the majority of my students try hard to be as accurate as possible about these cultural traits, traditions, and patterns, yet they still highlight stereotypes and misconceptions regarding each group. If these stereotypes and misconceptions are not challenged and corrected in their early years of college, that tends to make it more difficult for the average student to develop good, meaningful relationships with students who are different from them.

Another set of consequences associated with holding prejudicial views is that they naturally lead to ethnocentrism, racial prejudice, and negative racial attitudes. To reiterate, no one would admit that they have prejudicial, ethnocentric, racially prejudiced, or negative racial attitudes. The views of today's college students are often vastly different than their parents, in a positive way. But they often, literally do not know people of other races and ethnicities any more or better than their parents did.

The fact remains that a majority of today's college students know very little about other racial and ethnic groups. There is no doubt that a vast majority of colleges/universities are trying to educate and expose their student population to more diverse populations. Diversity enrichment, inclusion initiatives, and multicultural programming have significantly increased over the years and have had some positive impact on the views of the average college student.

Still, if you visit most college campuses today, you will find that a majority of students will prefer to be with their own race and ethnic group, know more about their own racial and ethnic group, and believe that their race and ethnic group is better or superior than others. Unfortunately, this perspective leads to our next negative consequence of poor race relations—discrimination.

Consequences of Discrimination

The second major consequence of poor race relations among college students is discrimination. As stated in chapter 3, discrimination refers to the actions or practices carried out by members of a dominant group or their representatives that have a differential and harmful impact on members of subordinate groups. Discrimination is actually the result of prejudicial views put into action against another group. It is what triggers discriminatory behavior.

Often associated with discrimination is discrimination power, where one uses his or her position to further demean a group via prejudicial views, and also reverse discrimination, where the initially discriminated group demeans the dominant group with harmful intent. In both cases, the intent is to deny, harm, and impact negatively the lives of the discriminated group.

Let's examine two practical examples of discriminatory acts among students that may occur on college campuses today.

Discriminatory Behavior #1

Socializing as a student is a very significant element of college life, all throughout college. From their very first days as freshmen, students are encouraged to socialize with as many students as possible and to make new friends. Socializing helps all students to get better adjusted and acclimated to this new college world. Yet socializing for some students is a bit more challenging, particularly for students of color who are attending predominantly mainstream white institutions.

For many students of color, it becomes very challenging to try to fit in and socialize with predominantly white students; also, it is challenging for some white students to socialize with students of color. Why does this still occur? The answer is simple: it is often the very first or one of the first few times in which a student of color or a white student is in a dorm/apartment/living quarters in which they have to interact on a daily basis and all are expected to socialize with each other. It's a challenge to bring students of various socioeconomic, religious, political, and sexual orientations from all regions of the country and educational levels together to live and socialize daily on a college campus, and the obvious, easily seen differences in race and ethnicity make it perhaps most challenging to bring different racial and ethnic groups together.

Today's mainstream college/universities sometimes have been very successful in managing many of these new student living arrangements and socializing issues for all students, particularly students of color.

Decades ago, as a freshman at a college in Ohio, I wanted to fit in and socialize. Initially, I naively thought that I could join one of these mainstream white fraternities during rush week. I saw friends having fun joining these fraternities, so I thought that I could do the same. I attended as many fraternity parties as possible and mingled with the members just like all my friends did, yet I did not get an invitation to become a pledge. In fact, whenever I showed up at the fraternity parties, many of the guys avoided me and would not have conversations with me. By the end of a couple of weeks, my closest friend from my dorm realized that I was being discriminated against because of my race. He felt sorry for me. At the time, we laughed it off and joked about it, yet both of us knew that it was wrong.

Indeed, it was discriminatory behavior typical of its time (1970s) on many college campuses, yet I am told by my college students today that it still happens. In fact, in my Honors Race Relations Seminar classes (2016 and 2017), many of my students stated that fraternities and sororities are still notorious for being very selective in the type of college students they recruit and select. One of the key criteria for selecting new members is their appearance and physical features, because some fraternities and sororities desire that their members look a certain way or have a certain image. This is not only true of fraternities/sororities but also of other college clubs and college groups affiliated with the college/university. Even among today's college students, many more types of students (including the poor, non-Christian, and gay) are experiencing subtle discriminatory behaviors and acts from college organizations, clubs, groups, or fraternities and sororities.

Discriminatory Behavior #2

Recruiting is a part of the essential fabric of all college and university departments, schools, and higher education institutions. Recruiting students for your institution, department, and program is a high priority simply because students keep our institutions, departments, and programs alive and functioning every year.

Recruiting qualified and academically high-achieving students is another set of challenging activities for any institution, department, and program. When recruiting for qualified and high-achieving students, we see institutions, departments, and programs sometimes become overselective and make vast assumptions about certain types of students based on certain criteria. Whether it's the potential student's socioeconomic status, religion, political affiliation, sexual orientation, region of the country, educational level, or race/ethnicity, administrators at some mainstream institutions avoid or do not take the extra effort in finding and recruiting students who may be different than the "typical" high-achieving, qualified college student.

This factor alone—assumptions—tends to influence recruitment strategies among college administrators and department chairpersons when they are searching for highly qualified and high-achieving college students. What is often said among some college administrators and department administrators when their ideal pool of college students tends to show little diversity year after year?

"There are just too few highly qualified and high-achieving minority students out there."

I have heard this statement time and time again over my 30 years in academia, yet it is far from the truth. Believe me: they are out there.

This statement is based on assumptions and a lack of effort in developing alternative strategies for recruiting more highly qualified and high-achieving college students who are diverse. Usually, it just takes an alternative strategy and little bit more time to find the highly qualified and high-achieving college students who happen to be persons of color and otherwise diverse. This is the very reason why certain mainstream public institutions, departments, and programs continue to consistently have low numbers of students of color and students of varying socioeconomic status, religion, political affiliation, sexual orientation, home regions of the country, and educational levels in their programs. Most importantly, this subtle discriminatory behavior is a practical negative consequence of poor race relations that institutions, departments, and programs have with diverse residents in their county, state, nation, and world.

Consequences of Segregation

The third major consequence of poor race relations among college students is segregation. Segregation refers to the separation or isolation of a race, class, or ethnic group by enforced or voluntary residence in a restricted area, by barriers to social interaction, by separated educational facilities, or by other discriminatory means (Kottak 2011).

In the context of colleges/universities, students are separated into specific groupings, either by an administrator, faculty, institution, or by themselves. Although we know that the overt institutionalization of segregation ended in the United States during the 1960s in most states, there still remain subtle signs of segregation activity and groupings on college campuses today.

For example, what has happened on many college and university campuses is there are designated buildings, centers, and areas on campus solely focused on minority and/or multicultural/diversity students. Because of the political, societal, and cultural pressures to mandate affirmative-action programming and initiatives for underserved students of color, these designated buildings, centers, and areas of campus have become known as the "[name the minority] building" or the "[name the minority] area." Students of all diverse backgrounds frequent these buildings, centers, and areas simply because many of their specific programs originate in these buildings and centers. These areas have also become known as a safe haven and congregation area for many diverse students on campus.

Therefore, the consequence of these well-intended, minority-focused programs, buildings, and centers has further segregated a segment of the student population from the majority of the student population. These subtly segregated areas on college campuses unfortunately produce some problems in race relations between those students who directly benefit from the programs and services affiliated with these buildings or centers and those who do not benefit from them.

As for the racial majority student, he or she may feel left out and accept that these programs and services are not for him or her, thereby avoiding these buildings and areas completely on campus. Yet at their core, these designated "underserved, minority-focused" programs, buildings, and centers are actually for all students, because a majority of students on college campuses usually fit within some category of underserved and minority status (socioeconomic, religion, sexual orientation, political affiliation, or educational level).

Conclusion

In this chapter, we made a broad examination of the negative consequences of poor race relations among college students and their potential outcomes. This is an issue that is seldom discussed, analyzed, and highlighted simply because very few college administrators want to think about this side of the issue as it relates to race relations. So the question remains: what really happens when a college student does not develop good relations with students who are of different racial and ethnic backgrounds or when an institution of higher learning does not invest appropriate resources or programs related to improving race relations?

The result is threefold. As shown throughout this chapter, poor race relations among student populations tend to

1. increase more prejudicial views among the student population;
2. increase the chances of subtle discriminatory behavior on campus; and
3. increase occurrences of segregated activity on campus.

All are interrelated, and all stem from an individual's misconceptions and stereotypes of individuals who may be different from the majority.

Thus, it becomes imperative that all of us who are a part of academia— whether as faculty, staff, administrators, or students of any racial and ethnic backgrounds—invest our time, resources, and energies in some fashion to improve race relations within our departments, programs, centers, and colleges, because it will dramatically reduce and potentially eliminate the negative consequences of poor race relations among our college students now and in the future. This calls for strategic plans that all colleges/universities should implement as soon as possible.

CHAPTER EIGHT

Positive Outcomes of Good Race and Ethnic Relations among College Students

It is always easier to document, list, or discuss the negative aspects of poor race and ethnic relations. What is more challenging, particularly with this topic, is to highlight the positive aspects and outcomes of good race and ethnic relations, especially as they relate to college students. We commonly assume that college students know the positive outcomes of good race and ethnic relations, but, in fact, many do not know or have not been taught answers to the question "What are the tangible and practical outcomes of good race and ethnic relations?"

This chapter highlights three major research studies showing the positive impact of good race and ethnic relations on the lives of a majority of college students, as well its effect on students of color. There are tremendous educational, professional, cultural, and personal benefits in developing good race and ethnic relations throughout one's college years.

Research Studies

Over the past couple of decades, there has been an increasing interest among scholars in what the key factors that influence a positive experience among college students during their undergraduate years are (Bowen and Bok 1998; Gurin et al. 2002; Hu and Kuh 2003; Hurtado 1998 and 2003). Much of the initial perception pool revolved around general and stereotypical views of college life: newfound freedom, partying with new friends, and participating in campus social events.

Yet many of these studies have not explored the factors among specific racial and ethnic college students that influence their positive experiences and outcomes. Why have scholars not investigated these issues among students of color? Is there an assumption that all college students respond similarly to university/campus social events? Fortunately, there are scholars who are investigating college life among students of color and feel that their experiences may be different than the typical college student.

Diversity Impact

In a final report, titled "Preparing College Students for a Diverse Democracy," to the U.S. Department of Education's Office of Education Research and Improvement, concerning its Field Initiated Studies Program, Hurtado (2003) examined quantitative and qualitative student data from nine public institutions with variations in their educational practices and diversity of student body and explored the following issues:

1. how colleges are creating diverse learning environments and actively preparing students to live and work in an increasingly diverse democracy;
2. the role of the diverse peer group in the acquisition of important cognitive, social, and democratic outcomes both inside and outside of the classroom; and
3. student outcomes that can be best achieved through specific kinds of initiatives designed to increase student engagement with diverse perspectives.

This Diverse Democracy Project consisted of data from over 4,700 students attending such public universities as UCLA, University of Washington, Arizona State University, University of Massachusetts at Amherst, University of Maryland, University of New Mexico, University of Vermont, University of Minnesota, and the University of Michigan.

The major findings from this Diversity Democracy Project demonstrated the following:

*   An "engaged campus" that integrates diversity and civic engagement as central to its mission makes a strong connection between institutional rhetoric (mission statements and priorities), practices (level and types of activity, rewards, and leadership support), and diversity outcomes (numbers of diverse students and faculty, community partnership activity).
*   Student gains on a host of educational outcomes are associated with informal interaction with diverse peers in the first two years of college.

- Campus practices that facilitate student interaction with diversity promote development of cognitive, social, and democratic skills.
- Student focus groups provided additional information about what students learn from interactions with diverse peers.
- Student focus groups also gave voice to racial/ethnic minority students who articulated contexts in which they faced the burden of educating others, including classrooms where diversity was a topic. (Hurtado 2003, iii–v)

Educational Impact

Establishing good race and ethnic relations among college students has a number of positive effects on the individual student and the entire student body on a college campus. Yet this is a general assumed outcome not often backed up with facts or evidence.

To better understand a potential positive outcome from having a racially diverse college campus, Chang (1999) reexamined the college student data (11,688 attending 371 four-year colleges and universities) from the Cooperative Institutional Research Program (CIRP) database and found the following:

1. Attending an institution that has a racially heterogeneous (diverse) student population increases the likelihood that a student will socialize with someone of a different race. The more students of color in the environment, the more likely students will be to socialize across racial groups.

2. Attending an institution that has a racially heterogeneous student population will increase the student's chances of discussing racial issues—the more students of color in the environment, the more likely students will discuss racial issues.

In conclusion, Chang stated that many educators view a racially diverse student body as an educational resource comparable in importance to faculty, a library, or science laboratories, citing ways in which diversity enhances the environment for learning. Accordingly, those students who do engage in diversity may be intellectually challenged by these unique activities and relationships, and the learning that occurs may well extend to other aspects of a student's academic life. In this way, a racially diverse student body does not only address the vestiges of past historical discrimination but is also a tool to achieve valued educational goals (Chang 1999, 392).

Self-Confidence Impact

Another potential positive outcome of good race and ethnic relations among college students is its effect on certain aspects of self or one's individual identity. According to Laird (2005), aspects of self or how an individual perceives himself or herself refers to particular ways one perceives one's roles, abilities, group memberships, and relationship with others. There is a continuum of modifications and changes an individual goes through as he or she successfully fulfills certain roles obligations as a college student, achieves certain accomplishments through college courses, participates and is accepted into college student organizations, and expands his or her social and friendship network.

Although Laird (2005) identified three major aspects of self (academic self-confidence, social agency, and critical-thinking disposition) in his study of 289 college students at the University of Michigan, he nonetheless found some supportive evidence as to the reasons why having good race and ethnic relations made a positive impact on an individual college student's self-confidence or individual identity. In particular, Laird (2005) found that those college students who had more experiences with diversity—either in course work or interactions with diverse peers—were

- more than likely to have more self-confidence and feel better about themselves;
- fulfilled more of their role obligations as college students;
- achieved certain accomplishments through college courses;
- participated in more college student organizations; and
- expanded their social and friendship network.

Summary of Research-Studies Impact

The three aforementioned studies provide supportive evidence that positive outcomes do occur when good race and ethnic relations are established among all types of college students. First, the Saenz, Ngai, and Hurtado (2007) study found that more racially and ethnically diverse institutions not only enhance opportunities for interactions generally but also generate more positive contexts for such interactions to occur. Thus a diverse student body increases cross-racial interactions, particularly for white students.

Secondly, Chang found that when college students attend a racially heterogeneous college/university, they are more than likely to not only socialize across racial groupings but also discuss racial issues during their college years. He further suggested that when students experience a diverse student body, it has a positive impact on their educational achievement as well as other aspects of their academic life.

Finally, Laird found that college students with more experiences with diversity, particularly enrollment in diversity courses and positive interactions with diverse peers, are more likely to score higher on academic self-confidence, social agency, and critical-thinking disposition. Laird also found evidence that all of these diverse experiences improve one's self-confidence and belief in oneself.

Practical Implications

With such positive outcomes highlighted from just the three aforementioned studies, some additional practical implications tend to occur when students experience a diverse, interactive, and engaging college life. There are four particular practical implications of note:

- language (i.e., slang terms),
- pop culture,
- music, and
- food.

Language (i.e., slang terms)

One place in which I regularly see and witness the impact of good race and ethnic relations among college students is in the classroom. As I have taught college classes for over 30 years—as a graduate student, assistant professor, associate professor, and now as a full professor—my college courses have greatly benefited from the interaction and engagement of my students, particularly when the class was racially and ethnically diverse.

For example, a regular class exercise that I do with my students in my undergraduate cultural-anthropology class has involved identifying that latest slang terms used by college students. I divide the class into five or six groups of students (about 10–12 students each) and then have each group develop a list of 5–10 slang terms that they use or have heard a friend use on a regular basis. After about 10–15 minutes, I then have each group assign a leader to come to the board to list their 5–10 slang terms.

Most often, as each group leader completes writing his or her list of slang terms on the board, the students in the classroom begin to laugh, giggle, joke, and talk among themselves about the displayed slang terms on the board. The immediate interaction and engagement of conversation among students of all various racial and ethnic backgrounds usually hits an all-time high in the classroom simply because they not only recognize most of the slang terms but also there are a portion of slang terms that some students cannot define. (As professor, I am usually clueless on 80–85 percent of the slang terms and their meanings.)

What is most rewarding about this class exercise is that once the individual group leader comes to the board, he or she has to pronounce the slang term out loud to the rest of the class and then state the meaning of the slang term. At this point, the entire class starts to laugh out loud and has fun with the correct pronunciation and meaning of the term.

What this class exercise actually does is to bring students of all different racial, ethnic, social, religious, sexual orientation, region of the country, educational, and political affiliation together because all of them can relate to the slang terms in different ways and, using humor in this way, allows college students to interrelate in a more positive, unique, and practical way. Indeed, language (i.e., slang terms) relates to college students in an especially practical way. I'm willing to bet some even adopt the slang terms presented by students of other races and ethnicities.

Pop Culture

Another strategy that I use in my undergraduate college class is to get students to interact and engage with one another by discussing pop culture. Today's pop culture, or mass culture, features cultural forms that have appeared and spread rapidly because of major changes in the material conditions of contemporary life—particularly work organization, transportation, and communications, including the media. Sports, movies, TV shows, amusement parks, and fast-food restaurants have become powerful elements of national (and international) culture. They provide a framework of common experiences and behavior overriding differences in region, class, formal religious affiliation, political sentiments, gender, place of residence, and ethnic group (Kottak 2011, 327).

Every generation of students is usually passionately connected to the latest pop-culture world and events. Whether its fashion, music, sports, celebrity icons, or music or entertainment events, pop culture is the entity that brings a majority of college students of all racial and ethnic backgrounds together.

Perhaps one of the most popular pop-culture icons of today is Beyoncé. Beyoncé, Ms. B. or Beyoncé Knowles, is a pop and R & B (rhythm and blues) singer, actress, entrepreneur, trend setter, mother of three (including twins), and married top rap artist. While married to business tycoon Jay Z, the two have created a mega industry of successes across several pop-culture outlets.

What makes Beyoncé unique, however, is that she has massive crossover appeal to several types of music and pop-culture fans from all racial and ethnic backgrounds. Beyoncé is also a very fashion-conscious superstar who is followed by millions of adoring fans, and she uses social media to keep them updated on all of her latest activities.

Within the past couple of years, Beyoncé has sparked mega attention to her music and brand, as when she appeared in the Super Bowl 50 halftime show, singing and dancing with her large group of African American women dancers in a way that a majority of mainstream viewers and media were unaccustomed to seeing her, a more militant and protest fashion (black beret, black boots, and tight black jump suit). Although this Super Bowl 50 half-time performance and the yearlong concert tour of her new album—*Lemonade*—caused mainstream media to be extra critical of her protest stance against police killings of black males and youths (e.g., Trayvon Martin and others), Beyoncé remained the number one pop icon among a majority of millennials, as well as an excellent pop icon who promotes good race and ethnic relations among college students.

Music

Closely related to our discussion of pop culture is music. Music is another topical discussion strategy that I use in my undergraduate cultural-anthropology class to get students to interact and engage with one another, because a vast majority of college students are intimately connected to music. Beyoncé, Lady Gaga, J Cole, and Chance the Rapper are musical artists and entertainers of today who have crossover appeal. Whether it's pop, rap, rock, country, or other types of music genres, music brings college students together.

Although I can no longer relate to the music artists today, I do remember that I used to have the same connection with the musical artists and bands during my college years (1970s). For example, when I attended college, there were a number of musical artists and bands that had crossover appeal. Such musical artists and bands as Earth, Wind & Fire, Stevie Wonder, Rufus and Chaka Khan, the Doobie Brothers, Elton John, and Peter Frampton crossed over with their music and attracted young black and white college audiences for many years.

Thus, as I experienced with my music preferences during my college years, college students today have musical artists and bands that have cross-over appeal to black and white college students, which can help to improve race and ethnic relations today. The fact that target audiences of today are far less racially segregated than they were a few decades ago enables musical artists to transform race and ethnic relations to a completely new level of collective togetherness.

Food

According to *Webster's Dictionary*, "food" is defined as "any substance that provides the nutrients necessary to maintain life and growth when ingested." When food is ingested and consumed in a regular pattern, we are referring to food habits. Food habits refer to the ways in which humans use food, how food is obtained and stored, how it is prepared, how it is served and to whom, and how it is consumed (Kittler and Sucher 2001, 2).

For college students in particular, food is another basic element of college life that they all share. Food and food habits are shared, experimented with, and used for all types of social, cultural, and sporting events on a daily, weekly, and monthly basis on every college campus in the United States. As many students say, if you want to bring more students to an event on campus, have food and the students will come!

Providing an opportunity in which each racial and ethnic group who has a particular tradition of foods, food preparation, and food habits enables students to not only share their foods with other students but most importantly engage with each other in a fun, delightful, and comforting way, which will allow more constructive and positive dialogue and learning from each other, thus resulting in another positive outcome of good race and ethnic relations.

Conclusion

Although our society tends to focus on the negative aspects of poor race and ethnic relations, this chapter showed the benefits and positive outcomes of good race and ethnic relations among college students. From the research studies showing how specific racial and ethnic groups are benefiting from better race and ethnic relations to its positive impact on a more diverse curriculum for college students, as well as the improved self-confidence that a college student receives after establishing good race and ethnic relations with other students, positive outcomes are well documented.

Additionally, this chapter provided practical strategies to get college instructors/professors to use today's pop culture, music, language (i.e., slang terms), and food to open up more dialogue about race and ethnic relations in a fun, interactive, and engaging way. Thus, establishing good race and ethnic relations among college students has very positive outcomes in the classroom as well as college students' overall college life.

PART 4

Solutions to Race- and Ethnic-Relations Issues

CHAPTER NINE

How College Students Can Solve Race- and Ethnic-Relations Issues

The primary goal of this book is to empower college students with practical approaches that result in improved race and ethnic relations. In order to get to this point, we have had to cover a wide array of topics that provided the framework for better understanding the multitude of issues influencing race relations. Although the topic has many serious elements to it, we have also discovered that there are positive and fun outcomes for college students when they have established good race and ethnic relations on their campus.

Now we will examine potential ways in which college students can play an integral part in addressing and solving both major and minor race-relations issues on their campus. The first portion of this chapter highlights an example of how college students worked with their administrators to improve their race and ethnic relations and some roots of my own personal strategies in addressing and solving race-relations situations by reviewing my own college years. The second half of the chapter examines specific types of solutions. The four levels of solutions are (1) individual strategies, (2) group strategies, (3) university strategies, and (4) societal strategies. Providing this practical four-level solutions framework will allow the average college student to select the solution strategy that best fits his or her individual race-relations situation. Therefore, there will be a greater chance that more college students will have direct and indirect impact on improving race-relations situations at their respective colleges and universities.

College Students Working with Administrators

Although it may initially be hard to imagine that college students can work with administrators at their respective colleges/universities, the national trend shows that more and more students are becoming intricately involved in the development, management, and operations of many campus-wide events and programs (Ruff 2016). Across the country, administrators at small and large colleges/universities are working with their students to help solve many of their day-to-day operational issues.

One example in which college students eventually worked with college administrators to address and implement a new race-relations and diversity initiative was at Emory University (Atlanta, Georgia) in 2016. This collaboration between administrators and students was initiated in part by the active student body at Emory University.

Emory University (Atlanta, Georgia)

In the *Chronicle of Higher Education* article "One University's Response to Students' Demands on Race: Radical Transparency," Ruff (2016) reported that in response to the demands of the Black Students of Emory movement and student activists to improve the racial climate on campus, Emory's senior vice president and dean of campus life, Mr. Ajay Nair, organized groups of students, faculty, and administrators consisting of at least a dozen or so folks to begin constructive, critical dialogue about how to improve the racial climate on Emory's campus. Each group met several times so that a majority were in agreement as to what their particular strategy should be. In fact, among the student group, there were some student protestors who had protested against the university yet now served on the student committee. Thus, the student concerns were actually heard among the student group committee. This small change in being inclusive to those who had previously protested against the university felt reassuring and empowering to the activists (Ruff 2016).

Once each committee (student, faculty, and administrators) arrived at some major conclusions on how to best address the racial climate on campus, they submitted their final report to a brand-new committee called the Next Steps Group. The directive for the Next Steps Group was to continue to discuss new ways of bettering Emory University's racial campus climate.

The major purpose of highlighting this Emory University race-relations incident is to show how students who were once protestors against their university could not only work with university administrators but also helped to guide future diversity initiatives to improve the racial climate on Emory University's campus. This is a model that should be duplicated at all other universities across the country.

Miami University (Oxford, Ohio)

Let me be clear: I am a very proud graduate and alumni of Miami University in Oxford, Ohio. More specifically, I attended Miami University from 1976 to 1977 for my freshman year. After transferring away from Miami University my sophomore year to Central State University (1977 to 1978), I nonetheless returned to Miami University for the remainder of my undergraduate years (1978 to 1980) and then attended graduate school in anthropology at Miami University for additional two years (1981 to 1983) to achieve my master's degree in anthropology.

I can remember like it was yesterday when I first stepped on Miami University's campus as a freshman. I was nervous like every other freshman and eager to start a new chapter of my life with completely new friends and new surroundings.

As stated earlier, I got along fairly well with a majority of my classmates, who happened to be white/Caucasian/Euro-American college students. Since there were so few students of color, particularly African American students, attending Miami University during those years, it was intimidating and very stressful for many African American college students. In fact, I knew of several African American students who could not adjust to being in a college setting with so many white/Caucasian/Euro-American college students, so they transferred out after one semester.

For me, however, I was used to this type of educational situation in which I would be the minority, primarily because of my prior years of education in the predominantly mainstream public-education school system of Xenia, Ohio. It was my years from 2nd grade (1965–66) to 12th grade (1975–76) attending Tecumseh Elementary, Warner Junior High, and Xenia High School, where I learned how to get along with kids who looked different than me yet enjoyed various aspects of school like I did. So it was these years of exposure and experiences, along with my parents' advice, that prepared me for this Miami University college experience.

Therefore, my strategies in dealing with race-relations issues at Miami University were more on an individual, one-on-one basis. Each situation was different, and each required a different strategy and approach, depending upon the situation and/or the individual.

For example, socializing is a key activity for all college students, particularly freshmen. When I decided to socialize on the weekend and attend the events at the uptown bars in Oxford where most of the college crowd congregated, I usually went with a dorm friend who could fit in and I could tag along. Some uptown bars were more inviting than others to persons of color. It did not take long to figure out which ones were more receptive to a mixed crowd. We therefore frequented the bars that were more receptive to a mixed crowd so that we could avoid any subtle or direct discriminatory behavior related to my race. This was an individual strategy that worked for me throughout my years at Miami University—find places and people who tended to be receptive, understanding, and comfortable around persons of color like myself.

College Students Solutions to Race and Ethnic Relations

One of the most difficult aspects of such a controversial and politically charged topic as race and ethnic relations is to conceive solutions when very few think that it is possible. Since most folks barely want to discuss race- and ethnic-relations issues, especially as it resonates with the increasing diversity of the college campuses across the country, it becomes even more pressing in developing practical solutions now more than ever.

In a practical sense, however, there are real-life issues that must be acknowledged, addressed, and confronted simply because all the various issues connected to race and ethnic relations are emotionally charged and highly divisive if not handled correctly. So there are practical step-by-step levels of general solutions that have a better chance of being supported and used by college students throughout their undergraduate and graduate years. It is called the College Student Race- and Ethnic-Relations Solutions (CSR-ERS) framework.

Specifically, the four levels of the CSRERS are as follows:

1. Individual strategies
2. Group strategies
3. University strategies
4. Societal strategies

By organizing the solution strategies in this four-tier framework, it allows all college students to become a part of the overall solution to better race and ethnic relations at their particular colleges/universities.

Individual Strategies

The College Student Race- and Ethnic-Relations Solutions (CSRERS) framework and specific strategies were derived from the class exercise activities associated with the two Honors Race Relations Seminars I taught at East Carolina University in 2016 and 2017. The first-level solution is referred to as individual strategies.

Individual strategies are strategies that each individual college student has used in his or her life to get along with persons of different racial and ethnic backgrounds. Although our society tends to focus primarily on the problems and difficulties that arise among different racial and ethnic groups, there are real-life, practical strategies that have been very effective for many college students.

For example, in my honors seminar race-relations class, I posed the following question: "What are some simple ways in which *you* can improve your interaction with students who are racially and ethnically different from you?"

Here are some of the responses:

- Student #1: "By acknowledging the fact that we are different and try to learn about these differences and understand their background. Often when someone is of a different background I do not bring up that fact in the conversation but instead stick to more common and safe topics such as classes, schedules, or day to day activities. If I were to say to a person that I understand they are of a different background and want to learn more about what is important to them and how they perceive their heritage, I think it could open up a new realm of conversation and lead to a deeper trust, understanding, and relationship. Even if not asked directly about their race or ethnicity, I think listening to people of different groups and really trying to get to know them could help me to improve interactions with those who are racially and ethnically different from me."

- Student #2: "Just to talk to them! It's not like because they are different from me there is some barrier that I have to first break through in order to speak to them. They are students just like me, and although we may be racially and ethnically different, I'm sure there is something that we have in common. Simply talking to people will also lead me to learning more about their racial and ethnic culture and I may learn something that I like and hopefully be able to make more friendships with my peers from this experience."

- Student #3: "I often find myself misjudging people based off outward appearance, but I have recently realized that looks are deceiving and conversation is really the best way to understand people. I really can miss out on befriending some great people when I am so closed minded, but that's not what I necessarily want to happen. I want to expand my friendship across borders and not have to worry about my friends being afraid or uncomfortable being upfront with me because they feel that I am judging them.

- Student #4: "To make sure I have a mindset free of stereotypes when we meet or talk. I try to keep stereotypes from my mind because I would hate for people to do that to me, but with the influence that media has to portray certain types of people, it can be difficult. If I can try and remind myself that stereotypes AREN'T the person, I'll open up to learning more about the PERSON and their personal background and not just assume I know them because of their skin. I could also try to go out of my way to try to interact with people of ethnicities that I don't usually hang out; this way I learn about their race through association and not the internet, the media, etc."

- Student #5: "Put myself in situations that expose me to students and situations that I normally wouldn't be exposed to. This could include sporting events, race-related events, and other campus activities. Generally speaking, I have positive interactions with all students that I come into contact with, regardless of their race or ethnicity. Because of this, I think that stepping out of my comfort zone and making a conscious effort to meet new people should be the first step for me in regards to improving my interactions with racially/ethnically different students." (Honors Race Relations Seminar, Spring 2017, East Carolina University)

One of the common themes from each of the individual strategies is to basically *begin talking* to individuals who are different, as well as *avoid stereotyping* others simply because they look a certain way. These are individual strategies that every college student can implement, and it only takes a simple presence of mind and action by the individual.

Yet this is a very significant starting point because today many students communicate with cell phones and devices, as opposed to simply talking directly to their fellow classmates or dorm mates who are different from them. Our CSRERS first-level strategy has a chance to restore basic communications and daily interactions among college students of all racial and ethnic backgrounds.

Group Strategies

The second level of the CSRERS framework focuses on group strategies. Group strategies are needed primarily because college students are automatically placed in a wide variety of categories based upon their gender, race, major, interests, and year of college. Since college students are usually placed into some type of category or group, it makes sense to develop group strategies as they relate to race- and ethnic-relations solutions.

On most college campuses, there are an abundance of student organizations each college student can join. It has become a pattern among many college administrators and college counselors to encourage all students to join a club or student organization. It is perceived that these clubs and student organizations will help the individual student to better adjust and adapt to college life.

Yet simply joining a particular club or student organization is not enough in accordance to our CSRERS framework. A college student should not only consider joining a club or student organization based upon his or her interests but more importantly a group that will intentionally and regularly try to work with, socialize with, and collaborate with other student organizations and groups on campus that are *different* from them, in a sincere effort in improving race and ethnic relations on campus.

A prime example of this group strategy occurred in my honors seminar class in 2016—the first year that I taught an honors seminar at East Carolina University. On completing my honors seminar course, my students realized that there was not a student organization on campus that regularly brought students together of all various racial and ethnic backgrounds in a concerted effort in improving race relations. So that was the reason for the creation of a brand-new student organization called the Coming Together Collective.

The Coming Together Collective (2016) is a student organization to get the conversation started about race relations. They want to create a community that fosters culture and the diversity it brings, by not being color-blind but by seeing our differences as the impetus for positive social and racial progress. Their main goal is, through starting the conversation, to create a more tight-knit and well-connected community that involves students in campus conversations on race relations and cultural appreciation.

The activities that the Coming Together Collective have organized and held on the university campus include

- Silent Protest March (on campus awareness for all students to come together)
- Breaking Stereotypes
- Drop the Mike Night
- Speed Friendly Night

Whether it's starting a new student organization or joining a group, the group strategy is for the college student to bring different groups of students together for the purpose of improving race and ethnic relations on campus. It is a feasible, manageable, and practical strategy to implement on a majority of college campuses in the United States.

University Strategies

The third level of the CSRERS framework focuses on university strategies. University strategies that are more student-focused and student-derived than the typical administrator-designed and administrator-implemented programs tend to be much more effective and supported by college students. Typically, college students respond better and support student-led programs than administrator-led programs simply because it is from their "student perspective" and not from a university "administrator perspective." No matter how much training the typical college administrator receives in his or her career or at the university, it will not normally match the perspective, approach, and design of a typical college student.

For example, in my race-relations seminar, I posed the following question to my students: "What are some practical ways in which East Carolina University (ECU) administrators can increase more integration and engagement among students of all racial and ethnic backgrounds as opposed to the current pluralism, cultural-pluralism, and separatism approach to everyday college life?"

Here were a few comments:

- Student #1: "I will start off by saying that ECU is starting to improve on how they promote different cultural events. However, they are not at the level that they should be at. This is because, as mentioned in class last week, events that are heavy in culture or come from cultural groups aren't publicized as much as 'traditional' ECU events like Polar Bear Plunge or other events of that nature. Administrators definitely need to change their ways and publicize more of these events so that ECU can definitely be considered a diverse campus."

- Student #2: "ECU administrators must continue to increase the diversity on campus while providing activities that incorporate people and cultures of different backgrounds. The ability to bring people together of different backgrounds cannot be completed without the people; therefore, ECU must continue to aggressively recruit and retain students of underserved and unrepresented communities."

- Student #3: "I think that directly speaking with those in administrative positions from the student perspective will show administrators how to gain direct insight from the community it is attempting to engage just as we are in this class (i.e., presenting solutions to the Chancellor, engaging with guest speakers, etc.). The increase of students from various backgrounds can also increase integration and engagement through stimulating a more diverse community. Within this, we could also reinforce the necessity of ECU students engaging individuals different from themselves; this way they are interacting with students and gaining knowledge of their culture/heritage that is rooted in their real lives rather than stereotypes."

- Student #4: "I think more passport events should be more cultural events, and instead of just making a couple of general education classes attend them, I think they should make all freshmen attend a certain number of these events. As they are mandatory for classes you know you will have a student audience, so why not use this already given platform and use it to teach incoming freshmen about their peers of different racial and ethnic backgrounds and teach them to appreciate it the very first year they are on campus?"

Interestingly, the comments from my students regarding some practical ways in which ECU administrators can increase integration and engagement among students of all racial and ethnic backgrounds emphasized that the university should

1. publicize and promote more of the cultural events on campus;
2. aggressively recruit and retain students of underserved and underrepresented communities;
3. reinforce the necessity of ECU students engaging individuals different from themselves; and
4. make all freshmen attend a certain number of cultural events so that they can engage with their peers of different racial and ethnic backgrounds.

All four of these student suggestions fit the third level of the CSRERS framework—university strategies.

Societal Strategies

The fourth level of the CSRERS framework focuses on societal strategies. Societal strategies are activities in which a student attempts to connect with the local community surrounding their college or university campus. On most college/university campuses today, this is referred to as service learning. Yet this strategy is more than service learning; it is designed for students to not only learn and serve for local organizations but also become a part of the organizations and community leadership to instill positive changes for the community in collaboration with the college/university. This way, the individual college student becomes a change agent to help local communities address their needs while also attempting to address such other societal issues as improving local race and ethnic relations.

Not surprisingly, most college students do not feel that they can make an impact on society while attending college. Yet this is a false assumption. Those students who are truly committed to making a societal impact while in college can do so, once they find and take the opportunity to connect with local organizations and serve in a leadership capacity with that organization.

For example, when I was a graduate student at Wayne State University, I volunteered at Henry Ford Hospital for some five years in their hypertension clinic. As a volunteer, I filed paperwork and medical files and most importantly spoke with individual patients about their health status. Yet I did not think about serving in a leadership role at all at the time.

A few years later, as an assistant professor at the University of Houston, however, I did volunteer with a local health department (Riverside Clinic) and also served in a leadership role as a community health organizer. In this additional leadership role, I became a positive change agent for the community because there was a definite need for improved health care and health education for the local community residents surrounding the University of Houston. Thus, working as a volunteer for a community organization, hospital, or health clinic—whether it is as an undergraduate or graduate student or even as an assistant professor, in my case—fulfills the societal-strategy objective of our CSRERS framework.

Conclusion

After teaching in academia for four decades (1983–2018), I always felt the students in my classes, if given an opportunity, could *solve* many of the world's problems, at least in their own part of the world. I know it may sound idealistic to some, yet it is the truth. The type of ideals, creativity, passion, commitment, sacrifice, and deep critical thinking that I have witnessed during lectures, exams, projects, and fieldwork papers over the years leads me to one simple conclusion—college students can solve serious real-life issues, such as race relations, if given an opportunity!

If given an opportunity—that is the key.

In 2016 and 2017, that is exactly what I gave undergraduate students in my Honors Race Relations Seminar—an opportunity to address this very serious race-relations issue on our campus. Here is the course description as listed in the honors college course description:

> Why is the United States still having major race relations problems in 2016 and 2017? Do you want to continue to sit along the sidelines or help solve this issue in our country, particularly here at East Carolina University? This course aims to examine, discuss, and debate the major concepts and frameworks associated with race relations in America. Students will not only gather background information on this issue through traditional research methods but also gather data by listening to key administrators at ECU and other NC state universities. After students gather this data, they will present their own race relations solutions to the Chancellor's Office at East Carolina University.

Not surprisingly, my students during year 1 and year 2 created and developed some amazing race-relations solutions for the university, which are strategically being incorporated into the university system.

College administrators and faculty should certainly include college students in all facets of the college/university operations, program planning, recruitment and retention strategies, and diversity outreach initiatives. The simple fact remains—the best solutions to problems for college students in a college/university setting can come from college students!

CHAPTER TEN

How Universities Can Solve Race- and Ethnic-Relations Issues

One of the most challenging aspects in addressing race and ethnic relations in the college/university setting is how to encourage college/university administrators to potentially modify, adjust, or even dramatically change their approach and programming of student initiatives targeted to address diversity and inclusiveness on individual campuses. Of course, this book is not stating that all current college/university student-diversity and race-relations initiatives need to be changed. What I contend is that there needs to be an opportunity for a set of new strategies to be tested and tried, to find out if we (faculty, administrators, staff) can get our current and future college students to think, behave, interact, and engage on a completely different level than what's currently occurring on college/university campuses.

We need them to think both critically and compassionately about the issue at hand. Since our campuses have increasingly become racially and ethnically diverse and will likely become more so in the years to come, it is imperative for college/university administrators to find new ways to teach, help, and inspire their college students of all backgrounds to interact and engage.

For those college/university administrators who want to *rethink* some of their future student-diversity initiatives, this chapter provides a framework and best-practices solution examples for engaging all students in a completely different way in which the entire college/university system and not just the multicultural affairs office or minority program office and their personnel is involved. This new framework is referred to as the Cultural Competency Engagement Initiative (CCEI).

Cultural Competency Engagement Initiative (CCEI)

As with all new initiatives in any institution or corporation, there are a set of definitions, terminology, and strategies that strive to inform, guide, direct, encourage, and motivate individuals to a certain frame of thinking and action. Once these sets of definitions, terminologies, and strategies are clearly explained and understood by individuals, then an initiative can be implemented. Thus, our first step with our new initiative is to explain the Cultural Competency Engagement Initiative.

First, we are not going to use all the so-called sophisticated, in-depth, and detailed jargon used by many administrators to describe a simple concept. Unfortunately, this happens all too often when administrators develop, design, and implement initiatives that only a handful of folks truly understand and appreciate.

I know this from experience because as a former federal government administrator, I had to learn "government-speak" to function effectively in my job while most folks outside of government could not understand what we government administrators actually meant. Thus, to avoid the confusion of administrative jargon, we are going to use plain language to describe our new initiative for all colleges/universities across the United States.

Cultural Competency Engagement Initiative (CCEI) means exactly this: "Every individual will strive to increase and improve his or her knowledge, attitude, skills, and engagement with a person who is racially and ethnic different from him or her."

Since the term "cultural competency" has continued to grow in its usage for all types of agendas, initiatives, and institutions during the past 20 years, I contend that one of the best usages of this concept originates in a public-health and medical textbook titled *Multicultural Medicine and Health Disparities* (Satcher and Pamies 2006) in a chapter from Ana Nunez and Candace Robertson.

Main Concepts

Here are the key concepts of cultural competency adapted to our usage for race and ethnic relations:

1. Knowledge: the ability of an individual to increase his or her knowledge and education about a racial and ethnic population that is different from him or her.

2.   Attitude: the ability of an individual to become more aware, improve, or change his or her values, opinions, and attitudes about a racial and ethnic population that is different from him or her.

3.   Skills: the ability of an individual to increase his or her skills in communicating, collaborating, working with, and socializing with a racial and ethnic population that is different from him or her.

4.   Engage: the ability of an individual to increase his or her interaction and engagement with a racial and ethnic population that is different from him or her.

All of us are familiar with these simple and straightforward concepts (knowledge, attitude, skills, and engagement). Yet when these four concepts are taken together, interconnected with each other, and then applied to the college setting and college students today, they take on a completely different meaning and outcome. As this chapter describes, these concepts—individually and collectively (as seen in the next section)—show why it is so important to adapt these approaches to our college/university setting as they relate to race- and ethnic-relations issues among college students.

College/University Programs and Initiatives

For a majority of college/university administrators, it is fairly easy to implement or introduce a new program for their student and faculty populations. It seems like every year (or every other year) college/university administrators implement and introduce a new program or initiative, whether college students and faculty like it or not.

Perhaps what is most challenging for administrators is to actually conceive or develop innovative programs and initiatives that directly address race and ethnic relations on their particular campuses. A lot of strategies and so-called new approaches to diversity initiatives have come and gone within many college/university systems during the past few decades. This college/university program and initiative however is different.

Cultural Competency Engagement—Knowledge Initiative

Without a doubt, every institution of higher learning fulfills this first component of the Cultural Competency Engagement Initiative of knowledge. Knowledge is the foundation of every educational system in primary school, middle school, high school, college, and postgraduate training. Yet knowledge that directly addresses race- and ethnic-relations issues in a cultural competency engagement strategy is different.

For example, East Carolina University accomplishes this CCE—Knowledge Initiative through their domestic- and global-diversity course-designation curriculum. Approved by the faculty senate (2012) and by the chancellor (2012), undergraduate students are required to complete two three-hour diversity courses: one course with a domestic-diversity focus and one with a global-diversity focus.

Domestic-diversity courses address understanding diversity within the United States in the context of problems faced by members of specific groups. Global diversity addresses understanding diversity in other cultures in the context of globalization.

More specifically, here are the course goals for each:

- Domestic-Diversity Course Goals
    1. Students understand problems that arise in the United States from differences in age, ethnicity, culture, national origin, ability, religion, sexual orientation, and gender identity in the context of their historical and contemporary causes and effects, including attempts to resolve these problems.
    2. Students demonstrate the ability to use critical-thinking skills to evaluate from different perspectives domestic problems arising from differences in age, ethnicity, culture, national origin, ability, religion, sexual orientation, and gender identity.
- Global-Diversity Course Goals
    1. Students understand how cultural beliefs and values shape people's perceptions and affect global decisions and actions.
    2. Students apply critical-thinking skills to evaluate global issues and events from multiple perspectives.

Overall, courses that address diversity provide opportunities for college students to learn about the beliefs, values, and achievements of people other than those of their own age, ethnicity, national origin, ability, religion, sexual orientation, and gender identity. These courses also give opportunities to learn how to deal constructively with these issues.

Although this is a good first step and example of fulfilling the CCE—Knowledge Initiative through university course offerings, it does not go far enough, simply because there is no requirement for interaction and engagement among students who are different from each other. New knowledge is not only gained through college courses, but I would contend that new cultural knowledge is acquired through actually interacting and engaging with individuals and groups of people who are different.

Thus, the second part of the Cultural Competency Engagement—Knowledge Initiative involves college/universities implementing a campus-wide housing policy for matching students of different racial and ethnic backgrounds to live together in their respective on-campus dorms. The daily interaction and engagement with each other from early morning to late night is the cultural competency engagement knowledge that all college students need to obtain.

An excellent example of this strategy is Elon University, in North Carolina. In the fall of 2010, university administrators organized undergraduate housing into "neighborhoods." The grouped housing brings together diverse populations of students and offers common social and study spaces. Faculty members also live among the students in each group, alongside residence-life staff members (Brown 2016a).

Elon University's Brooke Barnett—associate provost for inclusive community—explained: "Like our societies, we're a little more segregated than you'd think we'd be. People still tend to spend time with more people who are more like them than not" (Brown 2016a, 2). Yet she hopes that while on campus and through Elon University's Residential Campus Initiative students will mitigate that trend.

Cultural Competency Engagement—Attitude Initiative

Once students start to acquire new knowledge about different racial and ethnic groups (whether through coursework or living in campus dorms), their attitude will begin to change as well. It is simply not enough to gain new knowledge about different racial and ethnic groups anymore. The impact of this new knowledge must lead to a change of one's attitude—in other words, one's values, beliefs, and opinions that are the root cause for misconceptions, biases, and racial prejudice. That's why activities that reach or challenge the individual student's attitudes about various racial and ethnic populations should be implemented in some form of extracurricular activity for each student.

For example, at East Carolina University, the sole mission of the Coming Together Collective (the new student organization developed in 2016 highlighted in chapter 9) is to bring all racial and ethnic students together to address race-relations issues on campus. The Coming Together Collective wants to create a community that fosters culture and diversity, by not being color-blind but by seeing our differences as the impetus for positive social and racial progress. Their main goal is, through starting the conversation, to create a more tight-knit and well-connected community that involves students in campus conversations on race relations and cultural appreciation.

In fact, Coming Together Collective's president, Carly Judd, organized their first Peace Walk in the fall of 2016 and first Drop the Mike event in early 2017. The Drop the Mike event brought students of all racial and ethnic backgrounds together simply to talk about their race-related issues as a student in an open forum. As faculty advisor for the group and present during the event, I observed how each student—one by one—voiced his or her issue in a respectful and passionate way. It was not a session to blame other students or the university. It was simply an opportunity to share with the audience one's perspective and challenges regarding one's racial and ethnic identity on campus.

Organized by Coming Together Collective, this event helped to start a constructive dialogue to change students' attitudes about various racial and ethnic groups on campus. It also served as a constructive outlet for individual students to vent their frustrations, concerns, and emotions as a student who wants change as it relates to developing better race relations among all students on campus.

Cultural Competency Engagement—Skills Initiative

The third element to this Cultural Competency Engagement Initiative is skills—the ability of an individual to increase his or her skills in communicating, collaborating, working with, and socializing with a racial and ethnic population that is different from him or her.

An excellent example of improving one's skills as it relates to race relations is the new Dialogue 101 diversity-experience training program for students at the University of Oklahoma. The mandatory diversity-experience trainings are a five-hour training session for students in small groups to act out such real-life, day-to-day campus situations as getting acquainted with a new roommate or going to a social event on campus.

During the training sessions, students are paired off, learn skits, and then perform for other groups. What is unique about the skits and acting is that the students try to say what most likely a person would think about another person. Many times, generalizations and stereotyping occurs initially when students meet other students from different backgrounds for the first time.

For example, when meeting a roommate or an acquaintance for the first time, a person may ask, "Where are you from?" In actuality, they are thinking and wanting to say, "What is your race and/or ethnicity?" simply because the person looks different from others that he or she is accustomed to socializing with.

At that moment, the students not participating in the skit attempt to politely correct the misperception and suggest a more polite way of asking a more direct question about a student's race and ethnicity if that is an issue that needs to be addressed. Thus, students learn a new cultural competent engagement skill in communicating, working with, and socializing with students who may look different from them (Brown 2016b).

Cultural Competency Engagement—Engage Initiative

The final element of the Cultural Competency Engagement Initiative is engage—the ability of an individual to increase his or her interaction and engagement with a racial and ethnic population that is different from him or her. Although a majority of colleges/universities contend that their student populations engage and interact on a daily basis, and many do to a certain degree, most do not implement a university program that strives for and rewards students for cross-cultural engagement and interaction with students who are racially and ethnically different from them.

An example of this type of engage university initiative called the Cultural Explosion and Global Awareness Week originates from a brand-new university program developed by my honor students in 2017 at East Carolina University. As part of my honors seminar class titled Breaking the Boundaries of Race in America, my honor students were required to develop an end-of-the-semester project that attempted to address and solve some of the race-relations issues at East Carolina University. The outcome of their innovative project resulted in the support of the top administrators at East Carolina University and then implementation of it by the following academic year.

Originally called the Cultural Explosion and Global Awareness Week and revised to the Cultural Awareness and Global Explosion Event, it consists of a three-day event with student activities focused on bringing all students together to celebrate cultural global activities, which allow students to interact and engage in a whole new way. There are three major elements to this Cultural Awareness and Global Explosion Event:

1. All of the events within this week would be classed as passport events—therefore mandatory for many of the student body.
2. The events will be run by different organizations on campus that represent their respective cultural and ethnic backgrounds.
3. These events would also count toward the completion of the cultural competency engagement certificate that we plan to implement in order to give an incentive for people to become more active in different racial and cultural groups.

The weeklong events consist of such activities as a social-media takeover, student guest speakers, "Food Fun Fest," Panhellenic panel, and cultural awareness day, which involves all East Carolina University cultural groups performing on the mall (dancing, singing, artwork, oral histories, and music) in which students must take a selfie to show their participation and engagement with a cultural group that is different from them. This interaction and engagement with cultural groups that differ from the individual college student is the goal of this initiative and the overall goal of the CCEI.

Conclusion

This chapter presented a brand-new approach in solving race- and ethnic-relations issues on college campuses today. This new approach and framework, referred to as the Cultural Competency Engagement Initiative (CCEI), highlighted four key components—knowledge, attitude, skills, and engage. Working with these four key components in any college/university diversity-program initiative will allow college administrators to create a new cultural awareness and understanding for race and ethnic relations on any college/university campus. An example of this new framework can be seen in a fairly recent report by the American Association of American College and Universities (AAC&U).

In a 2005 report commissioned by the Association of American College and Universities titled "Making Diversity Work on Campus: A Research Based Perspective," Milem, Chang, and Antonio (2005) suggest that if college/university administrators truly want to make diversity work on their campuses, three principles of practices should be implemented:

1. Take a multidimensional approach;
2. Engage all students; and
3. Focus on process.

In other words, colleges and universities need to constantly encourage, motivate, and provide incentives for their student population to regularly increase their knowledge, improve their attitudes, acquire new skill sets, and engage with students who are different from them. Once colleges and universities institutionalize this initiative within their system, then we will truly see how colleges and universities can solve their own race- and ethnic-relations issues.

PART 5

Debate Issues

CHAPTER ELEVEN

Controversial Race-Relations Topics to Discuss and Debate

Race relations continues to be a very challenging topic to address, discuss, evaluate, understand, and solve. There are usually a wide range of opinions on each race-relations issue, which leads many to avoid the topic. This is one of the most unfortunate aspects of raising discussions of race relations. This issue tends to be highly polarizing and politically charged, so race relations remains a topic that requires serious, frank, and honest discussion, and, most importantly, respectful debate.

One of the foundations of academia and advantages of attending college is to provide students with a professional and intellectual setting for debate. Debating allows students of differing opinions to express verbally or written how they feel about a particular issue and gain an understanding of why someone else believes otherwise. Thus, it is healthy, empowering, and mind-expanding to debate. It is healthy to challenge the status quo. It is healthy to highlight the opinions of the underserved, underprivileged, minority, disabled, underrepresented, and persons of color. In essence, debating allows all individuals an opportunity to express their opinions and defend those opinions.

This is what this chapter is all about—debating race-relations issues that most people are hesitant or fearful to address, discuss, evaluate, understand, and solve.

Debate Issues: Pro, Con, and Potential Solution

Throughout one's college years, there are always a wide array of controversial race-relations topics that cause vigorous, opinionated, divisive yet healthy discussions among the student body on any campus. There are topics that strike a nerve and motivate even the most mild-mannered college student to speak out.

Here are a few topics that may cause a healthy debate on campuses:

- Removal of all Confederate depictions (statues, names, flags) on college campuses
- Protesting during the national anthem—for example, taking a knee—at college sporting events
- Protesting a top college administrator's office over a race-relations issue
- Making new immigrant college students assimilate to American cultural standards (language, dress, clothing) as soon as possible
- Limiting the number of specific racial and ethnic student organizations on campus
- Allowing controversial local or national personalities, scholars, or celebrities to speak on college campuses
- Protesting the U.S. president and/or U.S. policies
- Continuing affirmative-action programs for underserved and underrepresented college students
- Discontinuing specific and separate minority-focused programs on college campuses
- Allowing college students to carry a firearm

Removal of All Confederate Depictions on College Campuses (Statues, Names, Flags)

Pro

I support the removal of all Confederate depictions (statues, names, flags, and other) because they represent a time in our American history in which our country was divided primarily over the support of slavery by the South. Although I recognize that all Southerners did not support the institution of slavery, the symbolism of the Confederacy (whether through the hanging of the flag or erecting statues of Confederate soldiers) disrespects all African Americans—past and present—who have to be reminded daily of the hatred, history, and affliction it left for generations.

Con

I do not support the removal of all Confederate depictions (statues, names, flags, and other) because they represent a time in our American history in which our country decided to stand up for what it believed to be right and just for our society at the time, regardless of whether it separated our families and split our country in half. I may not agree with the principles, values, and institutions during that time in history, yet it is my family heritage and my individual history that I feel should continue to be recognized and not destroyed and rewritten. It happened and that's a fact.

Potential Solution

A potential compromise may be to remove a number of Confederate symbols, depictions, and statues yet agree on allowing at least one to remain. The primary purpose of keeping this one remaining Confederate symbol recognizes the Southern families who lived in this part of the country at that particular time period and that's it.

In addition, there could be multiple depictions and statues of African Americans and abolitionists who were pioneers and heroes in the South during the same period of time, who stood against the institution of slavery. These individuals and depictions would be visible in direct contrast to the one Confederate depiction, thereby compromising on a very politically charged, historical race-relations issue.

Protesting during the National Anthem at College Sporting Events

Pro

I support students protesting during the national anthem at college sporting events because it is their belief and right as a U.S. citizen to show their disagreement with a national issue. As long as the college student does a silent protest and does not offend the rights of other college students to support the national anthem, then he or she has the right to protest the national anthem.

Con

I do not support students protesting during the national anthem at college sporting events because as a U.S. citizen all of us should honor the rights and freedom of our American flag and the human sacrifice that all people, including all racial and ethnic groups in the United States, gave to our country. It is dishonorable for anyone, regardless of one's belief and the current problems facing a particular population, to protest the national anthem.

Potential Solution

In order for individual college students to exercise their democratic right for freedom of expression and protest as an American citizen—one of the founding principles of our country—perhaps make an announcement at the particular sporting event stating, "For those who want to protest, please participate at the first playing of the national anthem," so that all the protestors can be recognized. Then, play the national anthem a second time, and it's only for those who will not protest and who respect the national anthem. Therefore, give both audiences—protestors and nonprotestors—an opportunity to show and express their feelings publicly in a respectful way.

Protesting a Top College Administrator's Office over a Race-Relations Issue

Pro

I support students protesting a top college administrator's office over a race-relations issue because this may be the one and only way for a certain segment of the student body to get attention and a response from the administration concerning a race-relations issue that has been vastly overlooked, avoided, ignored, or escalated through a recent tragic event on campus. As long as the student protest of a top administrator's office does not harm anyone or stop the daily operations of the university, protesting over a race-relations issue should be allowed. In a majority of student protesting situations, all options have been utilized and exhausted, thereby leaving one final option—protest a top college administrator's office.

Con

I do not support students protesting a top college administrator's office over a race-relations issue because it only causes disruption on the college campus and does not resolve the particular race-relations issue. College students who protest an administrator's office tend to be self-serving for the needs of their own group, thereby ignoring the needs of the rest of the student population. Additionally, I do not support the protesting because it sends the wrong message to the college in which you are a student, indicating to others that you cannot be trusted to represent your particular college.

Potential Solution

When a particular race-relations issue occurs at a college, students have several other options besides holding a sit-in or protesting to get the top administrators' attention. First, it is more effective to raise awareness about the race-relations issue among your student base as a first step. Getting more students of all different racial and ethnic backgrounds involved, as opposed to just one group, is critically important.

Secondly, holding a rally on the student section of the university is more effective because it gets the attention one wants and motivates more of the student population to support the students' stance on a race-relations issue.

Finally, promote your stance on a race-relations issue by writing an article for the student newspaper, get an interview with local TV and radio news reporters, or use social media to raise awareness about the issue. These are constructive, practical, feasible, and manageable options for any college student population to call attention to and receive a response from top administrators at a college or university.

Making New Immigrant College Students Assimilate to American Cultural Standards (Language, Dress, and Clothing)

Pro

I support making new immigrant college students assimilate to American cultural standards as soon as possible because every student knows that there are a set of core values, expectations, and standards that are uniquely American, which helps a majority of college students on a campus to feel as one and safe. Immigrant students who consistently wear their traditional clothing and use their own language on American college campuses present to others a threat and cause concern to the average college student.

Con

I do not support making new immigrant college students assimilate to American cultural standards as soon as possible because it removes the uniqueness and diversity of the student population on campus. One of the advantages of a college experience is for average students to experience the diversity of their campuses through the diversity of their student populations. If there is a mandate or policy to make immigrant students fit in immediately, then it would be an unfortunate state of affairs for the college and the entire student body.

Potential Solution

Although there tends to be a divide between new immigrant, international students and native-born American college students, with the potential for misunderstanding, we must allow new immigrant students to be able to express themselves in their own cultural way (language, clothing, dress, and hairstyle) so that they can adjust to American customs. Once they do this, they are more likely to modify their cultural style to American cultural style.

Limiting the Number of Specific Racial and Ethnic Student Organizations on Campus

Pro

I support limiting the number of specific racial and ethnic student organizations on campus because if a college/university has too many racial and ethnic student organizations, then the college would lose its identity and history. Each college has an obligation to maintain the image and general look of its majority student population so that it does not get lost or overlooked despite the increase in diversity among the student population.

Con

I do not support limiting the number of specific racial and ethnic student organizations on campus because it would reduce the opportunity for minorities to express themselves on campus, and it would send the wrong message to the overall student population. Each college/university campus's major objective is to increase its diversity of students, particularly if it is a mainstream university planning to increase its student population.

Potential Solution

As colleges/universities try to keep up with the ever-changing landscape and increased diversity of its student population, student organizations are a way for students of all racial and ethnic backgrounds to find their place, support, and identity in the midst of a predominantly white student body.

Although we do understand that if each different racial/ethnic student group has its own organization, it may separate the overall student population into numerous separate subsections, thus becoming further disconnected from one another. On the other hand, as more diverse student organizations grow on a college campus, it actually reduces racial/ethnic tension and misunderstanding and improves race and ethnic relations. Thus, an unlimited number of specific racial and ethnic student organizations can only help a college/university student population.

Allowing Controversial Local or National Personalities, Scholars, or Celebrities to Speak on College Campuses

Pro

I support allowing controversial local or national personalities, scholars, or celebrities to speak on college campuses because it should be the credo or obligation of every public university to provide their student population with diverse perspectives and opinions, as long as they are conducted in a professional way. Whether or not the local or national personality holds unpopular opinions, as long as a clearly defined segment of the student population wants to hear this controversial speaker, the university should support their decision.

Con

I do not support allowing controversial local or national personalities to speak on college campuses because the speakers' major objective is to cause divisiveness and tension among college students on campus. I believe that any speaker whose main purpose is to instigate trouble or promote hate should not be given an audience on our campus. In addition, college/university administrators have the right to protect their students from any foreseen harmful campus events. That is why I do not support allowing controversial local or national personalities, scholars, or celebrities to speak on college campuses.

Potential Solution

Before the academic year begins, all student organizations on campus must provide a thorough list of all their invited guests to campus. The list of those speakers must also identify any speaker who is highly opinionated so that university committee members can make an equitable, fair, and just decision as to allow or not allow the speaker to come. In a majority of cases, the college administrators should fulfill their obligation to accept controversial speakers to campus. Only in the rarest occasion should a public university explore denying a controversial local or national personality, scholar, or celebrity, usually when there is major potential outbreak of violence, jeopardizing the welfare of any student on campus.

Protesting the U.S. President—Donald Trump

Pro

I support the protesting of the U.S. president Donald Trump because it is the civil right of every American citizen and college student to express his or her opinion about our U.S. government leaders, including our president. Although it may be an un-patriotic, I still have that right as an American citizen to protest the president because I am not in agreement with many of the policies and programs implemented during this administration. That's why I feel the need to allow college students to protest our president—Donald Trump.

Con

I do not support the protesting of the U.S. president Donald Trump pri-marily because it is un-American and simply the wrong thing to do. In the presidential election, the United States decides which candidate they want to be president, and whoever wins is the president for all Americans. That's why I feel that it would be un-American for anyone, even college students, to protest the U.S. president Donald Trump.

Potential Solution

In order for every student's voice to be heard, regardless of political affili-ation, and so adhere to freedom of speech, allow students to protest—or support—any U.S. president during designated times and places on campus. Both supporters and protestors get equal treatment and scrutiny of safety issues.

Continuing Affirmative-Action Policies and Programs for Underserved and Underrepresented College Students

Pro

I support continuing affirmative-action policies and programs for under-served and underrepresented college students because there are still not enough persons of color and minorities achieving the same status as nonmi-nority students. An affirmative-action amendment has recently been ruled in favor of and mandated by our federal court system, so it still makes sense to adhere to the affirmative-action policies and programs for our higher educa-tion institutions. Besides, it's the right thing to do.

Con

I do not support continuing affirmative-action policies and programs because we are no longer in an era of civil rights or the 1960s when these policies and programs needed to be implemented. Now that our colleges/universities have achieved an equal-opportunity status, it is no longer needed. In addition, since it is 2018 and affirmative-action programs have been in place for over 50 years, we are in a state of "equality" even though we know that all groups are not totally equal.

Potential Solution

Public institutions receiving state and federal funding are obligated to continue the policies and programs associated with the affirmative-action law. Although it may appear visibly on campus that many underserved and underrepresented college students are attending our university, the fact remains that their numbers are drastically lower than the majority students.

Discontinuing Specific and Separate Minority-Focused Programs on College Campuses

Pro

Although our colleges/universities must adhere to the federal affirmative-action policies and programs, I support discontinuing specific and separate minority-focused programs on our college campuses because they separate these groups from the rest of the college students, thereby giving them preferential treatment over other groups of students. Now that our institution is considered a culturally diverse institution of higher learning, we no longer need more specific and separate minority-focused programs on our campus.

Con

I do not support the discontinuation of specific and separate minority-focused programs on college campus because these groups will continue to need special support since they have traditionally been underrepresented and not a part of the mainstream portion of the university activities. So in order for these specific and separate minority groups to feel a part of the entire university system, there needs to be a continuation of specific and separate minority-focused programs on college campuses.

Potential Solution

Since our university/college must maintain as a budget-conscious, fiscal institution, we cannot fund and support every minority-focused program on campus. Therefore, establish a university committee made up of students, faculty, and administrators to determine a hierarchical priority system in which certain minority programs will be funded and others must be set at a lower priority or even be combined with other programs. This is the most practical, cost-efficient, and fiscally responsible solution.

Allowing College Students to Carry a Firearm

Pro

I support allowing college students to carry a firearm on campus because they are individual U.S. citizens first, and therefore they have the right as

21-year-old adult, regardless of how the local state or college/university may be against it. Moreover, the 21-year-old college student is considered a full-fledged, mature adult and must be treated as such. Finally, I support allowing 21-year-old college students to carry a licensed firearm because they have the right to defend themselves in the case of an armed threat on campus.

Con

I do not support allowing 21-year-old college students to carry a firearm on campus because it would increase the likelihood of students accidentally harming themselves on campus. Although 21-year-old college students are considered adults, they are nonetheless young adults who are often away from home for the first time. They are still learning about life and make too many mistakes at this stage of their lives. Additionally, college students often consume alcohol, and having college students carrying firearms may lead to additional problems on campus. I therefore do not support allowing 21-year-old college students with a license or any college student to carry a firearm on campus.

Potential Solution

Where state and local regulations allow carrying firearms, university/college administrators may set stipulations: select a number of designated, 21-year-old licensed and well-trained college students (e.g., campus safety interns, military professionals, and registered hunters) to carry firearms on campus. These select, designated student professionals can assist the campus police in any college/university campus setting, acting as a deterrent and preventing a major altercation on a peaceful college/university campus.

Conclusion

This chapter highlighted a few controversial race-relations topics in a debate format so that the reader can see that there are always two sides to each issue. Yet what is unique to this debate format was that I pressed for and presented some potential solutions to these very controversial topics. These potential solutions are the result of hearing out both sides—allowing both opposing sides to state their individual opinions, values, beliefs, and perspectives. Once each side is given this opportunity and forum, then a potential compromise and solution can result.

Of course, there are so many more controversial race-relations topics in the world today and on any particular college/university campus. Take the opportunity to not only express your opinions, values, beliefs, and perspectives in a constructive, professional, and civil way to such others as college administrators, faculty, other students, and family members about a particular topic, but most importantly listen and engage with other college students who are different from you so that you can form a more biopsychosociocultualinguistic perspective of race relations that will hopefully motivate students to engage with diverse college classmates in a more *culturally* competent way today and in the future. The world will be better for that.

PART 6

Teaching Strategies

CHAPTER TWELVE

Teaching a Race-Relations Seminar for the First Time: A Fieldwork Journal

Two of the greatest challenges with this topic are getting college students to enroll in a course focused on race relations and for the leader to design a college course, regularly lecture, and discuss and debate the topic in a guided, constructive manner throughout.

From January 2016 to April 2016, I taught my first race-relations seminar. After 14 weeks of lecturing, discussing, debating, and visiting another college campus, this race-relations seminar began proving itself a success. One indicator was the seven honor students who all completed the seminar with high grades and showed sound rationale as well as critical thinking.

Although I had planned lectures months in advance and refined my syllabus again and again, it was simply not enough, in light of what I experienced from the very first day of class. That introduction meant that I had to lecture about the very sensitive topic of race relations and also get my students (whom I did not know before) to open up and begin talking issues. The sensitive reality of this class immediately hit me. It's one thing to design a class and plan all the detailed topics to talk about in a nice syllabus but a completely different situation when you have to actually lead discussion, which can take on a life of its own, and head into unanticipated areas, discussions, and actions.

To capture typical, unique, and outstanding moments of this seminar, I kept a fieldwork journal for not only myself but also for the university, because it was a part of a new teaching strategy—to teach classes that involve more engagement with concepts and issues for students so that they could learn a different way to connect with scholarly issues. Thus, I and several other faculty members in my cohort taught courses that encouraged true engagement and innovative strategies to get students more involved with the issues. Less attention was paid to memorization of facts and far more to critical thinking, conversation, and problem solving.

What follows are weekly fieldwork journal notes from the race-relations seminar during the spring semester of 2016.

Fieldwork Journal Notes: Condensed

Day 1

It's day one for my new honors seminar course on race relations, and quite frankly, I am always a bit nervous to meet my brand-new class each semester, particularly this one—all honor students. No matter how long I have been teaching college classes, and this is year 30, I still feel anxious on the first day.

The classroom is located in our honors college. As I arrived in the building and walked into the seminar room, there were some of my students— seated toward the very back of the room. I greeted them and then quickly realized that I had to get situated at the front of the seminar room, thereby placing myself farther away from where the students were sitting. Once I got situated by the lectern and the interactive-whiteboard podium, I looked back at the students, and they were, yes, all definitely seated at the back of the seminar room.

So here was *the* moment at the very beginning of this class. Do I let the students stay seated toward the back of the seminar room or encourage them to move forward? They looked real comfortable sitting in their chairs and were chatting away with one another and did not even think about moving as I got situated.

Yet the most important issue of my seminar presented itself right then as well: "How are these students reacting to an African American professor?" Of course, they knew what I looked like from my photo that I'd posted on the course blackboard contact page, yet it is a completely different issue when students have to confront a person-of-color faculty member, particularly an African American male teaching race relations, where all of my students were Caucasian females—talk about a tenuous situation. I smiled, told a quick little joke, and asked the students to sit closer.

Fortunately, there was no hesitation on their part, and they collectively moved closer to where I was seated. So after they got situated, it was time for me to ease them more into how I teach, how I interact with students, and how we were going to examine and discuss such a sensitive topic—race relations—in this class.

Next, I told another quick joke about first-day classes, and I could tell that students were easing up more. That was another positive signal for me in that I was reducing their anxiety and helping them to perceive me as just another professor beginning to teach a new class.

I began to go over the syllabus and all the major requirements for the course. Before I went too far into the syllabus, I reminded myself to slow down even further in order to give my new students more background information about myself.

Sometimes I forget that this is the key for me as an instructor, particularly as an African American instructor, to spend extra time sharing my personal and professional background, allowing them to feel more at ease, comfortable, and relatable to me so that they can individually open up more about themselves much earlier in the semester.

Basically, what I shared with my students was that I came from a small midwestern town in Ohio and attended a mainstream mid-American university in which I was a part of a minority student population consisting of less than 1 percent of the total student population (approximately 20,000). This was my college situation throughout my undergraduate schooling and my first two years of graduate school.

At that point in the class, I said to my students, "I have always been in this situation in academia, and it's not a big deal to me. It's other people who make it a big deal."

Once I shared this story with my students, I could definitely see that all of them felt even more at ease with my lecture style and with me as a professor. Thus, I accomplished one of my major objectives for the first day—get the students to feel relaxed and ready to focus on the topic at hand, with a black professor.

My next major objective was to emphasize to my students about the uniqueness of this seminar and that they would have the opportunity to change how their university addressed race-relations issues, because they would share their ideas and solutions with the top administrator at East Carolina University—the chancellor.

Once I emphasized this key point, I could sense that they were genuinely excited about this potential outcome of the class. That's when I felt they were starting to commit themselves to the overall impact of this class.

Nonetheless, for us to actually get there, I also emphasized to my students that each student must become a leader in her own right by participating in class discussion, writing papers in which she must strongly express and justify her opinions, debate an issue with her colleagues, and interact with all the guest lecturers that came to our class, along with being fully involved when we took our field trip to a larger state university. I emphasized "individual leadership" first, because I felt that many students struggle with expressing themselves, particularly with this subject matter—race relations.

Then I emphasized "group leadership" because they would collectively develop their own race-relations solutions and present them to the dean of the college and then to the chancellor of the university. These race-relations solutions would represent the first set of ideals and strategies originating from ECU students—not administrators. It was clear they felt more empowered.

After completing these two major objectives of the first class, I gave the class a "fun" writing assignment consisting of only one to two pages. The assignment went as follows:

1. Discuss how you or your friends have been affected by race-relations issues here at ECU. (If you or your friends have not, just say "have not been affected at all.")
2. State whether or not we need a regular forum to talk about race-relations issues here at ECU.

Day 2

What a difference a week made. As soon as I walked into the seminar room, all of my students were in their chairs sitting close to my end of the seminar table and talking with each other in a very relaxed, lighthearted way. They were ready!

As I situated myself in front of the students, there were a few questions already from a couple of students regarding their first writing assignment. As the class began, I informed the students that the arrangement of class would change now that lectures were beginning. That is, for the first part of the class (about 45–50 minutes), I would highlight the major concepts and terms from our readings so that all of us had a similar understanding of the concepts and terms. Next, we would take a 5- to 10-minute break and then resume class, which would focus on our race-relations debate issues of the week. For the second half of the class, I expected to have the students share their personal experiences about race-relations issues that had affected them or others that they know.

I began to write the major basic race-relations concepts on the whiteboard, and we discussed each one of them:

*   Race
*   Racism

- Direct racism
- Indirect racism
- Internalized racism
- Ethnocentrism
- Cultural relativism
- Ethnic groups
- Racial groups
- Race relations

I was pleasantly surprised with the class discussion on each concept and the ways in which they shared their personal opinions about each one. Once they shared their individual comments, I interjected my own experiences as a college student, and my input helped students share even more of their individual experiences.

Next, we took a 10-minute break, and the students gradually left the seminar room. Yet within a couple of minutes, several of the students invited me to follow them into the next room, where there was leftover food from a reception that had just completed. I was pleasantly surprised they'd invited me. It may have seemed not to mean much, but it was heartening gesture, especially in light of the seminar topic.

As we began the second half of the class, I opened the floor and allowed each student to share her comments on her first writing assignment. The sincerity and seriousness of their comments showed that they really wanted to talk about this assignment and what it meant to them. They discussed their surprise at hearing other students speak derogatorily and tell discriminatory jokes about others on campus, on a fairly regular basis. I could tell that this was their first time talking about these very serious and sensitive issues, and they wanted some validation for sharing their opinions.

Once all the students shared portions of their comments related to the first writing assignment, class ended for the day. At that point, I explained our next week's writing assignment would focus on the debate topic "Have affirmative-action programs outlived their usefulness?"

Finally, at the end of class, one of my students asked me a question while everyone was busy getting ready to leave. She said, "What is the proper term to refer to blacks or African Americans?"

I thanked her for asking the question; then I responded, "It really depends on the person, but to be on the safe side and politically correct, you may want to use 'African American.'" I could tell that she was concerned and just wanted to know the correct term to use.

That moment meant a lot, because it gave an indication that my students were really thinking about the words that they used and not wanting to offend other races.

Day 3

I could tell my students were in a much more relaxed mode when we started class. Even though our topics were highly controversial, politically charged, and culturally sensitive, they appeared ready to discuss these issues in a more in-depth way. I truly appreciated it.

As I arrived in the seminar room, the entire class was seated and appeared ready to get started. To make sure we continued with the same format as last week, the first half of the class covered the major concepts related to race relations, and then I introduced the two major theories most often associated with race relations—pluralism and biculturalism.

After a break, the second half of the class covered the weekly debate topic in which each student shared her point of view. This weekly topic was "Have affirmative-action programs outlived their usefulness?"

Now that we were in the third week of this class with an established regular format, I believed that it allowed each one of my students to take the lead on expressing her views on a particular concept, provide examples on how it related to her, and then show her colleagues in the seminar how emotional many of these issues were to her individually.

For example, we covered the following race-relations concepts during the first half of the class:

- Race relations
- Race relations and behavior toward one another
- Acculturation
- Integration
- Assimilation
- Pluralism
- Cultural pluralism
- Structural pluralism
- Biculturalism

Not surprisingly, each one of these race-relations concepts motivated each student to talk about her individual interpretation of the concept, yet it was the topic of race relations and behavior toward one another that brought out the word "fear." All the students indicated that they were fearful of other races, particularly of black males.

This fear was heightened due to the fact that the university regularly sent out crime alerts for students and, frequently, when these notifications were sent out, a description of the accused perpetrator(s) on the campus criminal activity were black males. Therefore, each student indicated that on several occasions when she was walking on campus sometimes by herself, she took extra precaution when a group of black males got to close to her. Because the regular university crime alerts often highlighted black males as the perpetrators, they felt that they needed to take extra precaution.

I understood their feelings even though they were initially hesitant to share them because I am a black male. I understood their situation and agreed with their reactions. Once I conveyed my feedback with them, the students recognized that I appreciated their frankness and personal feelings on the topic, as well as how I was attempting to keep my own perspective out of the discussion so that they could feel even freer to express how they truly felt—not the "politically correct" thing to say.

During the second half of the class, each student commented on our weekly debate topic—the issue of affirmative-action programs. This discussion became the most highly charged and thought-provoking topic of the class thus far, primarily because most students talked about how this national policy had affected their lives or close friends' lives in their inability to receive funding for college. Several students indicated that they had worked extremely hard to get into the university and honors college, whereas as from their perspective minorities did not have to work as hard because of the affirmative-action policy.

Once I heard all of their comments and discussions with their fellow classmates, I countered with feedback for both sides of the debate. By the end of this session, I believe we came to the conclusion that the affirmative-action policy was, and still is, a necessary national policy as it relates to providing many underserved populations an opportunity for education and higher education, yet it does need to be reevaluated and revised based on the current set of political, sociodemographic, and cultural factors in our country.

By the end of this class, I felt students had gained more individual and group leadership skills simply because all the students took these issues personally and strived to express their views in a passionate yet professional manner. During this session, the students fulfilled many of the active learning and leadership themes:

• They reflected on what they were doing and understood themselves better.
• They shared their views with other students.
• They thought about the other student's and racial group perspectives.
• They stuck to their values and debated their stance.
• They learned the major theories related to race relations.
• They compromised some of their initial thoughts and beliefs after hearing from their colleague in class.
• They listened and worked with how I presented the race-relations concepts and provided personal examples of race-relations issues that directly related to our class discussion.

Day 4

As soon as I arrived in the seminar room, several students were laughing and telling stories of recent activities on campus. I greeted them, and they returned the greeting and then continued with their individual stories.

The reason that I always mention the first few moments of the class is that they gave me a subtle indication that the students were getting more and more relaxed with discussing the sensitive topics in our class. Even when they were not talking about race-relations issues, they were setting a more relaxed atmosphere in the seminar room and developed more comradery among themselves.

As I started the class, one student asked me: "Dr. Bailey, are we going to have an open forum soon?"

Fantastic idea! I responded, "Actually, next week, we are going to begin an open forum for the class to discuss a wide array of race-relations issues."

All the students looked pleased. At that moment, I knew they wanted to break away from my format and begin to venture into a brand-new seminar-oriented class discussion. I explained to the class the major reason I maintained this initial format was primarily because we needed to high-light and discuss the basic yet very sensitive concepts and theories related to race relations before we moved onto deeper areas of race-relations topics.

In this class period, the concepts were the most sensitive ones, and they revolved around prejudice and discrimination. Even the mention of these words caused a visual reaction among my students. I could tell just by their body language (e.g., moving around in their chairs, looking down at their notebooks, or folding their arms) that these concepts were the most sensitive ones thus far in the class.

I started my lecture by saying that *everyone* and *all groups* have varying degrees of prejudice and discrimination. No group is exempt, and all of us experience these feelings and behaviors. This statement was essential, because I wanted the class to know that we were not just talking about one group, but all groups and all individuals in this world having felt and some-times acted on various forms of prejudice and discrimination. Once I said this statement again and again, the students opened up and were ready to hear the specific definitions and consider practical examples of each concept related to prejudice and discrimination.

I placed the following major concepts on the board, and we addressed them individually:

- Prejudice—three definitions
- Racial prejudice

- Stereotypes
- Racial attitudes
- Explanations for racial prejudice
  1. Exploitation
  2. Ethnocentrism
  3. Structural opposition
  4. Psychological explanations
- Functions of racial prejudice

Each one of these concepts caused the students to share their individual experiences, and then they introduced the effects of the news media and how movies helped perpetrate stereotypes of various racial groups.

One particular part of the conversation brought to light another sensitive issue—stereotypes change over time, and the inappropriateness of certain words changes. Thus, words or sayings about a particular racial and/or ethnic group during the 1970s, 1980s, and 1990s may not be appropriate today because many racial/ethnic groups are more sensitive to these issues and desire to have more correct words used. Although a majority of the students agreed with my analogy, a couple did not because they questioned why a word or phrase accepted as appropriate earlier should be considered a poor choice now.

I emphasized that our society's cultural standards and each racial/ethnic groups' cultural standards change over time, so what may have been appropriate in a previous decade may not be appropriate now. The two students who initially disagreed simply shook their heads in confusion, and that was fine. They became aware that cultural standards change over time, and all of us need to be current on these shifting cultural standards.

After the break, I could tell that the students really wanted to talk about different issues. So I suggested a discussion of two particular race-relations issues that had arisen on our campus:

- The renaming of Aycock Dorm (because the name was connected to a former governor who exposed white supremacist views) and the development of Heritage Hall.
- Racist graffiti on campus

This caused another lively discussion. Students provided a wealth of background information and their personal feelings on how both issues had been handled by our campus administrators. Overall, the students conflicted with the administrators' strategies and felt that they'd reacted too fast.

At this point in the class, I felt that the students had accomplished the major objective of the day's seminar:

- They shared their views with other students.
- They thought about the other students' perspective.
- They thought about a particular racial and/or ethnic group's perspective on a race-relations issue.
- They stuck to their values and debated their stance.
- They learned the deeper context of certain race-relations concepts.
- They listened and worked with me on how I presented these new race-relations concepts.
- They appreciated personal examples of race-relations issues that directly related to our class discussion.

Although we did not get to our weekly debate topic—"Is the discussion about race and intelligence worthwhile?"—I felt that the students went as far as they could go for today's class. Moreover, since this seminar material was so sensitive, I felt that I shouldn't push certain topics too fast. My motto for this class in particular remained "One step at a time!"

Day 5

Once I was seated, my first comments were about how our seminar was going to change its format and our topic. The seminar would focus on a more open-forum format in which the students would bring up individual race-relations topics in the news or issues that had affected them while at the university. This open-forum format allowed students the freedom to express any particular topic of their choice and to share as much or as little about this issue in this open forum. It also allowed me to discover new race-relations topics that I was not aware of simply because I am an older African American male and not as in touch with student issues, which can go "hidden" for some time before they come to the attention of adults.

I recognized this from the very first day of class, so I wanted to be sure not to limit their opportunity to talk about their issues and share their unique perspectives. In general, I had to put my ego aside and acknowledge that, as a professor, I needed to learn as much as possible from these out-standing, inquisitive, caring, and committed students about *their* race-relations issues.

Once I emphasized this new format for the class and the open-forum dis-cussion, I got an immediate reaction from the students. They looked surprised yet very pleased and delighted that they'd have the opportunity to take charge and direct the topics of the day.

Immediately, they started talking about the Super Bowl football game featuring the Carolina Panthers and Denver Broncos and particularly the halftime performance by musical artist Beyoncé. Why Beyoncé's halftime performance? Beyoncé, along with the two other musical artists—Coldplay (a British band) and Bruno Mars (a multiracial American musical artist)—provided the halftime entertainment at Super Bowl 50. It was Beyoncé's performance that received a majority of the attention and *controversy* from fans and the media, due to the fact that she performed her newly released song in a very memorable way to send a message to the worldwide television-viewing audience.

This involved Beyoncé dressed in all black along with some 20 other African American women dancers also dressed in all-black short outfits with their hair in Afros and wearing berets. Their entire look and image were perceived by fans and the media as a sign of protest against U.S. mainstream society, particularly in the wake of protests against the killings of blacks by police officers during the past couple of years.

Two of my students voiced their opinion that they did not like her performance at all and wondered why Beyoncé had presented this image and protest message to the audience when the Super Bowl was supposed to be an American event in which all of us (all races) get along with each other. These students were perplexed, frustrated, and disappointed that race was put in the face of all viewing the Super Bowl show.

Some students reacted by commenting they initially were not even thinking about the symbolism of her performance or the protest message. They were just enjoying her dancing. And they wondered, what's wrong with a major international artist using this event that's seen worldwide to express her feelings through performance (dance and song) about discriminatory practices that police have committed against African Americans, an injustice that has not received proper attention from mainstream America?

Others defended Beyoncé's performance and stressed to their peers that race-relations issues are not properly dealt with in the United States even though we put up a great facade that says we all get along when, in fact, we do not.

Eventually, after frank conversation between those with the opposing perspectives on Beyoncé's performance, the first set of students somewhat agreed that it was okay for Beyoncé to have performed as she did during the Super Bowl. It was a very good discussion of differing opinions, along with an emotional debate, about a race-relations issue and eventually led to a compromise between the two sets of students in the class. I was proud of them.

We talked about other news-worthy race-relations topics throughout the remaining two hours of the class. Those topics included

- race relations and the United Nations,
- race relations and the generation gap,
- race relations and global discrimination practices,
- race relations and current national presidential politics, and
- racism and power.

They were topics I would not have covered if I didn't switch to an open-forum format.

After the break, the students and I talked about the last writing-assignment topic—"Is the discussion about race and intelligence worthwhile?" All the students agreed that this topic was worthwhile to continue talking about, because—among other issues—there needed to be an emphasis on how one's environment greatly influences one's intellectual ability far more than one's genetics.

At that point, I adjourned class and emphasized again that the remaining classes were going to be open format. I emphasized that our class would begin thinking about solutions to many of these race-relations issues that we'd discussed in the class thus far.

Day 6

Before class, all the students were excited and talking enthusiastically—always a good sign. Once class started, I reviewed all of the major topics discussed last week and then provided a reminder that we were going to have our first guest speaker—the ECU student president.

Next, I reiterated that our seminar course direction had changed, so we were not only going to introduce new race-relations topics of their choice during class, but they would also make points about how they could resolve these issues in a practical way. A couple of students said that they wished we had talked about solutions earlier in the course. I thanked them and under-stood that these honor students were accustomed to working on topics at a faster rate than other students. But I stressed to them that since we were discussing a number of very sensitive issues, I felt that we needed to take a little more time to go over the major concepts associated with race relations—such as prejudice, racial attitude, and racism—before we actually could attempt to solve these issues.

I explained that all of our future discussions on race relations would result in developing solutions or specific strategies to improve race relations. The four levels of solutions would be

- individual strategies,
- group strategies,
- university strategies, and
- societal strategies.

From that point until the end of the semester, students would be expected to think about the various strategies of how to resolve individual race-relations issues we had raised in class.

Our open-forum topics would include the controversial performances at the Grammys featuring the rapper Kendrick Lamar, the Super Bowl halftime show featuring Beyoncé (again) and Coldplay, and the university's new football head coach and his family. In the case of Kendrick Lamar, he performed his rap song in front of the Grammys audience while chained and in a set designed as a jail cell. As the students continued to discuss his performance, one decided to pull up the performance on her laptop and asked to show it to the class. We all sat around the table looking at Kendrick Lamar's controversial performance. Lively discussion followed.

After watching that performance, I asked the class what they thought the overall message was that he was attempting to communicate. Students agreed that he wanted to bring awareness to the unjust incarceration of black males to our society and to get more of mainstream America to start talking about it and potentially to do something about this unjust issue. They also stated that since Kendrick Lamar had always performed this way and has been committed to stopping all types of injustices against black people, it was fine for him to do this type of performance.

I immediately followed up their discussion and used Lamar's performance to illustrate our four-level solutions strategy framework. That is, Kendrick Lamar used his performance (individual strategy) to bring awareness to other racial groups in the United States, thereby bringing further awareness of this issue to society, our second (group) and fourth (societal) race-relations solutions strategies.

We moved the discussion away from national musical artists to issues here at the university, such as the hiring of a new football coach. The new football coach is an African American man with a wife and children; they have the potential to serve as new positive role models to the university community.

The students thought about how sports and the athletic department has so much support here among university students and the larger community that they could lead the charge to bring awareness to a number of race-relations issues on campus. We discussed the notion that if students, administrators, and faculty worked together, as opposed to separately, when a racial issue occurs on campus, the university could achieve individual, group, university, and societal solutions (four-level approach) to race-relations issues.

We finished our discussion by focusing on racism among fraternities and sororities and began to think about the type of strategies that could potentially work here with that issue. Although the class felt that this part of the university's institutions (fraternities and sororities) were untouchable, by the end, they agreed that we as an institution needed to begin a new strategy to reach them and change discriminatory practices among their members.

Finally, the class was reminded of our guest speaker for the next class and encouraged to challenge him by asking plenty of questions about his student race-relations strategies. One student proposed documenting his appearance in our class by taking a class selfie with him, so all could individually feel good about themselves, having participated in our overall plan to improve race relations at the university. She actually said, "We are the movement."

These students, it seemed, were committed to making a difference, becoming a "movement." And I believed that they would!

Day 7

Unfortunately, my plan to have our first guest speaker—the student government president—did not happen because of tornado warnings canceling all university classes after 1:00 p.m. that day.

Day 8

I reviewed and reminded students that our class had shifted its approach to concentrating on solutions to race-relations issues, as opposed to highlighting various race-relations issues in the news and on campus. The students were still eager to move to this approach, yet some were somewhat concerned about how we were going to accomplish this. I assured them that collectively we would develop a number of solutions and discuss them in detail. I could hear their sighs of relief. They definitely needed some guidance in this brand-new area of academic inquiry, and they wanted to accomplish an outstanding end product for this class.

Then it was open-forum time. I asked, "Are there any issues that the class would like to discuss that came up during the past couple of weeks?"

The two major news topics that students talked about were the Oscars and Republican presidential candidate Donald Trump, and the issues therein related to race relations.

The Oscars had aired, and the primary controversy surrounding the show was that there were no actors or actresses of color nominated for any award. Chris Rock, an African American comedian, hosted the Oscar show and joked about race-relations issues throughout the broadcast. A majority of students felt that he did an outstanding job handling a very sensitive topic, which became a national issue on race relations simply because the Academy of Motion Picture Arts and Sciences (the organization that gives out the awards), made up of predominantly white males, voted for only movies and actors/actresses that they were most familiar with and looked like the (white) academy members. Although there were a number of African American comedians/actresses and community-of-color organizations boycotting the Oscars show, Chris Rock did not and managed to raise the race issues.

My students all agreed and genuinely believed it unfair that the Oscars and the academy were so biased. They also realized that many of the race-relations issues that we had been talking about throughout the class involved opportunities that people of color wanted and should receive but were denied.

The second topic that my students wanted to talk about was the Republican presidential candidate Donald Trump. They couldn't believe that he was winning many of the Republican primaries and endorsements and felt so disappointed that such a large percentage of Americans supported him, even with his racist remarks. They were simply baffled, shocked, and sad.

This discussion went on extensively, and they concluded, "Race relations will be set back decades if he is elected." (We now know, since his victory nearly a year ago, that this seems absolutely true.)

We moved on to our discussion of solutions to race-relations issues, and I asked the class, "What are the top ten race-relations issues here on the university campus?" It took them a while, but the students developed a list of six issues:

- Fraternity/sorority issues
- Interracial dating
- Cliques
- Party/social life
- Social consciousness
- Military movements

From this list, I got the students to select one—cliques—and break out the solutions in the four-level solutions framework. The race-relations solutions framework, once again, consists of

- individual strategies,
- group strategies,
- university strategies, and
- societal strategies.

The entire group became energized and focused, critically thinking about each level of solutions as it related to cliques. In general, they sought to develop a plan about how to get university students to stop adhering to and staying in cliques throughout their years here. Their ideals were excellent, imaginative, creative, and inspirational.

After we completed this final activity, each of the students had shown leadership in wanting, taking charge of, and doing something about a race-relations issue on campus. I introduced an idea about how to continue our discussion and goals even after this class ended. The concept was articulated in the following formulation: #Coming Together—a Race-Relations Movement.

Day 9

After spring break, this was our last class. During the break, I'd worked on some of the ideas that these honor students and I developed in that previous class. I framed out what their PowerPoint presentation might look like. I started a new Facebook page titled "#ComingTogether," and I copyrighted our #ComingTogether concept. This was done so that they could see and feel that we'd truly developed something very special to begin a movement for better race relations.

When I arrived in the seminar room, one student immediately asked if we could have class outside that day—a great idea. Within minutes, we were outside and walking to the cupola in the middle of the campus. This was the class phase when we developed solutions and students prepared their Power-Point presentations for the dean and the chancellor.

All of us sat on the brick surface just out of the way of walking traffic and made a semicircular formation. As we got started, the conversation was immediately taken away by excitement over this next phase of the class—developing their PowerPoint presentation on our new group, #ComingTogether!

I shared that I'd copyrighted our #ComingTogether concept. Initially, they paused, and I repeated to them that I'd officially copyrighted our #Coming-Together concept so that we could get full credit for this very innovative idea. They were energized that now we were documenting each and every phase of their innovative concept to share with other students around the world. It also made them feel more empowered that they were a part of something that could truly change the lives of so many students if given a chance. I was fully committed to helping them take the concept to a completely higher level, even after the seminar class was over.

We spent an hour discussing details of the presentation. We brainstormed and brainstormed about how to present it, the major concepts, the major themes, and the overall message that we wanted the audience to take away from this presentation. I emphasized our initial audiences would be the dean of the college of arts and sciences and the chancellor of the university; it would be very important to find a way to get their attention at the very beginning of this presentation.

My students brainstormed again and bounced ideas back and forth. I simply gave encouraging ideas or asked questions of individual students to help them draw out their specifics, explanations, and rationales. They were "owning" it. Challenged with a real, relevant social problem and given time and encouragement to think creatively and outside the box, they developed phenomenal work!

Other students walked by, smiling at the obvious excitement, energy, and flurry of ideas. I believe my students knew that they were really lucky to be working to solve a serious problem, in a class somewhat unconventional yet enriching and important on a level of its own.

With this outside brainstorming activity, we covered the following topics and plans:

- PowerPoint presentation ideals
- Misconceptions about race relations
- Research on clubs on campus
- Make presentations entertaining
- Take-home messages for the presentation

  1. Educate to "bust" misconceptions
  2. Division is divisive
  3. To serve and lead, you must understand the people you serve and lead
  4. Creating community through celebrating culture

We'd had a very productive class, and they were on the way to developing a new college initiative specifically for students, not just at this university but for students at campuses across the United States.

Before my students left, I took a class selfie. They were overjoyed, and it showed in the image.

Day 10

We took a field trip to another university in the state, to visit their administrators in charge of diversity. Their excitement was loud and contagious as they settled into their individual seats in the van.

We arrived, walked into the building, and were greeted by a guide who walked us to our meeting room, where we met the top administrator in charge of diversity.

The administrator along with another senior administrator gave us a presentation on diversity initiatives there at the university. Both presentations were long, and both were the typical administrator's presentation. As each was talking to us, several of my students looked at me and just gazed as they got bored with the style of presentation and its overall theme. Fortunately, they completed their presentations, and it was soon time for my students to ask a few questions.

One stated that our class on race relations was so different than any other course because it could have a direct impact on the type of race-relations programming that occurs at other colleges and universities. I was pleasantly surprised.

Overall, the outcomes of this field trip—aside from my pride at these students' conduct, questions, listening, observations, and comments—was most importantly how they started to own their concepts and empower themselves with understanding and positive plans to deal with race-relations issues.

Day 11

This class was held in the student center.

What another surprising class today. In the Great Room at the student center, I had been speaking to the class all of two minutes when the vice-chancellor of student services appeared. For the next 45 minutes or so, the vice-chancellor spent time with my students asking them questions about their background, their thoughts on race relations, providing her insight on numerous race-related concepts, hearing about our new race-relations movement—#ComingTogether—and, most importantly, determining whether my students wanted to make our #ComingTogether concept a full-fledged university student group!

We covered a lot of topics within a short period of time, and by the end, my students were given the green light and approval from the vice-chancellor, who said that she would support their new student group at the university. The students were completely surprised and overjoyed. The vice-chancellor was very impressed by their sincerity, honesty, and passion to do something significant here at the university to resolve racial incidents.

My students needed a professional woman to talk to and relate to. The vice-chancellor was just the right woman; she inspired them, encouraged them, and motivated them to continue with their ideas and the concept of #ComingTogether. It was a special bonding among young college-aged Caucasian women and a middle-age professional woman of color that made this particular class meeting even more special.

Of course, we took photographs at the end.

Day 12

Now it was time to truly get the students moving forward on their final presentation of #ComingTogether! As I entered the seminar room, my students were actually working on their presentation before class started. They were excited yet nervous because now was the time to put all of their thoughts and ideas forward in a PowerPoint presentation. They started to share their ideas about their presentation.

One leading student had taken it upon herself to change the look and design of our #ComingTogether logo. It was much "hipper" and more "active looking" than my standard-font logo. I immediately agreed. I knew when to back off and let the students take charge. It is so refreshing and prideful to see students take charge and change things to amplify and invigorate a concept to better get the attention of and speak to their peers. I loved the new look of the #ComingTogether design; it changed the entire perception and visual impact of the concept!

For the next hour and a half, we mocked up the design of the PowerPoint presentation. Sometimes I wrote a few of their thoughts on the whiteboard in front of the class while the students wrote the bullet points in the Word document on their laptops.

The leader of the class took charge of typing all the major agreed-upon concepts in the PowerPoint presentation. Each student shared her opinion concerning which bullet points were to be included in the PowerPoint slide. They truly worked together discussing the key concepts.

My role was to listen, suggesting only a bit more of a framework and key messages needed in the presentation. In general, I followed their lead. When they did hit a standstill, I offered thoughts again to help them to the next facet of their presentation.

By the end of the class, everyone felt more comfortable with the key concepts and bullet points for the presentation. The students scheduled a weekend meeting on campus to work out more of the details. This was the first time that all of them had gotten together outside of class time to work on a class activity.

Day 13

This was the date of their first presentation in front of an administrator—the dean of the college of arts and sciences. As I arrived inside the college, the door to the seminar room was closed, but I heard the sounds of students talking inside. I opened the door to see my students all present and set up to make their presentation to the dean. They had the laptop computer connected to the projector, and the first slide of our presentation was on the wall. They were indeed ready!

Soon, the dean of the college of arts and sciences arrived, as did the (surprise) interim dean of the honors college. The deans took their seats, and I walked up along with my students to front of the room. I introduced myself and then let my students introduce themselves. My presentation provided an overview of the race-relations class and how my class arrived at their final thoughts about solving race-relations issues. I admitted it was definitely a challenge to begin lecturing about race-relations issues when my entire class consisted of young, white, Caucasian females. That was the first major challenge to overcome, and we did. I talked about this issue first because the dean of the college of arts and sciences asked about my class, prior to its start that day, and wondered how an "all-white, female" class could actually discuss race-relations issues. I told him that we'd addressed that issue at the very beginning of class, and this was how I summed that up: "I told them, don't apologize for being white because I am definitely not apologizing for being a black, African American male." I continued to tell my students, "You are who you are."

I also explained that these young, white, Caucasian females came with passion and deep interest to not only discuss these very sensitive issues but also develop very practical and thought-provoking solutions. The students chimed in to talk about their perspectives, recognizing that it might have limited their approach, yet they wanted to immerse themselves in the topics of race relations as best they could.

I sat down next to the laptop computer and managed the PowerPoint slides. Each one of my students had talking points with each slide, and I followed their step-by-step approach. As I sat there managing slides, I just listened to each student, overwhelmed with pride, for them and for their #ComingTogether initiative.

The dean of the college of arts and sciences immediately congratulated them on their work and then asked several key questions. Each question was answered with certainty and conviction.

The dean supported the students' #ComingTogether initiative and pledge that once they became a full-fledged student group in the fall semester, the college would invite them to many student events to share their message about coming together to address race-relations issues at the university.

We took a class selfie with the deans, to post on or #ComingTogether Facebook page and new #ComingTogether Twitter account. Indeed, it seemed they were going to make a difference at this university.

Day 14

The final day! This was the day our chancellor was scheduled to come. The students were all ready to present.

The chancellor arrived, as did administrators of the honors college who were also curious about my student's new initiative.

This time, the students' presentation included photos of themselves and photos of the university. Each student had a part to talk about, stating her major issue but most importantly elaborating on the issue and detailing how these race-relations issues personally affected her, her loved ones, and her friends. The students even politely challenged how the chancellor handled a recent racial incident on campus. In fact, they explained their opinion in a very politically correct manner, and the chancellor was impressed.

Wow. My students took a stance right then and there and made their politically correct suggestion to the chancellor. He appreciated it and followed up with one question after another. He indicated the most current racial incident caused the university administration to search for a new approach. And here he was in our class.

At the end, the chancellor and the honors-college administrators said that they would support my students' new #ComingTogether initiative as it grew and developed through the spring, summer, and next academic year.

After the chancellor and the honors-college administrators left, my students sat around the seminar table one last time. I gave each and every one of them my thanks, both verbally and with a written note.

I wanted them to know that each one of them was exceptional, that I expected that they would continue to believe in themselves and continue to work to improve race relations on campus and in their part of the world, wherever they were.

I believe each one of them took that to heart.

Race- and Ethnic-Relations Teaching Exercises

One of the most challenging aspects of teaching a race- and ethnic-relations course or lecturing about this topic in related courses is how to get college students engaged in the topic without feeling offended, targeted, apprehensive, stressed, or downright scared about saying the wrong thing to fellow classmates in a college course. Not only can this be an anxious, uncertain, and stressful situation for students but also uneasy for the instructor or professor.

For those who are new to teaching race- and ethnic-relations issues and those who feel somewhat uneasy, here are five teaching approaches that can start constructive dialogue, engagement, discussion, and fun interaction among students in the class.

1. Introduce Yourself

One of the first assignments for your class during the first week is to get your students to introduce themselves to the rest of the class. There are two ways in which students must introduce themselves. The first way is to introduce themselves online. By now, most college classes have some form of blackboard system in which the instructor communicates with the entire class with assignments and postings. If your university has some type of blackboard system, send out an assignment to all the students in the class to write a brief biosketch on themselves, covering such issues as their major, their extracurricular activities, and why they took this particular course. Get them to post their biosketch on the discussion board by the end of the first week so that the rest of the class can read it.

By week 2, spend 5 to 10 minutes at the beginning or end of each class for students to introduce themselves to the rest of the class. Usually, I individually select students and get them to stand up and talk about themselves to the rest of the class. This allows students to gradually get to know each other and to find out whether each student is consistent with the same biosketch that he or she posted online versus in the classroom.

Continue this same introductory session for the first month of class. By week 4, a majority of students will start to get more comfortable with each other and recognize that much of what they had posted online during week 1 truly matches the biosketch of the individual student or tended to stereotype the individual student even when he or she may not have known it.

2. Fieldwork on College Campus

One way that I get my students to recognize the diversity of the student population on campus is to get the entire class to go outside during class time and conduct an informal fieldwork observation of students on campus. Normally, I take my class out on this fieldwork observation during the early part of the semester, since the weather is usually pleasant, and students are still somewhat getting acquainted with my lecture style.

During the class period when we conduct the fieldwork observation, I arrive to the lecture hall like I normally do and surprise the class with an announcement that we would be going outside to conduct an observation. Next, the students take all their belongings, leave the lecture hall, and follow me outside to a designated place on the university campus (usually a shaded area close to our building).

Once all the students are seated on the campus grounds, I give them instructions as follows:

- During the next 10 minutes, observe all the various students walking on the campus ground in our area and evaluate any unique qualities that distinguishes them from other students.
- Pay close attention to everything that is associated with the particular individual student or the group of students.
- At the conclusion of 10 minutes, we will find out if you notice any particular pattern or distinguishing attributes from the students that you observed.

Once our observation period has ended, I simply ask my class, "What did you learn from your observation of students here on campus?"

Although there will be a wide variety of student observations, usually there is a pattern among students on this campus to walk together in groups of similar races/ethnicities. Whether it's a group of females or males or couples, we observe that students tend to walk and socialize with individuals who are similar to them racially and ethnically.

I then ask a very straightforward question: "Why do you think students tend to walk and socialize with individuals who are similar to them racially and ethnically?"

> That's when I get my class to recognize there may be some subtle preselection among a majority of students to primarily walk and socialize with others who are like them—racially and ethnically. More than likely, it's unintentional, yet when my students actually see it occur again and again and again during this informal fieldwork observation, that's when they recognize that race-relations patterns are being practiced each and every moment on campus.

3. Identifying Cultural Traits and Patterns among the Major Racial and Ethnic Populations in the United States

This is a class exercise that usually enlightens all the students on how much they thought they knew about themselves and other major racial and ethnic populations, but more importantly it sheds a new awareness on the types of stereotypes that all students have about other groups.

As soon as I arrive in the classroom, I divide the class into five major groups. Since I have a fairly large introductory class, usually each group consists of approximately 20 students. Immediately, the students start to talk among themselves wondering what is going to happen.

Next, I write on the lecture whiteboard the following:

- Identify the major CULTURAL TRAITS and CULTURAL PATTERNS associated with your assigned racial and ethnic population.

Then I assign each group to a racial and ethnic population. The major U.S. racial and ethnic populations are

- African Americans/black,
- Hispanic/Latino,
- Asian Americans and Pacific Islanders,
- American Indian and Alaskan Natives, and
- Caucasian/white.

For the next 10 to 15 minutes, the students get together in their assigned racial and ethnic groups and develop a list of 5 to 10 major cultural traits and cultural patterns for their group without using their iPhones or laptops to look online or Google for specific information on their group. After the time is up, I then ask each group to assign a group leader to come to the white-board and place their list of cultural traits and cultural patterns on the board so that the *entire* class can see their responses.

After each group leader places their responses on the board, I then ask each group leader to explain or elaborate upon the cultural traits and cultural patterns. This is where the students get a little cautious, uncertain, and hesitant to state these traits and patterns simply because they are not absolutely sure. Furthermore, I ask the rest of the class if they are satisfied with each group's cultural traits and patterns that they have identified.

Often, I get really good feedback and responses from the classroom, particularly the individuals who are actually a member of the identified group. Each response provides more clarity and deeper understanding about the particular cultural trait and cultural pattern associated with the particular group.

Students also laugh, giggle, and smirk in the classroom when they review the individual traits. The major reason for their reaction is that all of them start to realize that these cultural traits and cultural patterns tend to be stereotypical for each group and that they do not know nearly as much about each group as they originally thought.

Once the students arrive at this stage of the exercise, I reaffirm the major outcomes of this class exercise:

- A majority of the cultural traits and cultural patterns that we associate with particular racial and ethnic populations are stereotypical.
- All of us lack a better understanding and deeper appreciation of the cultural traits and cultural patterns associated with the major racial and ethnic populations in the United States.

4. Solutions for Improving Race Relations on Campus

This is a class exercise in which students are given an opportunity to solve an actual problem/issue that has occurred on campus during the past semester. Whatever the race-relations issue is, the students will talk about it, analyze it, and then develop a solution for it. The primary purpose of this class exercise is to empower all the students in my class so that they know they have the power to change how the university administrators and their policy may need to be changed in order to come up with better and more effective solutions.

As soon as I arrive in the classroom, I divide the class into six major groups. In my introductory class, usually each group consists of approximately 20 students. Immediately, the students start to talk among themselves, wondering what is going to happen again.

Next, I write on the whiteboard the following:

• Identify 5 to 10 race-relations issues here at the university that are of concern to your group, and identify ways in which your group can solve them.

For the next 10 to 15 minutes, each group talks among themselves, identifies the race-relations issues, and then arrives at a decision as to the best ways to solve these issues. Then a group leader is selected, and he or she comes to the board and places their responses on the whiteboard so that the entire class can see.

After each group leader places their responses on the board, I then ask each group leader to elaborate upon the list of problems of race relations that their group identified on campus and explain their given solutions. Oftentimes, this is the part of the class exercise in which it gets fairly serious, particularly when the group leader attempts to explain the problem of race relations, and the rest of the class gets surprised by many of the situations that have occurred on campus. Most of the issues identified are often very subtle incidents of stereotyping or discrimination at a campus event or dorm party, which goes undetected. Yet when they are explained in this manner in front of the entire class by the group leader, the race-relations problems become even more significant.

What is even more surprising, however, are the solutions that each group provides. Many of the solutions are imaginative, innovative, and downright simple. Yet they address the race-relations issue directly and show how easily they can be corrected. Once each group leader provides their solutions, the class finally recognizes how easily many of these race-relations issues can be resolved. That's truly the reward of this class exercise because it subtly empowers not only the class in examining these practical race-relations issues but also empowers each individual student to be an active participant regardless of their race and ethnicity.

5. Speed Friending to Improve Race Relations

Here is a new class exercise that I have added to my introductory classes, which I got from my student organization, the Coming Together Collective. After witnessing how effectively the Coming Together Collective used this group strategy during one of their monthly events with students on campus, I wanted to see if it would fit my introductory class of students. Indeed, it does.

Here is the procedure:

- As soon as I arrive in the classroom, I tell the class that we are going to do a class exercise in which you will have to talk to your classmate who is seated next to you and others who are seated near you.
- Once I place a question on the lecture hall whiteboard, each student is to respond to the question by talking to the student who is closest to them.
- During the five minutes, each student is to respond to the question on the lecture whiteboard.
- After five minutes, each student changes chairs and moves to the next student in class.
- Then I place the next question on the lecture whiteboard, and each student responds to the next question for the next five minutes.
- We continue this strategy 10 times to get through 10 questions that I have for the entire class period.
- Here are the 10 questions:

  What type of ice cream would you be?

  What is one thing you would change about the world?

  What was the last deep conversation you had?

  If you were a household appliance, what would you be?

  What is the first thing you would buy if you had a million dollars?

  Where is the farthest you've been?

  What song are you jamming to right now?

  What is your biggest issue at our university?

  If you could live anywhere, where would you live and why?

  Who do you look up to the most and why?

It is truly a pleasant surprise when you see your students finding a new way to interact, engage, and learn something novel about their classmates. By the end of the class exercise, students who would have never spoken to each other are laughing together and engaging in a completely different dialogue about subjects that they might never otherwise have ventured to discuss with another student.

This is exactly the approach that allows any student, regardless of racial and ethnic background, to engage with another student, thereby improving their ability to enact better race relations within their given network, the rest of the university's diverse college student community, and hopefully beyond.

References

Chapter 1

Bauer-Wolf, Jeremy. "Arrest of U of Maryland Student in Stabbing Death of Bowie State Student Shakes Both Campuses." *Inside Higher Ed*, May 23, 2017. https://www.insidehighered.com/news/2017/05/23/arrest-u-maryland -student-stabbing-death-bowie-state-student-shakes-both-campuses (accessed June 18, 2018).

Black Lives Matter. "About the Black Lives Matter Network." August 6, 2016. http://blacklivesmatter.com/about.

Harris, Gardiner, and Mark Landler. "Obama Tells Mourning Dallas 'We Are Not as Divided as We Seem.'" *New York Times*, July 11, 2016. https://www .nytimes.com/2016/07/13/us/politics/obama-dallas-attacks-speech.htm (accessed June 18, 2018).

Jaschik, Scott. "Supreme Court Upholds Consideration of Race in Admissions." *Inside Higher Ed*, June 24, 2016. https://www.insidehighered.com/news /2016/06/24/supreme-court-upholds-consideration-race-admissions (accessed June 18, 2018).

Pearson, Michael. "A Timeline of the University of Missouri Protests." *CNN.com*, November 10, 2015. https://www.cnn.com/2015/11/09/us/missouri-protest -timeline/index.html (accessed June 18, 2018).

Schmidt, Rose. "University of Missouri President Quits after Faculty Walks Out." *USA Today College,* November 9, 2015. http://college.usatoday.com/2015 /11/09/university-of-missouri-president-quits-after-faculty-walks-out/ (accessed June 18, 2018).

Tampa Bay Times. "A Review of the Evidence Released in the Trayvon Martin Case." *Orlando Sentinel/Miami Herald*, May 17, 2012.

U.S. Department of Commerce, United States Census 2010. *Overview of Race and Hispanic Origin: 2010: 2010 Census Briefs.* Washington, DC: Economics and Statistics Administration, March 2011.

USA Today College Staff. "Racism on College Campuses: Students on Where We Are Now." *USA Today College*, February 26, 2016. http://college

.usatoday.com/2016/02/26/racism-on-college-campuses-students-on-where-we-are-now/ (accessed June 18, 2018).

Vogue, Ariane de. "Supreme Court Upholds University of Texas Affirmative Action Plan." *CNN.com*, June 23, 2016. https://www.cnn.com/2016/06/23/politics/supreme-court-abortion-affirmative-action-texas-immigration/index.html (accessed June 18, 2018).

WFAA. "TD Jakes: 'Tragedy We Ignore Today Will Be on Our Doorstep Tomorrow." July 11, 2016. https://www.wfaa.com/entertainment/tele vision/televison/programs/jake-bishop-td-jakes-speaks/267862656 (accessed June 18, 2018).

Wolf, Richard. "Supreme Court Upholds Affirmative Action in University Admissions." *USATODAY.com*, June 23, 2016. https://www.usatoday.com/story/news/politics/2016/06/23/supreme-court-university-texas-affirmative-action-race/83239790/ (accessed June 18, 2018).

The World Factbook. The Central Intelligence Agency (CIA). U.S. Government Printing, 2016.

The World Factbook. The Central Intelligence Agency (CIA). U.S. Government Printing, 2017.

Chapter 2

Ancis, Julie, William Sedlacek, and Jonathan Mohr. "Student Perceptions of Campus Cultural Climate by Race." *Journal of Counseling and Development* 78, no. 2 (2000): 180–85.

Bailey, Eric. *Medical Anthropology and African American Health*. Westport, CT: Bergin & Garvey, 2000.

Bauer-Wolf, Jeremy. "Arrest of U of Maryland Student in Stabbing Death of Bowie State Student Shakes Both Campuses." *Inside Higher Ed*, May 23, 2017. https://www.insidehighered.com/news/2017/05/23/arrest-u-maryland-student-stabbing-death-bowie-state-student-shakes-both-campuses (accessed June 18, 2018).

Corcoran, C. B., and A. Thompson. "'What's Race Got to Do with It?' Denial of Racism on Predominantly White College Campuses." In *The Psychology of Prejudice and Discrimination: Racism in America*, vol. 1, edited by J. L. Chin, 137–76. Westport, CT: Praeger, 2004.

DaCosta, Kimberly McClain. *Making Multiracials: State, Family, and Market in the Redrawing of the Color Line*. Stanford, CA: Stanford University Press, 2007.

Dennis, Rutledge. *Biculturalism, Self Identity and Societal Transformation*. London: Emerald Group, 2008.

Garam, Bernadette, and Jeneve Brooks. "Students' Perceptions of Race and Ethnic Relations Post Obama's Election: A Preliminary Analysis." *Race, Gender and Class* 17 (2010): 64–80.

Gonzales, Juan. "Race Relations in the United States." *Humboldt Journal of Social Relations* 12, no. 2 (1993): 39–68.

Hurtado, S., E. Dey, P. Gurin, and G. Gurin. "College Environments, Diversity, and Student Learning." In *Higher Education: Handbook of Theory and Research,* edited by J. C. Smart, 145–90. Lonon: Kluwer Academic, 2003.

Jaschik, Scott. "Epidemic of Racist Incidents." *Inside Higher Ed*, September 26, 2016. https://www.insidehigheredu.com/news/2016/09/26/campuses-see-flurry-racist-incidents-and-protests-against-racism (accessed June 18, 2018).

Kallen, Horace. *Culture and Democracy in the United States.* New York: Moni and Liveright, 1929. As quoted by Milton M. Gordon, *Assimilation in American Life.* New York: Oxford University Press, 1964, 142–43.

Laird, Thomas. "College Students' Experiences with Diversity and Their Effects on Academic Self-Confidence, Social Agency, and Disposition toward Critical Thinking." *Research in Higher Education* 46, no. 4 (2005): 365–87.

Lederman, Doug, and Scott Jaschik. "Race on Campus, Nontraditional Leaders, Rising Confidence: A Survey of Presidents." *Inside Higher Ed*, March 9, 2016. https://www.insidehighered.com/news/survey/race-campus-nontraditional-leaders-rising-confidence-survey-presidents

Lowery, B., C. Hardin, and S. Sinclair. "Social Influences Effects on Automatic Racial Prejudice." *Journal of Personality and Social Psychology* 81 (2001): 842–55.

Mack, D., T. Tucker, R. Archuleta, G. DeGroot, A. Hernandez, and S. Oh. "Intraethnic Relations on Campus: Can't We All Get Along?" *Journal of Multicultural Counseling and Development* 25 (1997): 256–68.

Martin, Judith, Alison Trego, and Thomas Nakayama. "College Students' Racial Attitudes and Friendship Diversity." *Howard Journal of Communications* 21 (2010): 97–118.

McCormack, A. "The Changing Nature of Racism on College Campuses: Study of Discrimination at a Northeastern Public University." *College Student Journal* 29 (1995): 150–56.

Milem, Jeffrey, Mitchell Chang, and Anthony Antonio. "Making Diversity Work on Campus: A Research-Based Perspective." Washington, DC: Association of American Colleges and University, 2005.

Pantoja, Antonia, Wilhelmina Perry, and Barbara Blourock. "Towards the Development of Theory: Cultural Pluralism Redefined." *Journal of Sociology and Social Welfare* 4, no. 1 (2014): 124–46.

Pettigrew, T. "Intergroup Contact Theory." *Annual Review Psychology* 48 (1998): 65–85.

"Race Relations on Campus." *Journal of Blacks in Higher Education* 1 (Autumn 1993): 106–8.

Root, Maria. *The Multiracial Experience: Racial Borders as the New Frontier.* Thousand Oaks, CA: Sage Publications, 1996.

Sanday, Peggy. "The Application of the Concept of Cultural Pluralism to the United States Domestic Social Policy," revised version of a paper presented at the 69th Annual Meeting of the American Anthropological Association, San Diego, California, November 1970.

Santos, Silvia, Alejandro Morales, Anna Ortiz, and Monica Rosales. "The Relationship between Campus Diversity, Students' Ethnic Identity and College Adjustment: A Qualitative Study." *Cultural Diversity and Ethnic Minority Psychology* 13, no. 2 (2007): 104–14.

Schmitt, Eric. "Analysis of Census Finds Segregation Along with Diversity." *New York Times*, April 4, 2001: A15.

Smith, Timothy, Raquel Bowman, and Sungti Hsu. "Racial Attitudes among Asian and European American College Students: A Cross-Cultural Examination." *College Student Journal* 41, no. 2 (2007): 436–43.

Sydell, E., and S. Nelson. "Modern Racism on Campus: A Survey of Attitudes and Perceptions." *Social Science Journal* 37 (2000): 627–35.

Torres, Kimberly. "Culture Shock: Black Students Account for Their Distinctiveness at an Elite College." *Ethnic and Racial Studies* 32, no. 5 (2009): 883–905.

U.S. Department of Commerce. United States Census 2000. *The Two or More Races Population: 2000.* Washington, DC: Economics and Statistics Administration, November 2001.

Van Laar, C., J. Sidanius, J. Rabinowitz, and S. Sinclair. "The Three Rs of Academic Achievement: Reading, Riting, and Racism." *Personality and Social Psychology Bulletin* 25 (1999): 139–51.

Chapter 3

Bailey, Eric. *The Cultural Rights Movement: Fulfilling the Promise of Civil Rights for African Americans.* Santa Barbara, CA: Praeger, 2010.

Bailey, Gloria. "Analyzing Present and Future Effects of Civil Rights Legislation and Diversity in Human Resource Planning and Management," paper printed in the Proceedings of Humanities, 2008.

Berry, Mary Frances, and John W. Blassingame. *Long Memory: The Black Experience in America.* New York: Oxford, 1982.

Chisholm, Shirley. *Chisholm 72—Unbought and Unbossed: Expanded 40th Anniversary Edition.* Washington, DC: Take Root Media, 2010.

Cosby, Camille, and Renee Poussaint. *A Wealth of Wisdom: Legendary African American Elders Speak.* New York: Atria Books, 2004, 70.

Franklin, John Hope, and J. Alfred Moss. *From Slavery to Freedom: A History of Negro Americans,* 14th ed. New York: Alfred A. Knopf, 1988.

Freeman, Jo. "Shirley Chisholm's 1972 Presidential Campaign." Jo Freeman website, 2009. https://www.jofreeman.com/polhistory/chisholm.htm (accessed May 28, 2018).

Gutgold, Nichola. *Paving the Way for Madam President.* New York: Rowman & Littlefield, 2006, 51–52.

Hunter, Desiree. "Johnnie Carr, 97: A Civil Rights 'Spark Plug.'" *Washington Post,* February 25, 2008.

Kitano, Harry. *Race Relations.* Upper Saddle River, NJ: Prentice Hall, 1997.

Kottak, Conrad. *Cultural Anthropology: Appreciating Cultural Diversity,* 14th ed. New York: McGraw-Hill, 2011.

Mindel, Charles, and Robert Habenstein. *Ethnic Families in America: Patterns and Variations,* 2nd ed. New York: Elsevier, 1981.

Molnar, Stephens. *Races, Types and Ethnic Groups: The Problem of Human Variation.* Englewood Cliffs, NJ: Prentice Hall, 1975.

Page, Susan, William Risser, and USA TODAY. "Obama's Rise Spotlights Gains in Race Relations." *ABC News,* September 22, 2008. https://abcnews.go .com/Politics/story?id=5862293&page=1

Parham, Sandra. *Barbara Jordan: Selected Speeches.* Washington, DC: Howard University Press, 1999.

Robinson, Robert. "How Far We Have Come." *USATODAY,* November 7, 2008.

Rousseau, Paul. "Native-American Elders: Health Care Status." *Clinics in Geriatric Medicine* 11 (1995): 83–95.

Scarborough, Megan. *A Voice That Could Not Be Stilled.* Austin: University of Texas Archives, 2003.

Scupin, Raymond. *Race and Ethnicity: The United States and the World,* 2nd ed. Boston: Pearson, 2012.

U.S. Department of Commerce. United States Census 2010. *Overview of Race and Hispanic Origin: 2010: 2010 Census Briefs.* Washington, DC: Economics and Statistics Administration, March 2011.

U.S. Department of Commerce. *We the First Americans.* Washington, DC: Economics and Statistics Administration, Bureau of Census, 1993.

Williams, Juan. *Eyes on the Prize: America's Civil Rights Years, 1954–1965.* New York: Penguin Books, 1987.

Chapter 4

American Anthropological Association. "American Anthropological Association Statement on Race." May 1998. http://www.virginia.edu/woodson/courses /aas102 (spring01)/articles/aaa_race.html (accessed May 28, 2018).

Ancis, Julie, William Sedlacek, and Jonathan Mohr. "Student Perceptions of Campus Cultural Climate by Race." *Journal of Counseling and Development* 78, no. 2 (2000): 180–85.

Bailey, Eric. *The Cultural Rights Movement: Fulfilling the Promise of Civil Rights for African Americans.* Santa Barbara, CA: Praeger, 2010.

Bailey, Eric. *Medical Anthropology and African American Health.* Westport, CT: Bergin & Garvey, 2000.

Boas, Franz. *Race, Language and Culture.* New York: MacMillan Company, 1940.

Corcoran, C. B., and A. Thompson. "'What's Race Got to Do with It?' Denial of Racism on Predominantly White College Campuses." In *The Psychology of Prejudice and Discrimination: Racism in America,* vol. 1, edited by J. L. Chin, 137–76. Westport, CT: Praeger, 2004.

Dennis, Rutledge. *Biculturalism, Self Identity and Societal Transformation.* London: Emerald Group Publishing, 2008.

Du Bois, W. E. B. *The Autobiography of W. E. B. DuBois: A Soliloquy on Viewing My Life from the Last Decade of Its First Century.* Washington, DC: International Publishers, 1968.

Foner, Philip. *W. E. B. Du Bois Speaks: Speeches and Addresses 1890–1919.* New York: Pathfinder, 1970.

Garam, Bernadette, and Jeneve Brooks. "Students' Perceptions of Race and Ethnic Relations Post Obama's Election: A Preliminary Analysis." *Race, Gender and Class* 17 (2010): 64–80.

Gates, Henry Louis, and K.A. Appaiah. *Zora Neale Hurston: Critical Perspectives Past and Present.* New York: Amistad, 1993.

Gonzales, Juan. "Race Relations in the United States." *Humboldt Journal of Social Relations* 12, no. 2 (1993): 39–68.

Hurston, Zora Neale. *Mules and Men.* New York: Harper Collins, 1935.

Kallen, Horace. *Culture and Democracy in the United States.* New York: Moni and Liveright, 1929. As quoted by Milton M. Gordon, *Assimilation in American Life.* New York: Oxford University Press, 1964, 142–43.

Kottak, Conrad. *Cultural Anthropology: Appreciating Cultural Diversity.* New York: McGraw-Hill, 2014.

Laird, Thomas. "College Students' Experiences with Diversity and Their Effects on Academic Self-Confidence, Social Agency, and Disposition toward Critical Thinking." *Research in Higher Education* 46, no. 4 (2005): 365–87.

Lowery, B., C. Hardin, and S. Sinclair. "Social Influences Effects on Automatic Racial Prejudice." *Journal of Personality and Social Psychology* 81 (2001): 842–55.

Mack, D., T. Tucker, R. Archuleta, G. DeGroot, A. Hernandez, and S. Oh. "Intraethnic Relations on Campus: Can't We All Get Along?" *Journal of Multicultural Counseling and Development* 25 (1997): 256–68.

Marable, Manning. *W.E.B. DuBois: Black Radical Democrat.* Boston: Twayne, 1986.

Martin, Judith, Alison Trego, and Thomas Nakayama. "College Students' Racial Attitudes and Friendship Diversity." *Howard Journal of Communications* 21 (2010): 97–118.

McCormack, A. "The Changing Nature of Racism on College Campuses: Study of Discrimination at a Northeastern Public University." *College Student Journal* 29 (1995): 150–56.

Mead, Margaret. *Coming of Age in Samoa.* New York: William Morrow, 1928.

Pantoja, Antonia, Wilhelmina Perry, and Barbara Blourock. "Towards the Development of Theory: Cultural Pluralism Redefined." *Journal of Sociology and Social Welfare* 4, no. 1 (2014): 124–46.

Pettigrew, T. "Intergroup Contact Theory." *Annual Review Psychology* 48 (1998): 65–85.

Sanday, Peggy. "The Application of the Concept of Cultural Pluralism to the United States Domestic Social Policy," revised version of a paper presented at the 69th Annual Meeting of the American Anthropological Association, San Diego, California, November 1970.

Santos, Silvia, Alejandro Morales, Anna Ortiz, and Monica Rosales. "The Relationship between Campus Diversity, Students' Ethnic Identity and College Adjustment: A Qualitative Study." *Cultural Diversity and Ethnic Minority Psychology* 13, no. 2 (2007): 104–14.

Scupin, Raymond. *Race and Ethnicity: The United States and the World*, 2nd ed. Boston: Pearson, 2012.

Smedley, Audrey, and Brian Smedley. *Race in North America: Origin and Evolution of a Worldview*, 14th ed. Boulder, CO: Westview Press, 2012.

Smith, M.G. *Pluralism in Africa*. Edited by Leo Kuper and M.G. Smith. Berkeley: University of California Press, 1969.

Smith, Timothy, Raquel Bowman, and Sungti Hsu. "Racial Attitudes among Asian and European American College Students: A Cross-Cultural Examination." *College Student Journal* 41, no. 2 (2007): 436–43.

Sydell, E., and S. Nelson. "Modern Racism on Campus: A Survey of Attitudes and Perceptions." *Social Science Journal* 37 (2000): 627–35.

Torres, Kimberly. "Culture Shock: Black Students Account for Their Distinctiveness at an Elite College." *Ethnic and Racial Studies* 32, no. 5 (2009): 883–905.

Van Laar, C., J. Sidanius, J. Rabinowitz, and S. Sinclair. "The Three Rs of Academic Achievement: Reading, Riting, and Racism." *Personality and Social Psychology Bulletin* 25 (1999): 139–51.

Chapter 5

Alderman, Bruce. *Interracial Relationships*. Detroit: Greenhaven Press, 2007.

Baird-Olson, Karen. "Colonization, Cultural Imperialism, and the Social Construction of American Indian Mixed-Blood Identity." In *New Faces in a Changing America: Multiracial Identity in the 21st Century*, edited by Loretta Winters and Herman DeBose, 194–221. Thousand Oaks, CA: Sage Publications, 2003.

Harris, Marvin. *Patterns of Race in the Americas*. Westport, CT: Greenwood, 1964.

Ifekwunigwe, Jayne. *Mixed Race Studies*. New York: Routledge, 2004.

Molnar, Stephens. *Races, Types and Ethnic Groups: The Problem of Human Variation*. Englewood Cliffs, NJ: Prentice Hall, 1975.

Morning, Ann. "New Faces, Old Faces: Counting the Multiracial Population Past and Present." In *New Faces in a Changing America: Multiracial Identity in the 21st Century*, edited by Loretta Winters and Herman DeBose, 41–67. Thousand Oaks, CA: Sage Publications, 2003.

Murphy, Christopher. *Black and White: The Relevance of Race: Unfinished Business*. Research paper, Augusta State University, Department of History and Anthropology, October 5, 2001.

Nimmons, Svenya. *Just Because I'm Mixed Doesn't Mean I'm Confused: Empowering within and Discovering Your Heritage*. Lexington, KY: Swirlpower, 2011.

Sanabria, Harry. *The Anthropology of Latin America and the Caribbean*. Boston: Pearson, 2007.

Sweet, Frank. *Legal History of the Color Line: The Rise and Triumph of the One-Drop Rule*. Palm Coast, FL: Backintyme Publications, 2005.

U.S. Census Bureau. *Population and Housing Inquiries in U.S. Decennial Census, 1790–1970*. Washington, DC: U.S. Government Printing Office, 1973.

Velazco Y Trianosky, Gregory. "Beyond Mestizaje: The Future of Race in America." In *New Faces in a Changing America: Multiracial Identity in the 21st Century*, edited by Loretta Winters and Herman DeBose, 176–93. Thousand Oaks, CA: Sage Publications, 2003.

Williamson, Joel. *New People: Miscegenation and Mulattoes in the United States*. Baton Rouge: Louisiana State University Press, 1980.

Winters, Loretta, and Herman DeBose. *New Faces in a Changing America: Multiracial Identity in the 21st Century*. Thousand Oaks, CA: Sage Publications, 2003.

Zack, Naomi. *Race and Mixed Race*. Philadelphia: Temple University Press, 1993.

Chapter 6

Clinton, Bill. *My Life*. New York: Alfred A. Knopf, 2004.

Clinton, Bill. "One America in the 21st Century: The President's Initiative on Race." 2009. https://clintonwhitehouse4.archives.gov/media/pdf/PIR.pdf (accessed May 28, 2018).

Cottman, Michael. "Analysis: Has Trump Improved Race Relations in the First 100 Days?" *NBC News*, April 29, 2017. https://www.nbcnews.com/storyline/president-trumps-first-100-days/analysis-has-trump-improved-race-relations-first-100-days-n749926 (accessed June 18, 2018).

Dumain, Emma, and Anita Kumar. "After Oval Office Meeting, Tim Scott Says Trump 'Got It' on Charlottesville." *Idaho Statesman*, September 13, 2017.

Gallup. "Americans' Worries about Race Relations at Record High." March 15, 2017.

Holmes, Steven. "Clinton Panel on Race Urges Variety of Modest Measures." *New York Times*, September 18, 1998.

Irwin, Neil. "Trump Says More Jobs Will Help Race Relations. If Only It Were So Simple." *New York Times*, August 18, 2017.

Kottak, Conrad. *Cultural Anthropology: Appreciating Cultural Diversity*. New York: McGraw-Hill, 2014.

Obama, Barack. *The Audacity of Hope: Thoughts on Reclaiming the American Dream*. New York: Three Rivers Press, 2006.

Obama, Barack. *Dreams from My Father: A Story of Race and Inheritance*. New York: Three Rivers Press, 2004.

Obama, Barack. "Obama Race Speech." *Huffington Post*, November 17, 2008. https://www.huffingtonpost.com/2008/03/18/obama-race-speech-read-th_n_92077.html (accessed May 28, 2018).

Office of Management and Budget. *Budget of the U.S. Government—A New Foundation for American Greatness: Fiscal Year 2018*. Washington, DC: U.S. Government Printing, 2017.

Page, Susan, and William Risser. "Poll: Racial Divide Narrowing but Persists." *USATODAY*, July 23, 2008.

Robinson, Eugene. "The Moment of This Messenger?" *Washington Post*, March 13, 2007.

Robinson, Robert. "How Far We Have Come." *USATODAY*, November 7, 2008.

Struyk, Rryan. "Blacks and Whites See Racism in the United States Very, Very Differently." *CNN Politics, CNN Politics Data*, August 18, 2017.

Washington, Jessee. "African Americans See Painful Truths in Trump Victory." *Undefeated*, November 10, 2016.

Chapter 7

Kottak, Conrad. *Cultural Anthropology: Appreciating Cultural Diversity*, 14th ed. New York: McGraw-Hill, 2011.

LaVeist, Thomas. *Minority Populations and Health: An Introduction to Health Disparities in the United States*. San Francisco: Jossey-Bass, 2005.

Chapter 8

Bowen, W., and D. Bok. *The Shape of the River: Long-Term Consequences of Considering Race in College and University Admissions*. Princeton, NJ: Princeton University Press, 1998.

Chang, Mitchell. "Does Racial Diversity Matter? The Educational Impact of a Racially Diverse Undergraduate Population." *Journal of College Student Development* 40, no. 4 (July/August 1999): 377–95.

Denson, Nida, and Mitchell Chang. "Racial Diversity Matters: The Impact of Diversity-Related Student Engagement and Institutional Context." *American Educational Research Journal* 46, no. 2 (2009): 322–53.

Gurin, P., E. Dey, S. Hurtado, and G. Gurin. "Diversity and Higher Education: Theory and Impact on Education Outcomes." *Harvard Educational Review* 72, no. 3 (2002): 330–66.

Hu, S., and G. Kuh. "Diversity Experiences and College Student Learning and Personal Development." *Journal of College Student Development* 44, no. 3 (2003): 320–34.

Hurtado, S. "Enhancing Campus Climates for Racial/Ethnic Diversity: Educational Policy and Practice." *Review of Higher Education* 21, no. 3 (1998): 279–302.

Hurtado, S. *Preparing College Students for a Diverse Democracy*. Ann Arbor: University of Michigan, Center for the Study of Higher and Postsecondary Education, 2003.

Kittler, P., and K. Sucher. *Food and Culture*. Belmont, CA: Wadsworth Thomson Learning, 2001.

Kottak, Conrad. *Cultural Anthropology: Appreciating Cultural Diversity*, 14th ed. New York: McGraw-Hill, 2011.

Laird, Thomas. "College Students' Experiences with Diversity and Their Effects on Academic Self-Confidence, Social Agency, and Disposition toward Critical Thinking." *Research in Higher Education* 46, no. 4 (2005): 365–87.

Saenz, Victor, Hoi Ning Ngai, and Sylvia Hurtado. "Factors Influencing Positive Interactions across Race for African American, Asian American, Latino, and White College Students." *Research in Higher Education* 48, no. 1 (2007): 1–38.

Chapter 9

Bailey, Eric. *Personal Experience in College at Miami University* (Oxford, OH), 1976–83.

College Students Race and Ethnic Relations Solutions (CSRERS). Breaking the Boundaries of Race in America: Developing Race Relations Solutions for East Carolina University. Honors seminar course at East Carolina University, 2016 and 2017.

Coming Together Collective. *Student Organization at East Carolina University*. 2016.

Ruff, Corinne. "One University's Response to Students' Demands on Race: Radical Transparency." *Chronicle of Higher Education*, April 21, 2016.

Chapter 10

Brown, Sarah. "At Elon, Living Differently Together." *Chronicle of Higher Education*, May 15, 2016a.

Brown, Sarah. "Required for All New Students: Dialogue 101." *Chronicle of Higher Education*, May 15, 2016b.

Cultural Competency Engagement Initiative. Cultural Awareness and Global Explosion and Breaking the Boundaries of Race in America: Developing Race Relations Solutions for East Carolina University. Honors seminar courses at East Carolina University, 2016, 2017, and 2018.

Milem, Jeffrey, Mitchell Chang, and Anthony Antonio. "Making Diversity Work on Campus: A Research-Based Perspective." Washington, DC: Association of American Colleges and University, 2005.

Satcher, David, and Ruben Pamies. *Multicultural Medicine and Health Disparities*. New York: McGraw-Hill, 2006.

Chapter 11

Bailey, Eric. Cultural Awareness and Global Explosion and Breaking the Boundaries of Race in America: Developing Race Relations Solutions for East Carolina University. Honors seminar courses at East Carolina University, 2016, 2017, and 2018.

Chapter 12

Bailey, Eric. Breaking the Boundaries of Race in America: Developing Race Relations Solutions for East Carolina University. Honors seminar course at East Carolina University and a BB&T University Leadership Grant initiative for Faculty, 2016.

Appendix

Bailey, Eric. Introduction to Anthropology, Cultural Anthropology, African American Culture, Seminar in African American Culture, Breaking the Boundaries of Race in America, and Race and Ethnic Relations: Discovering New Solutions. College Courses taught 1983–2018 at Wayne State University (Detroit, MI), Indiana University, Purdue University at Indianapolis–IUPUI (Indianapolis, IN), University of Houston, and East Carolina University (Greenville, NC), 2018.

Index

About the Author

Eric J. Bailey, PhD, MPH, MA, BA (PhD 1988 Wayne State University, MPH, 1996 Emory University, MA and BA 1983 and 1980 Miami University, Oxford, OH) is joint-appointed Professor of Anthropology and Public Health at East Carolina University (North Carolina). Bailey is Director of the Ethnic and Rural Health Disparities (ERHD) Graduate Certificate Online Program (www.ecu .edu/erhd) and Director of the new Global Public Health Study Abroad program in the Department of Public Health (http://piratesabroad.ecu.edu/?go =MPHGlobal). He teaches undergraduate courses in the Department of Anthropology, including Cultural Anthropology, Introductory to Ethnic Studies, Medical Anthropology, Professional Development Anthropology, and Race and Ethnic Relations: Discovering New Solutions, along with seminar courses in the honors college: Breaking Barriers of Race in America and Cultural Awareness and Global Explosion. The graduate courses that he teaches in the Department of Public Health include African American Health, Ethnic Health and Health Disparities, Global Public Health, Capstone Experience in Ethnic Health and Health Disparities, and Global Public Health Study Abroad Experience. Trained as an applied cultural and medical anthropologist, Bailey has broad-based research experience in several health issues and chronic diseases, including hypertension, diabetes, prenatal care, cancer, alternative medicine, and HIV/ AIDS, and has published research findings in scholarly journals and lectured for the past 30 years on issues related to medical anthropology, multicultural and multiethnic health care utilization, alternative medicine, ethnic health and health disparities, community health, race and ethnic relations, and culturally competent health programs. Bailey was former Assistant and Associate Professor at the University of Houston, Indiana University–Purdue University at Indianapolis (IUPUI), the University of Arkansas Medical Sciences (UAMS), and Charles Drew University of Medicine and Science. At IUPUI, he also served as Interim Director of the Afro-American Studies Program. Dr. Bailey has also worked outside of academia. Dr. Bailey worked for the National Institutes of Health (1999–2004) as a Health Scientist Administrator and Program Director in the National Cancer Institute (NCI) Comprehensive Minority Biomedical Branch (CMBB) and the National Center on Minority Health and Health Disparities (NCMHD) in Bethesda, Maryland. Bailey has received federal funding to assist in the training of health professionals in the ERHD program and conducted public-health training programs for program directors at the Centers for Disease Control and Prevention in Atlanta. He has authored 14 peer-reviewed articles and seven books, including *Urban African American Health Care*, as well as the Praeger titles *The New Face of America: How the Emerging Multiracial, Multiethnic Majority Is Changing the United States*; *The Cultural Rights Movement: Fulfilling the Promise of Civil Rights for African Americans*; *Black America, Body Beautiful: How the African American Image Is Changing Fashion, Fitness, and Other Industries*; *Food Choice and Obesity in Black America: Creating a New Cultural Diet*; *African American Alternative Medicine: Using Alternative Medicine to Prevent and Control Chronic Diseases*; and *Medical Anthropology and African American Health*.